OFF TH[illegible]
TRACK

OFF THE TRACK

AMAZING BUT TRUE RACING STORIES FROM ALL AROUND THE WORLD

BARRY & ALAN WOOD

The Five Mile Press

The Five Mile Press Pty Ltd
1 Centre Road, Scoresby
Victoria 3179 Australia
www.fivemile.com.au

First published 2012

Printed in Australia at Griffin Press.
Only wood grown from sustainable regrowth forests is used in the manufacture of paper found in this book.

Page design and layout by Shaun Jury
Cover design by Luke Causby
Cover illustration: iStock/Gokcen Yener
Cartoons by Brian Doyle

National Library of Australia Cataloguing-in-Publication entry
Wood, Barry.
Off the Track: amazing but true racing stories from all around the world / Barry and Alan Wood.
ISBN: 9781743005323 (pbk.)
Subjects: Horse racing.
Race horses.
Thoroughbred horse.
Wood, Alan.
798.4

The authors will donate a percentage from their sales of this book to *beyondblue*.

This book could not have been written without that spark from a dear friend, and the purpose and memory of a dear son, whose silent urging has kept our shoulders to the wheel. We would like to dedicate this to Darren, much-loved son and nephew, who struggled with life's journey in his later years.

FOREWORD

It's not often that something, in a literary sense, illuminates and surprises. But here we have two brothers obsessed with racing trivia and racetrack stories in general. That is one thing. But to be able to translate such an 'obsession' into a form that is both revealing and entertaining is an art which I'm sure Barry and Alan Wood surprised even themselves by refining.

To some of us the stories are well known. To others they present the challenge of reaching into the past and experiencing events with an excitement and sense of anticipation that we missed by not being part of, or aware of, the original event.

Barry and Alan Wood are correct when they say that there are such wonderful stories about horses, jockeys and trainers, famous and infamous, that they deserve not to be ignored.

The authors have balanced stories from all over the world. They've fashioned different chapters for different countries. They retell the great triumphs and racing tragedies from far-flung parts of the world.

We are regaled with quirky and thoughtful horse names (and let's face it, nothing is more difficult than the naming of a horse) and racing trivia, often so extraordinary as to make you believe it's fictional.

And with all of this, they then have to confront the ultimate challenge of holding the attention of the sporting public who sometimes, let us be honest, have the attention span of a goldfish!

For something that has been a labour of love for over two years and for something that percolated for a long time in the brain of Barry Wood, now all has come to fruition. These are two fairly straightforward blokes who've spent their lives looking for another hill to climb. They have chosen an Everest in research here.

The racing industry challenges us, satisfies us, but equally frustrates us as no other industry can. But we can all live vicariously through these wonderful and true stories. We can live important episodes of racing history all over again. For me, the most extraordinary thing is not so much in the telling (a remarkable accomplishment in itself) but also in the fact that every story is true; and, in many instances, the files have been dusted off and what was old becomes new again.

This is a literary and sporting journey that deserves recognition. The ultimate recognition sought by Barry and Alan Wood is that you read it, enjoy it and boast a little in the retelling of some of the stories as if they were yours in the first place. And I'm delighted to say, there may be more to come.

If you love racing, you'll love this and I sense that the love of what is between the covers of this book will be the ultimate reward for its authors.

Alan Jones AO
Broadcaster Radio 2GB & Channel 7

CONTENTS

INTRODUCTION

I suppose you could call this a journey of discovery for two retired brothers. We have written this as a combined effort, but when we started typing, we didn't realise the implications of this journey.

Barry and I were baby boomers of the mid-1940s, and enjoyed the basic primary-school system in Brisbane, Queensland. We both went on to complete two years of secondary education and left the safety of the school system to join the workforce at the age of fourteen.

Barry went on to own his own company in the screenprinting and display field and was a very successful and creative innovator for his craft and his industry in general. I followed a similar path and joined the printing industry as an apprentice, and eventually went on to be the state manager of an Australasian paper company; the position I held until my retirement in January 2010. Ill health in 1996 forced Barry into early retirement, and his company was sold in early 2000. We have always enjoyed the love and support from our respective families throughout the years: Barry with wife Sandra, son Darren and daughter Kelly, and myself with wife Beth and our daughters Peta and Karly.

Unfortunately, Barry and Sandra's son Darren could not outrun the 'black dog' of depression late in 2008, which explains the dedication we have made at the beginning of this book. Our commitment is to donate a portion of our proceeds from the sale of *Off the Track* to *beyondblue*. The memory of Darren, the loving son and nephew, the man and the larrikin, kept our shoulders to the wheel and at the end of the day, we know he too has been a major part of this journey and our lives.

It was in August 2009 that someone stoked the furnace that led to where we are today. A life-long friend of ours, Rolf Westin, was endeavouring to put together some trivia questions about horse racing for a local trivia night at his club. Knowing Barry's keen interest in horses, he asked him if he could send some questions and answers to him.

Now IT was not Barry's strong point, so with all of the patience that a long-supportive wife has, Sandra slowly introduced Barry to the wonderful world of emails. Rolf was the recipient of a treasure trove of tidbits, so much so that he rang Barry and uttered these words: 'Gee, Baz, you should write a book.'

That was the real beginning, for without Rolf making that statement, we may never have made the journey. It was in March 2010 that Barry and I sat at his kitchen table and shook hands to support a collective effort in writing a number of stories to see how far we could get. When there is a commitment to work closely and honestly, you find out your own strengths and weaknesses. On reflection now, at the end of this three-year journey, it's clear the team we formed evolved as 'The Ideas Man' and 'The Engineer and Architect'.

Barry has always said that the book needs to be short stories because the average bloke 'has the attention span of a goldfish' – and he is right. We have included many original cartoons from our close friend Brian Doyle throughout the book to lighten up the stories because, as Doyley has always said, some of us just like to 'look at the pictures'.

People close to us say that what we have achieved does not happen in real life: you don't just write a book and get it published. Well we did, and we have, so to that end, Barry and I are deeply indebted to those who have supported us and the great (and very patient) team at The Five Mile Press.

... once a passion, always a passion.

Alan Wood

Where it all began – baby sister Carol introducted big brothers Barry (*left*) and Alan (*right*) way back in 1951.

CHAPTER 1
Australia

Are we ready to race yet?

... no, the tide is still in!

For 92 years, the people of Brisbane were privileged to have a very unusual racecourse.

The Albion Park Racecourse was established in 1889. What made this track so different from its Brisbane rivals at Eagle Farm and Doomben was that it was sand. The racetrack is situated just a few hundred metres from Breakfast Creek, a meandering tidal waterhole that winds its way from the Brisbane River through the suburb of

Albion Park. Typical of good old Australian colloquialism, the track soon had a nickname – 'The Creek' – and horses that raced there regularly were known as 'Creekers'.

The final meeting was held on 30 December 1981, with Lyre News winning the last race. He was trained by Jim Atkins and ridden by Mike Pelling.

Some of the great 'Creekers' of yesteryear included Amberdown (winner of the 1916 Stradbroke Handicap as a two-year-old), Auction, Lucky Ring and Red Seas. Lucky Ring also showed his versatility by winning the 1949 and 1950 Stradbroke Handicap at Eagle Farm, while Auction also won the 1942 Doomben 10,000.

Another thing that made Albion Park so unique was that nature had a funny way of upsetting some of the race day meetings ... with king tides. Sometimes, when a king tide occurred, parts of the racecourse and car park would flood. However, there was never any question of abandoning a race meeting. All one had to do was to wait until the stewards gave the all clear to resume racing 'on the outgoing tide'.

By far the most popular way for the patrons to show their patience was to head straight to the bar and have a few 'malt sandwiches'. Once the meeting resumed, the horses were never in any danger when racing as the surface of the wet, compacted sand was as safe as a 'good track'.

'The Creek' is now the headquarters for harness and greyhound racing in Brisbane.

Blue's Finito

... what's in a name? A lot, apparently!

We often wonder about how a horse gets its name, and one interesting example is Blue's Finito.

He was a very successful horse that won the Doomben 10,000 in 1978 and went on to have an outstanding career at stud, where one of his offspring was the excellent sprinter Tiny's Finito.

Blue's Finito was by the successful stallion Bluescope, and his dam was Lowland Lady. Bluescope was by Helioscope out of the mare Blue Jeans, so you can see at first glance how Bluescope was named. Obviously 'Blue' figured prominently in the naming of the sire's side. Therefore, you would think a colt by Bluescope may have a name like 'Blue Boy' or similar – but why Blue's 'Finito'? Under the circumstances, it is perfect.

'Finito' is the Italian vernacular for 'dead' – and that was exactly what Bluescope did on the very day the colt was born. Yep, the poor bugger dropped dead just as his strapping young offspring arrived. So it now makes perfectly good sense that the youngster was named Blue's Finito – the first of the 'Finitos'!

The 1948 Melbourne Cup

... and the Great Debate continues!

History books record the following result in the 1948 Melbourne Cup:

1st: Rimfire (ridden by R Neville carrying 45.5 kg at 80/1)
2nd: Dark Marne
3rd: Saxony

The official winning time recorded was 3.21 flat ... or was it?

The 1948 Melbourne Cup was the first time a photo finish camera was used. It was groundbreaking technology for the day and a giant leap forward in determining the place-getters in close finishes. The officials thought all controversy would be left behind, since the accuracy of a photo finish was unquestionable. But they were sadly mistaken.

As most Cups are, the 1948 race was a torrid affair with Rimfire, the bookies' hope at 80/1, desperately trying to hold off all challengers. The bookmakers were cheering their hearts out trying to get this long shot to the line and, in doing so, line their pockets with riches. Then along came a devastating finish by the well-fancied Dark Marne.

They went to the line seemingly locked together, but all the good punting judges near the finishing post believed Dark Marne had claimed Rimfire in the last bound to win the Cup. Dark Marne's jockey, Jack Thompson, had his tuppence' worth and waved his whip in the air, convinced that his fast-finishing mount had claimed the 'roughie' in the shadows of the post.

Apparently the photo finish camera was the perfect judge, so it was to the bewilderment of all and sundry, especially those near the finishing post, that the photo showed Rimfire beating Dark Marne by the narrowest of margins, with Saxony third.

Many there that day asked to see a copy of the photo just to convince themselves that they weren't seeing things, and many left the course shaking their heads in disbelief. After all, *the photo doesn't lie.*

Some things just don't leave some people's minds, and a Sydney journalist who had witnessed that Melbourne Cup started to theorise about what could have gone wrong at the finish in 1948. He didn't conclude that dark conspiracy theories were at play, despite the 'bookmakers' result'. After all, you can't just up and doctor the photo at such short notice. The following year, in the autumn of 1949 – some six months after the Cup was run and won – the journalist found time to closely inspect the finishing line at Flemington.

The reporter discovered the unthinkable. The mirror and the finishing post camera that combine to give us the accurate image did not line up! The Flemington racecourse officials were advised and shown the error, but although an alteration to the alignment was made, not a lot of publicity was undertaken to explain away their photo finish camera debacle.

You cannot rewrite history after the horse has bolted, so to speak, and it was certainly too late for Dark Marne's connections and punters to dispute the result. Would it have been a different outcome if the device had been calibrated correctly? Many who were near the post that fateful Melbourne Cup day believed so, but what could be done?

Dark Marne first, Rimfire second . . . what could have and possibly *should* have been!

LKS Mackinnon

... a great racing man who made one error of judgement

Here is the tale of one of the great characters and supporters of Australian racing, a man who shaped the destiny of some great races during one of the most important times on the racing calendar, the Spring Carnival in Melbourne. His legacy is etched in the mighty Group 1 LKS Mackinnon Stakes. He also gave us a bizarre decision that brought about rule changes that stopped the likes of Phar Lap contesting the VRC Derby. Geldings, you see, could not contest the VRC Derby from 1931 until 1956.

Lauchlan Kenneth Scobie Mackinnon was born on the Isle of Skye and emigrated to Melbourne in 1884, where he became a partner at Blake & Riggall Solicitors. He was a respected company director and a long-serving member of the Victoria Racing Club. Just before his death in 1935, LKS was made Chairman of the VRC after serving many years of prominent and influential service on the committee.

The Melbourne Stakes was first run in 1869, but was renamed in honour of the late Mackinnon in 1936. The LKS Mackinnon Stakes is a Victorian Racing Club Group 1 horse race held at the Flemington Racecourse in Melbourne each October, on the Saturday before the running of the Melbourne Cup. The weight-for-age race over 2000 metres has prize money of around $1 million and it's proven as a reliable lead-up guide to the form of horses running in the Cup. The mare Tranquil Star is the only horse to have won the race on three occasions, in 1942, 1944 and 1945; the fastest time ever recorded was 2.00.30 by Rogan Josh in 1999.

Being a successful racehorse owner, LKS Mackinnon was no stranger to the purses of some of Australia's great races. In 1914 he was the owner of Kingsburgh, winner of the Melbourne Cup. Kingsburgh carried 12 lb (43.54 kg), was ridden by G Meddick and trained by a Mr I Foulsham. He started at the generous odds of 20/1 and covered the distance in 3.26.00. The prize money of £9890 was a king's ransom in 1915 and it was rumoured that LKS picked up a further £14,000 in bets.

The Victoria Derby is a Group 1 race also traditionally run on the Saturday before the Melbourne Cup, on the same meeting as the LKS Mackinnon Stakes. It was originally run over one and a half miles. However, in 1972, to conform with the metric system, the race distance was changed to 2400 metres. The problem then arose that this distance represented a danger in having too short a run to the first turn, so in 1973 it was extended to 2500 metres.

LKS Mackinnon owned a very good two-year-old colt in 1928 called Carradale, whose early wins included victory in the Easter Stakes over 1200 metres, beating a little-known gelding called Phar Lap, who came in eleventh. You could imagine the high hopes and expectations that LKS must have had for his colt and he was not alone in assessing Carradale as a big chance in the derbies on the 1929 racing calendar.

However, greatness has a way of shattering dreams. In October 1929, the gelding Phar Lap won the AJC Derby over one and a half miles, beating Carradale into second place. Just to prove that there was no luck involved, the peerless Phar Lap then produced a champion's effort in November by taking out the Victoria Derby, also over one and a half miles. You guessed it: Carradale was again beaten into second by the champ.

Surprise, surprise, after Phar Lap's victory in the 1929 Victoria Derby, officialdom placed an unnecessary emphasis on whether geldings should race against colts in the future Derbies. It may have taken twelve months or so but commencing in 1931, the VRC Committee – with LKS a central figure – dictated that all geldings were banned from racing against colts in the VRC Derby. Amazing! Common sense and fairness did not prevail until the 1956 VRC Derby, when geldings and colts could again compete against each other in this prestigious event for three-year-olds at set weights.

LKS was always intent upon turning the tables on Phar Lap. In the 1929 Melbourne Cup, Phar Lap ran third behind Nightmarch and poor old Carradale ran last. In the 1930 Melbourne Cup, the now legendary Phar Lap won in fine style, leaving the hapless Carradale (and its disgruntled owner) to bring up the rear yet again.

So here we go once more! Phar Lap was nominated for the Melbourne Cup in 1931 and he was promptly given a whopping

10 lb (68 kg) by the VRC handicapper (I wonder if LKS was on that committee as well?). When Phar Lap's connections asked that their horse be scratched because of the weight allocated to him, they were astonished to be advised by the honourable VRC Committee that if Phar Lap did not contest the Cup, he would be ineligible to contest any other races during the Spring Carnival.

Well, Phar Lap did start in the 1931 Melbourne Cup under the staggering 68 kg and ran a gallant eighth, in what was the last time we saw this supreme horse race on Australian soil. We all know what happened soon after in the United States.

Thus is the tale about LKS Mackinnon, Phar Lap, Carradale, the geldings, the Victoria Derby and the very 'honourable' Members of the VRC Committee!

Four Mighty Warriors

... and a very Special 'K'

Mustard

On 19 December 2009, the second-last race on the Randwick program in Sydney was an Open Handicap of 1400 metres. It was run and won by Mustard, having his 100th start in a race. A great effort for a horse that competed for such a long time and clocked up so many kilometres during his career.

Mustard was a twelve-year-old gelding at the time and struck a great blow for 'the older brigade'. What was more incredible was that he took his earnings to over $700,000 with that win. Well, the old fellow kept on racing but added only a few more placings to his CV. Surely the time had come to put him out to pasture and a well-deserved life of luxury?

Unlike a lot of old racehorses, Mustard refused to be pensioned off and remained so full of energy that he was put back into training. The birthday buzz of turning the ripe old age of thirteen must have excited the old bloke, because on Saturday 14 August 2010, he won at his 108th start in the Merrylands RSL Handicap over 1100 metres at Rosehill. This took his earnings to over $771,000.

However, there was more to come. On Saturday 22 January 2011,

Mustard ran third in the 1300-metre Myer Handicap at Rosehill, to take his earnings to $800,817. *At his 117th start!*

In December 2011 and at his 126th start, fourteen-year-old Mustard finished in the prize money to take his earnings to $807,617. Surely it was time for his 'pension' days now.

Has the Australian turf ever seen a sprinter of that age win that amount of money? We don't think so!

Taos Pleasure

What a way to start 2010. On 16 January, the eleven-year-old gelding Taos Pleasure won an open handicap at the Morphetville racecourse in Adelaide at his 110th start in a race. This was his nineteenth win and took his career earnings to over $473,000. As the prize money in Adelaide doesn't compare to the money offered in Sydney, this was an amazing effort.

But did the story stop there? No siree! One week later, the old stager won his 20th race and took his earnings to $499,955; an elusive $45 short of the magic half-million dollar mark. Was Taos Pleasure going to be Adelaide's oldest sprinter to reach that great achievement?

The following week saw the eleven-year-old line up in a $50,000 handicap race over 1200 metres, and fate smiled on the senior citizen, because prize money was allocated right down to tenth place. By running seventh in a field of nine, 'Old Taos' picked up $400 and took his prize-money earnings to $500,395, a terrific accomplishment. Congratulations to John Hickmont on a marvellous training achievement. Just as well the old bloke didn't suffer any arthritic attack prior to the critical race. Taos Pleasure that is – not John.

At the age of eleven, was Taos Pleasure the oldest horse in Australia to win two open City Handicap races on consecutive Saturdays? Prove us wrong, but our money is on that stat being correct.

Sensational Swing

The third warrior on our list is the twelve-year-old 'youngster', Sensational Swing.

Not to be outdone by Mustard, he too won at his 100th start at the Sale races in December 2009, to take his earnings to a very respectable $205,000. Nearly two years later in November 2011, twelve-year-old Sensational Swing lined up at Cranbourne in an Open Handicap. At his 120th race start, he unfortunately could not improve on his $220,275 racetrack earnings. Those of us who've owned and raced many a slow horse would love to brag about that sort of prize money!

This old warrior may not have had the talent of his two mates, but he had something going for him that others didn't have. You see, Sensational Swing has been trained in all his 120 starts by Dianne Wynne and has been ridden in all 120 by Dianne's daughter Sally. How wonderfully unusual is that?

Without a doubt, this sounds like a 'Ripley's Believe It or Not' moment and it is one racing statistic that we are confident will not find an equal. Sensational Swing, and Dianne and Sally Wynne, are Guinness World Record nominations for sure.

Karasi: the very special 'K'

We are definitely not talking about a breakfast cereal here; rather, a special little horse. Bred in Ireland, he was not much bigger than a pit pony. His pedigree suggested he was an ideal horse to run in a Melbourne Cup, but he gained his fame and fortune by becoming our greatest ever prize money-winning steeplechaser – Karasi, affectionately known as the 'pocket rocket'.

Before being trained for jumping events, the gelding had a luckless but nonetheless imposing staying record in Australian flat distance races. His notable achievements were:

- 2000: 2nd in the Group 1 Adelaide Cup
- 2000: 3rd in the Group 1 Brisbane Cup
- 2001: 3rd in the Group 1 Brisbane Cup
- 2001: 1st in the Group 3 Geelong Cup
- 2001: 4th behind Ethereal in the Melbourne Cup

You can see that he was always ultra competitive in staying races on the flat and won over $500,000 in prize money. His owners then decided to switch him to jumping races, initially in hurdle races, then in a natural progression to steeplechase races. Steeplechase races are run at a slightly slower pace, with the obstacles a little higher than in the hurdles. Karasi's initial achievements in Australian premier races over the jumps were a third in the Grand National Hurdle and a third in the Hiskins Steeple, both in 2004.

However, his greatest claim to fame was to happen a long way from Australia, in Japan. In 2005, the owners made the courageous decision to take Karasi overseas to compete against the best international jumpers of the time. He was to run in the formidable 4250-metre Nakayama Grand Jump, the richest jumps race in the world.

This old warrior, trained by Eric Musgrave and ridden by Brett Scott, must have really loved the month of April because he won this great event in three consecutive years – 2005, 2006 and 2007. It took many combined efforts to achieve these great results, none better than Musgrave's wonderful conditioning of the horse, and Scott's three magnificent rides ... take a bow, gentlemen.

In all that Karasi achieved, it is important to remember that old saying: 'It is not the size of the dog in the fight, but the size of the fight in the dog'. Karasi left our shores as a tough, honest little campaigner, but came back a legend, the only horse to win three Nakayama Grand Jumps – the world's richest steeplechase race.

At the age of thirteen, the veteran campaigner suffered a career-ending injury in Japan while being prepared for the 2008 race. Karasi was retired, having earned more money than any other twelve-year-old racehorse in Australia's racing history – in excess of $3 million. It is an unlikely and magnificent career record.

Karasi, Mustard, Taos Pleasure and Sensational Swing: these four mighty old warhorses all champions and legends of the Australian turf ... in their owners', trainers' and riders' eyes, that's for sure.

The classic ring-in

... but the result stood and you have to wonder why!

The year was 1928. The race: the AJC Derby, run at Randwick Racecourse in Sydney.

Official records of the race are as follows:

1st: Prince Humphrey (by Duke Humphrey out of Princess Hazel)
2nd: Mollison
3rd: Oatendale

The record books show that was the finishing order; however, Prince Humphrey was not the winner. *He was not even in the race*. The winner was Cragsman, also a horse by Duke Humphrey but from a different mare. Some months later, a Mr Dick Tate of Toowoomba, Queensland, saw a picture of the Derby winner, and soon realised that the AJC might have a problem on their hands.

At one time Dick had been employed by Woodlands Stud, and he knew that Prince Humphrey had white feet and white markings on his face, and what's more, he had a photograph to prove it. The embarrassed hierarchy of the AJC admitted that they hadn't checked the brands properly and it was too late to rewrite the record books. They didn't even attempt to right a wrong.

What about the connections of the second horse, Mollinson? One can bet they never received the first-place purse.

Yes, brands are checked more thoroughly now.

Be wary of Mr Connolly!

... there's something in the wind

The time: the Depression years of the 1920s and 1930s
The signs: alarm bells are ringing
The punter: Eric Connolly
The catchphrase: 'Money lost, nothing lost; courage lost, everything lost'
The bookies: 'God, what is he up to now?'

Eric Connolly's motto for life was 'money lost, nothing lost; courage lost, everything lost'.

During the 1920s and 1930s, wages were pretty skinny even if you could find work, and the best you could hope for was a few pounds a week. Eric Connolly was an astute gambler and he won many thousands of dollars during this time of great hardship, and whenever he appeared on a racecourse, the bookies were scratching their heads trying to work out his next move.

His first foray into the world of professional punting was at the Flemington races in 1904, where he walked into the gate with 10 shillings ($1) and walked out later in the day with £4200 ($8400), multiplying his original investment 8400 times.

One of Connolly's greatest plunges occurred in the early spring of 1929. The four-year-old Nightmarch was entered for the 13-furlong (2600-metre) Metropolitan Handicap, as well as the 1-mile (1600-metre) Epsom Handicap. Because of the horse's superior staying ability, many people, including the bookies, thought that the longer race was going to be the horse's focus.

Eric Connolly had a quiet whisper to the owner of Nightmarch, Mr A Lousson, and suggested that the horse might be better off starting in the shorter race, the Epsom Handicap; the owner probably had his doubts but thought, 'What's in it for me?' Well, the very persuasive Connolly got his way, and on race day, he let loose on the bookies, backing Nightmarch for a fortune to win the Epsom Handicap. The plunge came off when Nightmarch, ridden by Roy Reed, brilliantly won the Epsom Handicap from barrier 23. The horse had been backed in from 20/1 to 3/1. Besides the prize money for first place, one wonders what was in it for the owner, Mr Lousson ... quite a few quid, we suspect.

Dave Davis, the owner of Phar Lap, was also known to have a bit of a punt, and both he and Eric Connolly let loose on the bookies and duly collected when Phar Lap won the Rosehill Guineas in a lead-up race to the Melbourne Cup.

Phar Lap was a brilliant three-year-old and along the way to the Cup also won the AJC and VRC Derbies. He was so short in Melbourne Cup betting that it looked like he was going to start the shortest-priced favourite in the history of the Cup. Due to his effortless wins in the three-year-old classics, and with the luxury weight of 7 stone 6 pounds (47 kilograms), the public could not see their idol being beaten. Since his regular rider, Jim Pike, could not make the weight, he was replaced by the 51-year-old veteran Bobby Lewis. It was seen as a great choice of rider, as Lewis had already won a record four Melbourne Cups.

Enter the astute Mr Eric Connolly. Was he going to get on the Phar Lap bandwagon? It was obvious that Connolly had done his homework, right down to the last minor detail.

The four-year-old Nightmarch was seen as a more seasoned horse than the one-year-younger Phar Lap, but did have a good horse's weight of 9 stone 1 pounds (57.5 kilograms), giving away to Phar Lap a very handy 1 stone 9 pounds (9.5 kilograms). He also had the services of his regular rider, Roy Reed, the same jockey who had been part of that very successful Epsom Handicap plunge.

Before Melbourne Cup day, Connolly started to put his plan in motion. He thought that the young, headstrong Phar Lap, without his regular rider Jim Pike, might be too hard to handle for the veteran Bobby Lewis, and that in the closing stages of the race, this may be a telling factor. History shows that jockey Jim Pike also liked to have a bet occasionally, and he may have had a whisper in Connolly's ear. Who knows, anything could have been on the agenda. The race turned out as predicted, and Phar Lap gave Bobby Lewis a nightmare of a ride; he was reefing and pulling and just would not settle in the field of fourteen. Nightmarch responded to Roy Reed's hard riding, cruised past Phar Lap, and duly won the 1929 Melbourne Cup, with the tiring Phar Lap in third place.

Nightmarch, due to the Eric Connolly's influence, was backed in from 20/1 to 6/1. The amount of money the public wagered on Phar Lap was so great that he still started an even-money favourite.

The 1930 autumn carnival races were run and won, and everyone was looking forward to the forthcoming Melbourne Spring Carnival. This was the year the mighty Phar Lap was virtually unbeatable, and was understandably very short in the Caulfield Cup and Melbourne Cup betting. With his brilliant record so far that year, why wouldn't he be? There was no value for the professional punters as he was short odds in both races, as well as the Cup's doubles.

A plan was being put into place, and leading the charge was the scourge of all bookmakers far and wide: Eric Connolly. The people Connolly brought into his little scheme were Phar Lap's owner Dave Davis, the horse's regular rider Jim Pike, one of Australia's fearsome female punters Maude Vandenberg, and Harry Telford, Phar Lap's trainer. Another person to figure in the end result, but not for the right reasons, was one of Australia's leading and most flamboyant bookmakers, Andy Kerr, who went by the nickname 'The Coogee Bunyip'.

Under Connolly's guidance, vast sums of money were wagered on the Cup's doubles, and with Phar Lap's presence in the Caulfield Cup, his opposition started to dwindle; one of the scratchings was the previous year's Melbourne Cup winner, Nightmarch. Phar Lap's price was getting shorter and shorter as no-one thought that the great horse could be beaten.

Eric Connolly's team certainly observed a code of silence, as there was never any intention of running Phar Lap in the Caulfield Cup. For Eric's team there was much more money to be won on the punt. Phar Lap was sensationally scratched from the Caulfield Cup, and with only fourteen horses left in the field, the mastermind Eric Connolly declared Amounis a near certainty in the race.

Now, we know that Connolly and the owner of Nightmarch, Lousson, had hatched some very well-planned plunges the previous year, so the question was, did the Nightmarch camp play a part in this operation as well?

The team, led by Eric Connolly, had secured 20/1 for the Amounis/ Phar Lap Caulfield Cup and Melbourne Cup double. When the eight-year-old Amounis won the Caulfield Cup, you could just imagine how the bookies felt... sick, sick, sick. How the hell was Phar Lap going to get beaten in the second leg, the Melbourne Cup? Would Lady Luck intervene for the hapless bookies?

Lady Luck was nearly on their side, because just a few days prior to the Melbourne Cup, an attempt was made on Phar Lap's life. On the way back to his stables, a car sped past and shots were fired at the great horse, but fortunately no-one was injured. To this day, no-one knows who was behind this attempt at stopping the great horse running in the Melbourne Cup, but what we do know is that the bookies were in for some astronomical payouts if Phar Lap won ... yes, the old conspiracy theory.

The 1930 Melbourne Cup was brilliantly won by the 'wonder horse' Phar Lap, carrying 9 stone 12 lb (62.5 kg) and starting at 11/8 on, still the shortest-priced favourite in the history of the race. The 20/1 Amounis/Phar Lap double was far more lucrative than taking a Phar Lap/Phar Lap 2/1 double if he had started in both Cups and won. It was reported that the bookies were up for a payout to Connolly's team of the equivalent of $400,000, which was a king's ransom way back in 1930.

Everything was legal, but the bookies had their suspicions that something was smelly about the whole outcome when such people as Eric Connolly, Dave Davis (Phar Lap's owner) and Maude Vandenberg were involved. The Aboriginal word *coogee* means smelly seaweed, so maybe poor old Andy Kerr, the Coogee Bunyip, should have smelt something was not right that day, when Connolly's little band of commissioners let loose on the Amounis/Phar Lap double with him. When Amounis won the first leg of the double, no doubt the bells were ringing in Kerr's head and he probably knew by then that he was part of the Connolly sting. Andy Kerr was broke for quite a few months after that, but in time he was back to his flamboyant bookmaking best. Even the best can be stung by the best.

In 1929, Nightmarch won the Epsom Handicap, the WS Cox Plate and the Melbourne Cup, and after that, he never got within cooee of Phar Lap whenever they raced each other again.

Roy Reed, Nightmarch's rider who was involved in two of those successful betting plunges, was killed in a race fall in Trentham (New Zealand) in 1936. Eric Connolly, the leviathan punter, died in 1944 with an estate the equivalent of $12,000, a very respectable amount back then, but definitely a far cry from his halcyon days 'on the punt'.

Money lost, nothing lost; courage lost, everything lost.

Gloaming

... an apple a day keeps a champion at play!

We breed a great horse in Australia and let him do all of his racing in the Land of the Long White Cloud – and it is only fair that we can pay him back occasionally.

It is quite possible that we could have been writing about 'the great racehorse Celestial' but the first name offered to the racing authorities was unavailable, so connections had to settle for their second choice in Gloaming. He was a bay gelding born in Australia in 1915, bred by a Mr E Clarke and owned by George Greenwood, who, according to the record books, bought him for only 230 guineas; he was trained by Dick Mason and did most of his racing in New Zealand. The interesting thing about his breeding was that his future was a bit of an each-way bet as his dam, Light, was unplaced but his paternal grandsire, Flying Fox, was an English Triple Crown winner. He is recorded as standing only 15.3 hands tall.

Gloaming's remarkable racing statistics were 67 starts for 57 wins and nine seconds, and he fell in his only other race start. He raced through until he was a very competitive ten-year-old and amassed a fortune in prize money of £43,100 in the early 1920s. His remarkable career was frequently overshadowed, however, by the success of Australasia's other beloved heroes at that time, in Carbine and Phar Lap.

Gloaming raced in the years just after World War I, and his consistency and durability made him a hero to the people at a time when the two nations had lost a generation of young men.

Here are some of his major race wins:

Wanganui Guineas: 1918
New Zealand Derby Stakes: 1918
Arc Islington Plate: 1918, 1919, 1920
Chelmsford Stakes: 1918
AJC Derby: 1918
WRC Wellington Stakes: 1919
WANGJC Jackson Plate: 1919, 1921, 1922, 1924
Craven Plate: 1919, 1922, 1924

New Zealand Derby: 1918
Great Northern Derby: 1919
Hill Stakes: 1922
Ormond Memorial Gold Cup: 1922, 1925
Melbourne Stakes: 1924
AJC Spring Stakes: 1924

He beat the very best horses Australia and New Zealand could put against him and, judging by his record, was a very elite athlete even as he got on in age. At the age of nine, he held the Australasian record of nineteen successive wins jointly with Desert Gold. He was successful at distances from 4 furlongs (800 metres) to 12 furlongs (2400 metres). Gloaming still held the record for 4 furlongs at the time that metric distances were introduced.

In 1925, the up and coming champion The Hawk was set to race against Gloaming in a two-horse war, the Hawke's Bay JD Ormond Memorial Gold Cup at Hastings, run over 7 furlongs (1400 metres). At this time, The Hawk had come off seven consecutive victories, and it was a case of the old bull at nine years of age racing against the young bull, The Hawk. The British Bloodstock Review of 1925 best describes the struggle between these two outstanding competitors:

> ... The two horses got away on equal terms, both carrying 9 stone 10 lb (nearly 61.5 kg) over the mile.
>
> At the end of three furlongs, The Hawk was leading by 2 lengths. A furlong further on Gloaming had drawn level and shortly thereafter, got his head in front. Whilst traversing the six furlong mark, The Hawk was once more in front but only slightly. He was now under the whip, while Gloaming was being ridden hands and heels.
>
> In the final furlong, Gloaming got the upper hand and gradually drew away to win by a length. The enthusiasm of the great crowd that had assembled to witness the contest was tremendous. The result was in accordance with the desire of the vast majority, but the gallant effort The Hawk had made against his big-striding conqueror, was heartily recognized and so he to, received an ovation.

Gloaming was an intelligent horse with a gentle disposition, and was a bit of a 'guzzle guts'. Such was his appetite that he wanted to eat everything in sight. They even had to put a muzzle on him to stop him from eating his straw bedding at the stable. Apples were his favourite and he was awarded one after every victory, asking for it by way of a nudge to his handler. He was well aware when he didn't win a race because on those occasions he never begged for his favourite treat. However, on one occasion, despite being beaten, the grand old horse virtually begged for an apple, and that was following his fall in the 1919 North Island Challenge Stakes. He was given one that day.

After his racing career had ended, Gloaming lived a life of leisure at owner George Greenwood's farm at Teviotdale, North Canterbury. He died at the age of seventeen in May 1932. This was only a month after the mysterious death in the United States of Australia's racing hero, the great Phar Lap. His gravesite became known as Gloaming's Hill. One in, all in, because sadly, his owner G D Greenwood and trainer Dick Mason died the same year.

He was a truly remarkable champion.

The double sting of the century

... and it wasn't Fine Cotton!

A lot has been written about the Fine Cotton ring-in affair, but there is a theory with some substance attached to it that we only know half of what actually happened – there were too many variables to line up in perfect order for it to come off. So here is the story. 'The Real Sting' – and it wasn't Fine Cotton.

There is no doubt that what transpired back in August 1985 was controlled by a very tight band of brothers who knew the parts they had to play and the jobs they had to do. In every operation, there has to be the element of chance and every contingency needs to be covered to be successful – whether by design or by accident, there is no doubt that we will never know all of the truth behind what unfolded. One thing we can be sure of is that in the planning there were puppets, but there was also a very competent gentleman who we shall call the Puppet Master, who pulled all of the strings.

Before we are familiarised with the facts that are a matter of public record, there are two very important questions that should be posed. First, has anybody identified or interviewed the person who commenced the 'ring-in, ring-in' chorus in the crowd at Eagle Farm that day, when Fine Cotton was being led back to scales after his win? And second, why did Hayden Haitana, the trainer of Fine Cotton and one who was supposedly involved in the sting, allegedly have his hard-earned money invested on the second place-getter, Harbour Gold?

Keep those two questions in mind as we relive that infamous event.

Fact: Saturday 18 August 1985 was to be the running of the Commerce Novice over 1500 metres at Eagle Farm Racecourse in Brisbane.

Fact: The short-priced favourite for that race was Harbour Gold. Friday's race guide had another horse in the field, Fine Cotton, quoted to start at 33/1 – both prices were indicative of both horses' chances.

Fact: The horse Dashing Soltaire was purchased for the sole reason of replacing the real Fine Cotton in this race as a ring-in, but in preparation for the sting, he was injured.

Fact: As the preparation for the sting reached the point of no return, another horse, Bold Personality, was purchased to replace Dashing Soltaire as the ring-in.

Fact: Bold Personality was an ex-Sydney galloper and in his heyday was trained by Tommy Smith, but now, as a seven-year-old, he was doing his racing around the tracks in northern New South Wales.

Fact: Fine Cotton was an eight-year-old brown gelding with white markings on his two hind legs, while Bold Personality was an almost black gelding with no white marks on him whatsoever.

Fact: The Friday before the race, Bold Personality was floated from northern New South Wales, towed by a small four-cylinder vehicle, and was initially dropped off at a property at Beenleigh, about an hour's drive from Eagle Farm Racecourse.

Late on Friday 17 August, Bold Personality arrived at Beenleigh in a very distressed state of dehydration and it was decided that the horse be given a saline drench to restore his salt levels. As they were acquiring the necessary equipment to rehydrate the horse, the conspirators gave Bold Personality a quick colour dye wash to try and get his coat colour closer to that of Fine Cotton. Remember, Bold Personality was black and Fine Cotton was brown. As the saline drench was being attempted, a blood vessel was ruptured during the procedure and pretty soon everyone was knee-deep in blood. A senior member then took charge and applied cold towels to the horse's nostrils and the blood flow eventually stopped.

Upon inspecting Bold Personality very early on race day at Beenleigh, it was discovered that the dye had failed miserably, so after a quick call to a mystery man, they were directed to take the horse to a suburban property in Weller's Hill, less than 30 minutes from the Eagle Farm Racecourse. At this property, another dye was applied but still the match wasn't really what they wanted, and because they were running out of time, the 'hairdresser' carried on like a 'frog in a sock' and called it quits. However, there still remained one other small problem: Bold Personality did not have any white markings on his hind legs. This merry band then trumped everything they had done so far and asked each other in turn, 'Right, who brought the peroxide with them?'

This classic comedy scene was going from bad to worse because they had left it behind at Beenleigh. One of the brains trust then made a mad dash to the garden shed and came back with a spray can of white enamel paint – brilliant. Anyone who has used a turps-based enamel knows that the painted area needs two or three coats for the finished product to be acceptable and it needs six to eight hours' drying time between coats. Yes, one could definitely see a train wreck on the horizon with this lot. Here we have a quiet street in suburbia, a horse tied to a fence, and grown men applying colour wash and then doing a bit of spray painting on the hind legs of a racehorse ... sort of a giveaway for the neighbours, don't you think?

To the average punter, preparing a horse to be involved in a ring-in would be a very serious affair and you would have to have a pretty

good match to proceed. The fact was the overall colour wasn't right and the white enamel markings on the horse's hind legs were not dry, so it would appear that the sting was doomed for failure ... or was it? Well, in for a penny or in for a pound: it was now a quick trip to Eagle Farm. This had all the ingredients of the old Marx Brothers movie *A Day at the Races*.

In the saddling enclosure prior to the running of the race, apprentice jockey Gus Philpot was legged up. It must be said that investigative authorities cleared young Gus of any wrongdoing and having any knowledge of the ring-in whatsoever.

Fine Cotton was backed like a living certainty all over Australia, in from 33/1 to 7/2. Anyone who has been to the races would know how quickly word can spread about a tip or a good thing. The punters came from everywhere to back Fine Cotton. With the right words in the right ears in the major capital cities on the morning of the race, a betting bushfire began. Because the plunge on Fine Cotton was so immense, bookmakers in the major betting rings all over Australia were starting to smell a rat – a possible ring-in.

The race was run and won and as it turned out, Bold Personality, alias Fine Cotton, had a ding-dong battle down the straight with the previous short-price favourite, Harbour Gold, with Fine Cotton falling in by a nose. Harbour Gold started at the very generous odds of 5/1, such was the volume of money that went on Fine Cotton.

Mr Anonymous in the crowd yells out, 'Ring-in, ring-in,' and when Fine Cotton came back to scale, the single voice was now drowned out by a chorus of contempt. The stewards had no option but to suspend correct weight and try to make some sense of the calamitous scene.

The inevitable train wreck

The stewards tracked down Fine Cotton's trainer Hayden Haitana on course, and requested that he immediately go and get Fine Cotton's registration papers. 'Not a problem, sir, I will get them straight away.' Haitana made his way to the course stable area where his papers were kept with his gear, and, when out of sight of the authorities, he was off, and was not to be seen for over two weeks.

Fact: After exhaustive inquiries were held, the people responsible (supposedly) for the sting were arrested, and some were sent to jail.

Fact: Leading Sydney bookmakers Bill and Robbie Waterhouse lost their betting licences, but years later they were renewed.

Fact: Other people involved were warned off racecourses for life.

Fact: Probably thanks to the Fine Cotton affair, far more stringent procedures were put in place in checking horses' identification before racing. The tremors of change were felt all over Australia, not just in Queensland.

The above may well be the reported outcome, but just consider again the two questions posed at the beginning of this story.

Interstate punters only heard about a red-hot tip that would win, and so they all had a slice of the price. But those closest, knowing what a debacle it was getting their charge to the races, must have had second thoughts and in no way could they have treated their horse as a certainty. How many things had to go right for Fine Cotton (Bold Personality) to win in that field, beating the original red-hot favourite for the race? Just how many things had to line up? Why did

Hayden Haitana allegedly have his $50 on the pre-post favourite, Harbour Gold? Did he finally realise how farsical the whole 'sting' really was?

Could it have been a double sting? Could that inevitable train wreck have been orchestrated by the Puppet Master? It certainly makes one think.

Authorities never interviewed that knowledgeable larrikin who started the chorus of 'ring-in, ring-in' when Fine Cotton was being led back to scale after his win. Maybe they couldn't find him, or just maybe he did not want to be found. After all, leading a cheer squad in the chorus of 'ring-in, ring-in' would certainly attract attention, something that our cheerleader could probably well have done without. Neither the newspapers nor the magazines could find our mystery man. However, there is no doubt that a lot of other people in Australia would dearly love to have had a yarn with our cheerleader.

Why did Hayden Haitana allegedly have his money on the horse that ran second and the original red-hot favourite for the race in Harbour Gold? Maybe it was a saver bet!

On 23 May 2010, nearly 25 years after the Fine Cotton/Bold Personality debacle, it was reported in the Brisbane press that one of the masterminds involved that day (for the benefit of this story called the Puppet Master) stated that it was in fact a double sting. He claimed that despite a $2 million national betting plunge on Fine Cotton that took his price from 33/1 to 7/2, the horse was never supposed to win, and the eventual winner, Harbour Gold, was the real target.

Harbour Gold had drifted out from very short odds on the day of the plunge, to a very generous 5/1 because of the weight of money wagered on Fine Cotton. The weight of the public money backing Fine Cotton after the word was out about a red-hot tip was ingeniously used to inflate the price of Harbour Gold, the real 'go' in the race, and this is where the educated money from the Puppet Master and his lieutenants went. After 25 years, it was reported that within a couple of days of this double sting, one of this elite group lodged his $1.8 million winnings on Harbour Gold into an offshore account.

Doesn't it all make sense? Remember those two very important questions. One could assume that Mr Anonymous, who started the 'ring-in, ring-in' chorus, was part of the elite group, and as insurance against Fine Cotton winning rather than Harbour Gold, he then started the firestorm of protest and melted back into the crowd.

Maybe it also follows that the Puppet Master had a fairly good idea that those he had put together to groom Bold Personality were collectively as sharp as a bowling ball, so all contingencies were covered and they had their safety net. Harbour Gold would win at the generous odds of 5/1 or Fine Cotton would get the money over the original favourite, and with the help of the 'ring-in' chorus everything would be revealed about the substitution and the race awarded to Harbour Gold.

Now there still is that second question: why did Hayden Haitana, Fine Cotton's trainer, allegedly have his money on Harbour Gold?

Hoofnote: What if Dashing Soltaire had not been injured originally? He was a good performer and had very similar markings to those of Fine Cotton. Was that the original sting, or was the Puppet Master forced to have an each-way bet when the 'Keystone Kops' were preparing Bold Personality?

With that, we will leave you to ponder another insight on the Fine Cotton saga.

Hayden Haitana, Frank Pearson and me

This is where the last part of my story begins. As we all know, every Friday afternoon after a very long week, the public bar of just about every suburban pub in Australia is full of tradies, factory workers, office workers and knockabouts from all walks of life, who take off their hats and put on their armchair expert head gear and discuss everything sport: the races, the footy, the cricket, the motor racing, the expert selections, and critical comment on all and sundry.

One of the most important discussions in any public bar on a Friday is without a doubt the form guide racing selections for all the race meetings on Saturday, from Darwin to Hobart, and Brisbane to Perth. But can they compare with our selections? We have found the lay-down misère specials, the absolute certainties, the horses that just cannot be beaten. Our expertise in this field will eventually take us from this life of hard yakka to the life of a respected professional punter and all of the trappings that go with it. Of course, as the afternoon rolls on and the malt sandwiches just keep on arriving, we, the Friday Afternoon Experts, reveal ourselves. Nothing changes.

It was the Friday after the Fine Cotton ring-in attempt and I was having a quiet beer with one of my long-time mates, Frank Pearson, at a hotel on the south side of Brisbane. Unfortunately for Frank, he had just been given his marching orders for the third time from his local footy club, so it was the local watering hole and not the footy club where we got together.

There we were, enjoying a cold malt sandwich at the public bar, when a news flash came over the bar's TV screen with words to this effect: 'Queensland police have an established lead that the notorious trainer of Fine Cotton, Hayden Haitana, has been sighted in Adelaide, and we shall keep you updated as this story unfolds.' They then proceeded to show photographs of Hayden, with the voice=over saying, 'If anyone knows the whereabouts …'

Fair enough, the establishment had their job to do, and when I turned back to face Frank, he was just sitting there with a smile on his face like the cat that swallowed the canary. I said, 'What's so bloody funny?' He said, 'Turn around and have a bloody look who is sitting right beside you.' There, also watching the TV, was Hayden Haitana, the so-called mastermind of the Fine Cotton affair and the man who just a minute earlier had been reported on a TV news flash to have been seen in Adelaide.

Frank, who is not backward in coming forward, turned to Hayden and said to him, 'Bad luck mate, you nearly pulled that off, better luck next time.' Hayden replied, with a cheeky grin from ear to ear, 'I don't think there will be a next time.' We left him alone with his thoughts, and after another beer he quietly slipped away. It was about two weeks later that the police finally caught up with Hayden Haitana in Adelaide, and charged him over his involvement in the Fine Cotton affair.

To this day, Frank and I will swear on a stack of Bibles that it was definitely Hayden Haitana who was sitting beside us at the pub. If it wasn't him with his face plastered all over the TV, then the bloke we spoke to did a bang-up job of impersonating him.

Old Fine Cotton, totally oblivious to his infamy, lived the life of Riley for the rest of his years at Stanton's property and on 20 February 2009, he passed away at the ripe old age of 31. Didn't he cause a stir back in 1985? Well, he and his mate Bold Personality did, with a cameo appearance by Dashing Soltaire. With a supporting cast reminiscent of a Keystone Kops movie, the double sting now makes much more sense of the Keystone Kops version of how to paint a racehorse, doesn't it?

Did it really happen?

... Yes it did

Here are two pieces of trivia for the Guinness World Records.

What opposition?

How would you like to go to the races knowing that you would definitely train at least one winner on the program? You know which race it is, and there is certainly nothing underhanded going on.

On Saturday 9 October 2010, race 5 at Mackay in Queensland seemed to be just an ordinary restricted class race with a field of eight runners. However, this field of eight were all trained by local trainer John Manzelmann. When asked how this freaky circumstance came about, Manzelmann simply replied, 'Well, no-one else nominated.' All the horses in the race were owned in partnership with his wife. Just for the record, the winner was $4.60 chance Taupin, ridden by Trinity Barron.

The handicapper's dream

On Monday 20 December 2010, nine horses faced the starter in the final race of the day at Dubbo in New South Wales. At the end of the 1600-metre journey, the race handicapper must have had a grin from ear to ear, and probably shouted himself a couple of double scotches.

Had he done the impossible? The horses finished in race book order...

1st: No. 1, Miss Reed
2nd: No. 2, Hinterland
3rd: No. 3, Flash Academy
4th: No. 4, Happy Henry
5th: No. 5, Tompeppa
6th: No. 6, Ornithology
7th: No. 7, Seatune
8th: No. 8, Grand Chime
9th: No. 9, Roughshot

The odds of this happening are 362,880/1 – believe it or not.

I had a dream!

... Walter Craig, Australian hotelier and racehorse owner, 1870

Everyone has dreams, but do we dream of horses winning races? Maybe some of us do.

Over 140 years ago, a Ballarat hotelier by the name of Walter Craig was fortunate enough to have a runner in the 1870 Melbourne Cup. Then the strangest of things happened. Prior to the running of the great race, Mr Craig dreamt that his horse Nimblefoot won the Cup by a very short margin. Imagine that: his horse winning our greatest race, the Melbourne Cup – a dream too good to be true.

However, there was one thing that disturbed him. Every time he thought about the dream, he kept seeing all the jockeys wearing black armbands. He spoke of his dream to a friend, bookmaker Jeremiah Slack, but the bookie thought so little of the horse's chances in the Cup that he offered Mr Craig the odds of £1000 ($2000) to three cigars. This probably put a dampener on Mr Craig's aspirations of being a Cup owner, but he accepted the bet.

Unfortunately, Mr Craig never saw how his horse would perform, because prior to the running of the Melbourne Cup, he took ill and died from pneumonia. The possibility of jockeys wearing black armbands, and Nimblefoot still taking his place in the Cup, might have left Jeremiah Slack thinking about the hotelier's dream, and that maybe the dream was a prophecy. With that, he laid bets to win himself £15,000 ($30,000).

History tells us that Nimblefoot did win the 1870 Melbourne Cup by the narrowest of margins, and that his jockey John Day did wear a black armband. After the race, there might have been two things that went through Jeremiah's mind:

- Even though Walter Craig was dead, should he honour the bet and pay Craig's widow the £1000?
- Should he hold on to the £1000 and forget about the wager?

But then his thoughts may have turned to Walter Craig waiting for him outside the Pearly Gates with arms wide open, welcoming him inside. There was no way the honourable bookmaker Mr Jeremiah Slack was going to test himself in that way, because he duly paid Walter Craig's widow the £1000.

Here are some very interesting facts about Craig's Hotel in Ballarat, Victoria:

- Walter Craig purchased Bath's Hotel in 1857, and renamed it Craig's Hotel.
- The CSS *Shenandoah*, described as an American Confederate cruiser, visited the city of Melbourne in 1865. The *Shenandoah*'s mission was to enlist recruits for the Confederate army, and one of their functions was held in the main dining room of Craig's Hotel in Ballarat.
- In 1867, Prince Alfred, Queen Victoria's second son, visited Ballarat, and roomed in quarters specially prepared at Craig's Hotel.
- In 1867, one of Australia's most noted poets and horseman, Adam Lindsay Gordon, entered into an arrangement with

William Craig to conduct the stables at the hotel. In Gordon's poem *The Banker's Dream*, he makes reference to 'Craig's pony'.

- In 1881, Prince Albert Victor and his younger brother Prince George were guests at Craig's Hotel.
- In 1908, Dame Nellie Melba, Australia's noted opera singer, performed from the balcony of the hotel's Reading Room.
- Other famous guests in the early 1900s included the Duke of Windsor, Lord Kitchener, and the Duke and Duchess of York, who later became King George V and Queen Mary.

However, our story does not end there. Back in October 1895, an American gentleman of note was on a world speaking tour and stayed at Craig's Hotel. He was then invited as guest of honour to attend the running of the famous Melbourne Cup. Was he disappointed in what he saw? He later penned the following about his visit, which appeared in all the nation's newspapers of the day: *'Nowhere in this world have I encountered a festival of people that has such a magnificent appeal to the whole nation – the Cup astonishes me.'*

That person who witnessed Auraria's 1895 Melbourne Cup win was none other than Mark Twain.

Skinny Thomas

... and his very lucky seven

The year 1929 proved to be a calamitous one. The unimaginable and unthinkable happened when the stock market on Wall Street, New York, the home of the United States' financial empire, crashed. In history it will always be known as 'Black Tuesday'. It was also the year that Nightmarch won the Melbourne Cup.

Probably more important in the memory of north Queensland's Thomas family, Skinny Thomas rode the card at the Townsville racecourse at Cluden Park, a lucky seven out of seven for this unheralded jockey.

The eldest of six sons and one daughter, William 'Skinny' Thomas was born in 1898 at Charters Towers, a mining town in central Queensland. His parents were William Edwin and Florence Thomas.

Back then, the only means of transport were either by 'shanks' pony' (walking), a train or horse. As a horseman, Skinny Thomas showed a lot of natural ability. One day, at the age of 27, Skinny's life changed forever when he struck up a conversation with the local horse trainer, Tom Salmon. He was asked if he was prepared to ride in a race against professional jockeys. Skinny accepted and would you believe it, he won on his very first ride.

It was the start of a thirteen-year career, and one day he would repay Tom Salmon in a very generous way.

On 29 June 1929, Skinny made his way to the racecourse at Townsville where he had a full book of seven rides, and on that day, William 'Skinny' Thomas rode himself into the record books by riding the full card on the program. He became the first jockey in the history of Australian racing to ride seven out of seven winners. His winners were Own King, Kingsman, Constant Boy, Greengold, Pageacre, Northern King and Night Flame.

On his very last race ride before hanging up his saddle, Skinny was legged up on a horse owned by Tom Salmon, the man who had given him his start in the racing industry. As fortune had it, he won that final race for his former master.

Skinny's record was held for more than 43 years, until Geoff Prouse rode all seven winners on the program at Elwick in Tasmania on 22 January 1972. They were joined at the top by J Kinninmont on 18 June 1983, when he also won on all seven races on the program at Laverton in Western Australia.

William 'Skinny' Thomas became the first ever to achieve this rare distinction, and although he has since been joined by two more great horsemen, the record has never been beaten. Well done, William 'Skinny' Thomas; he holds a special place in the history of thoroughbred racing in Australia.

Magic Millions

... a special piece of history

In January and February 2010, two $1 million Magic Millions races were held in the Southern Hemisphere, with the Gold Coast Magic Millions in Queensland, Australia, and the Karaka Magic Millions at Ellerslie in New Zealand. Both races were for two-year-old graduates of the Magic Millions sales.

Here are some very interesting statistics from those two races in 2010:

- Both race winners were fillies.
- Both fillies were bred in their respective countries.
- Both fillies were trained in Queensland, Australia.
- Both fillies were sired by General Nediym.
- Military Rose was trained on the Gold Coast by Gillian Heinrich and won the Gold Coast Magic Millions.
- Sister Havana was trained in Brisbane by Liam Birchley, and won the Karaka Magic Millions in New Zealand.
- Both fillies were ridden by the late Brisbane jockey Stathi Katsidas.

General Nediym was king for the day when he won the 1997 Gold Coast Magic Millions. He will also be remembered as being 'king of the kids' (two-year-olds) in Magic Millions races in Australasia. His last crop raced in the 2011/12 season. While he did not have a winner or placegetter in Australia, Warhorse did him proud by running third in the 2012 New Zealand Magic Millions. It seemed quite ironic that General Nediym passed away in January 2009, the month that his progeny tasted their great success. Here are his winners and placegetters, with Warhorse being the only colt:

1st: 2003 Regimental Gal (Gold Coast)
1st: 2010 Military Rose (Gold Coast)
1st: 2010 Sister Havana (New Zealand)
2nd: 2009 Paprika (Gold Coast)
2nd: 2011 Combat Kitty (Gold Coast)
3rd: 2012 Warhorse (New Zealand)

At the end of the 2011/2012 racing season, General Nediym was the only winner in the 24-year history of the $1 million Magic Millions races to have won and to have sired a winner, let alone three. His record may stand for quite a few years.

A real five-star general.

The Craiglea invasion

... a world record and an outstanding contribution to the racing industry!

Stan and Marilyn Johnson run the very successful Craiglea Stud on Queensland's Sunshine Coast, just north of Brisbane. It is not unusual to see their horses week after week competing at many metropolitan and provincial race meetings throughout the state. They own and race a huge number of horses that are easily identified, as their names all begin with the prefix 'Craiglea'.

The Rockhampton race program on 29 December 2009 had eleven Craiglea horses nominated for eight races, with one race having six Craiglea horses out of the eight starters. Was this a world record, having a race with so many horses' names beginning with the same word? And was it going to be a race caller's greatest nightmare? Well, we never knew the outcome of the race because the meeting was abandoned due to wet weather and an unsafe track.

Two weeks later on 15 January 2010, eleven Craiglea horses were nominated for a race meeting at Mackay. After the scratching of one horse in race four, a field of eight starters remained, with seven Craigleas to do battle. They were Craiglea Rawie, Craiglea Gal, Craiglea Smokie, Craiglea Edge, Craiglea Matilda, Craiglea Tina and Craiglea Royale. All horses had the same coloured silks, with the colour of the jockeys' skull caps the only thing to differentiate them in running. Race caller Tony McMahon probably thought, 'Why me, what have I done to deserve this?' Was he was about to go down in history with one of the great race calls of his life, in one of the most tongue-tied attempts to try to call seven Craiglea horses by their correct name, their correct position in running and the correct finishing order? He had every right prior to the running of the race to think to himself that if he got the first four right as they crossed the line, then he wouldn't give a 'Craiglea' about the rest of the field.

Those of us who had the honour of listening to that historic event no doubt marvelled at the fantastic job the race caller did in applying his craft. Tony McMahon called the horses superbly in running, and incredibly called them in correct finishing order, 1-2-3-4-5-6-7. Craiglea Royale won, with the odd one out, Willy Nic, running last.

Take a bow, sir, for what is surely a world first in race calling.

The Craiglea Show didn't stop there; it only got better. Here are some other interesting statistics:

- 29 January 2010, Mackay: five Craiglea horses faced the starter in race 3. Four of the five finished 1-2-3-4, to give the stable their second 'first 4' in two weeks, with the winner being Craiglea Edge.
- 6 July 2010, Mackay: In a field of nine, another four Craiglea horses faced the starter and finished 1-2-3-4, giving them their third 'first 4' for the year, with the winner being Craiglea Tina.
- 18 January 2011, Toowoomba: The invasion kept rolling along. At the twilight meeting, and having his 109th start, ten-year-old Craiglea Warrior lived up to his name by running second and taking his earnings to a very respectable $300,150. He was definitely their leader of the pack.
- 25 January 2011, Townsville: Ten Craiglea horses faced the starter in three races, for one second and one third.
- 10 February 2011, Mackay: Nine Craiglea horses faced the starter in four races for one win.
- 15 February 2011, Townsville: The Craiglea invaders hit the jackpot once again. They had six starters for the day in the one race. Once again, the course broadcaster applied his craft by correctly calling the place-getters, with Craiglea Romeo leading the procession home to finish 1-2-3-4-5-7, giving the stable their fourth 'first 4', and first for the new year.
- 2 December 2011, Rockhampton: Six horses faced the starter in race 1. However, just before they jumped, the siren sounded to signal a late scratching. A piece of history was in the making. All

five horses left in the race were owned by Craiglea Stud, all five were trained by Peter Fleming, and once again all five had their name beginning with the prefix 'Craiglea'. As they crossed the finishing line, there was a three-way photo, with the eventual winner being Craiglea Mandy. Yes, a nice result: 1-2-3-4-5, and another 'first 4' – or should we say 'first 5'. Once again, the race broadcaster deserved a bouquet for another precise race call.

Here are some interesting facts about the Craiglea organisation:

- As at 31 December 2011, there have been a staggering 192 horses with the prefix 'Craiglea' registered in Australia ... incredible.
- In the 24 months from 1 January 2010 to 31 December 2011, there were a total of 465 'Craiglea' horses to race at registered TAB meetings in Queensland. That equates to just over nineteen horses a month.
- In December 2010, 29 'Craiglea' horses faced the starter at registered TAB meetings in Queensland ... now that is really supporting the racing industry.

Has any other racing stable worldwide raced a number of horses with the same prefix in their name? One doesn't think so!

All those associated with the Craiglea Stud racing team are doing a great job supporting the Queensland racing industry. Who knows, maybe one day Stan and Marilyn Johnson might receive a gong in the Queen's Birthday Honours list. It certainly would not be out of place, and nor would a race called 'The Craiglea Handicap', open to all Craiglea horses who have finished behind a Craiglea winner. No doubt there would be dozens of nominations.

What's in a name? ... Craiglea, obviously.

Hoofnote: In January 2012, the stud set a world record when 33 Craiglea-named horses faced the starter. Pretty good considering there were only 31 days in the month.

Our mighty Bernborough

... we never saw how good he really was

Right next door to the Jondaryan Shire Council chambers in Oakey, a little town on the Darling Downs in south-east Queensland, stands a life-size statue of one of Australia's most famous post-war champion race horses. There is a plaque at the base of the statue that reads:

> Bernborough
> This statue was sponsored by the Oakey Chamber of Commerce with the help of the Citizens of the Darling Downs to commemorate Queensland's Greatest Racehorse.
> Opened by Hon. M Hodges MLA 29th October 1977.

Keith Noud, Queensland's great race caller, who fully understood the limited opportunities given to Bernborough, recalls his great wins in the Doomben 10,000 and, just one week later, the Doomben Cup in 1946. Recalling that these were two of the greatest wins he had ever seen on a racetrack, he unashamedly shed a tear when Bernborough's number came up on the on-course semaphore.

The strangest part about this great horse was that the racing officials did not allow him to race outside of Toowoomba until he was a six-year-old. While we cannot criticise them for their actions, all we can do is lay out the facts so you can be the judge.

Controversy surrounding Bernborough and the Queensland Turf Club (QTC) started very early. Record books show that Bernborough, foaled in 1939, was by the sire Emborough from the dam Bern Maid. However, it was stated by a well-respected local stud owner that the day Bern Maid was served, the sire Emborough was nowhere in sight. In those early days we did not have the luxury of blood typing or DNA, so in very rare circumstances what was on the official pedigree paperwork did not necessarily match reality.

If the offspring were successful, then the documented sire (whether an ordinary or good performer) would have his stud fees increased based on the offspring's success. Therefore, if we consider that the paperwork states a non-performing sire and a good dam, but in reality it was a good sire and a good dam, then the offspring's success would put the spotlight on the non-performing sire and his fees would increase markedly. A genuine false favourite, if you know what we mean.

There must have been a few other rumours making the rounds about this young colt, because after he was sold to Frank and John Bach for 150 guineas (just over $300), the QTC would not accept any nomination from the Bachs. Pre-empting the official edict, the Bachs onsold Bernborough to a Mr A Hawden.

However, the QTC did not believe that transaction was legitimate either, stating that they believed the Bachs were working in collusion with Mr Hawden, and with that, the QTC kept the ban on Bernborough racing outside Toowoomba. You can just imagine the handicapper's task in awarding such a good horse the right weight, as he won race after race. Finally, his record in Toowoomba was nineteen starts for eleven wins and he remained there in isolation until he was a six-year-old.

Enough was enough for the owners of Bernborough, so they finally relented and sold him. He was bought by Sydney restaurant owner Azzalin Romano, who in turn offered the horse to Harry Plant to train. One can only imagine that the original owners thought that as a six-year-old, his best racing was behind him, but now he was given his greatest opportunity.

His first run in Sydney saw him running on well down the outside to finish fourth, and his placing was put down to an inexcusable jockey error so this unlucky individual was sacked from any future riding engagements on Bernborough. Athol Mulley was then appointed as his jockey and he won his next three runs in Sydney. He was then sent to run in Melbourne to contest the 1946 Futurity Stakes, and with a staggering weight of 10 stone 2 pounds (64.5 kilograms), he easily beat the star-studded field by five lengths. Next on the agenda was the Newmarket Handicap, and in a field of 28 runners, carrying 9 stone 13 pounds (63 kilograms), he was the first one home. Bernborough returned to Sydney and continued on his winning way with the Rawson Stakes, Chipping Norton Stakes and the All Aged Stakes. That made a total of five Group 1 races in a row.

Stop for a minute and consider the following. It is suggested that most horses reach their full potential as a four- and five-year-old, and by the time they reach the grand old age of six, most would have already experienced their performance peak. Here Bernborough was a six-year-old winning five Group 1 races in a row against the best in the land. How good was he?

His next mission was to go to sunny Brisbane and contest the Doomben 10,000 and the Doomben Cup, just one week apart. He was given a hefty 10 stone 5 lb (65.5 kg) to carry in the 10,000 in what was considered a very smart field. In typical Bernborough fashion, he came from last in a field of 27 and swamped them in the straight to win, going away in a course record time.

The win was considered so significant by the handicapper that his weight for the Doomben Cup was adjusted up by a further 6 lb (3 kg), making the weight he had to carry in this classic a staggering 10 stone 11 lb (68.5 kg). The Doomben Cup was a tactically run race and Bernborough was put in a pocket with no way out. Having full confidence in his mount, Athol Mulley simply went out the back door, so to speak. Going back to the tail of the field, Mulley pulled him wide, and Bernborough came down the outside at what seemed to be a million miles an hour to win running away.

He had everything against him, a pocket and 68.5 kg, but he had everything going for him, his unbelievable talent and a great jockey. Hardened racegoers that day couldn't believe their eyes and one and all knew they had just witnessed something only a champion could do.

Returning to Sydney, he followed up with wins in the Warwick Stakes, the Chelmsford Stakes and the Hill Stakes. Next in his planned assault were the Caulfield Cup and the Melbourne Cup. The handicappers didn't miss him, allotting 10 stone 10 lb (68 kg) in the Caulfield Cup and 10 stone 9 lb (67.5 kg) in the Melbourne Cup. The connections were not happy with Athol Mulley's fifth place in the Caulfield Cup, stating that he did not ride to instructions, so Athol was sacked and a new jockey Billy Briscoe was appointed for the rest of the campaign. Up until his fifth placing in the Caulfield Cup, he had won fifteen races in a row. His next lead-up run was the Mackinnon Stakes and tragically, during the running of the Stakes, he fractured his sesamoid bone.

After recuperating from this injury, Bernborough was sent to the United States for stud duties to stand at Spendthrift Farm in Kentucky, where he finally died in 1960. He produced two very good horses in Berseem, Champion USA Sprinter of the Year, and Bernwood, who held the 1-mile (1600 metres) world record of 1.33.8 for a period of time. While his progeny fell far short of his championship status, he was ultra-consistent and produced winners of more than 950 races in the United States. His personal record stood at 37 starts for 26 wins and two placings. We always wonder about how good Bernborough was, considering he never got his real opportunities until he was six years old.

After Bernborough recovered from his sesamoid injury and was sent to the United States, the question was often asked: why didn't he stand at stud in Australia? Remember, he was exiled to race in Toowoomba up until he was a six-year-old because of the dark cloud hanging over his pedigree right from the start. It can only be assumed that the governing body in Australia still held the belief that this was still a very contentious issue and therefore they could not guarantee his pedigree and any subsequent registration of offspring in Australia. American authorities had no issue in accepting him and his stated pedigree into United States' breeding barns.

Bernborough's name does not appear too many times in the history of the Australian breeding industry. However, the imported Danzig stallion Langhfur, who stood for quite a few years in Australia, carried the Bernborough bloodline through his dam Sweet Briar Too. The Australian sire Biscawong is believed to be the only successful stallion to carry the Bernborough cross, and his most important victory was the 1979 Group 3 Shorts Handicap.

Born in 1975, Biscawong was by Biscay out of the imported mare, Gay Wendy, whose sire Hook Money was a son of the mighty Bernborough. Of his 276 progeny to race, he produced very few Black Type winners, the best being the 1985 Group 1 AJC Sires Produce Stakes winner Wonga Prince, and Our Horizon, which won the 1990 Group 2 Coca-Cola Classic and the Group 3 Skyline Stakes.

I think the officials got it right – don't you?

Lou Robertson – not again!

... the story of the could-be Cups King

Lou Robertson was born in New Zealand in 1874, and started his trade in the sport of harness racing. Moving to Australia in the early 1900s, he was granted a trainer's licence by the Victoria Racing Club in 1908. In a remarkable career, he was to win many of Melbourne's top racing trophies. Nicknamed by the press of the day as 'Oyster', he certainly knew how to get a horse ready for all the rich pickings. One of his earliest successes was Wingarara in the 1912 Grand National Hurdle at Flemington. In 1914, he won the Adelaide Cup with Hamburg Belle.

Listed are some major wins, including his multiple race wins. These have now been converted to their Black Type status.

- one VRC Melbourne Cup (Group 1)
- three VRC Derbies (Group 1)
- three VRC Oaks Stakes (Group 1)
- three VRC Newmarket Handicaps (Group 1)
- two VATC Caulfield Cups (Group 1)
- three VATC Oakleigh Plates (Group 1)
- five VATC Futurity Stakes (Group 1)
- two VATC Toorak Handicaps (Group 1)
- six VATC Williamstown Cups (Group 2) (now the Sandown Classic)
- five VRC Sires Produce Stakes (Group 2)
- five VRC St Leger Stakes (Listed)

As of 2011, Bart Cummings had trained twelve Melbourne Cup and seven Caulfield Cup winners, while back in the late 1880s, the great Etienne de Mestre had trained five Melbourne Cup winners.

One must feel sorry for Lou Robertson, because listed here are his training feats in our two greatest races, which could prompt the question: 'What if?'

VRC Melbourne Cup	VATC Caulfield Cup
1st: 1935 – Marabou	1st: 1915 – Lavendo
2nd: 1926 – Naos	1st: 1949 – Lincoln
2nd: 1928 – Strephon	2nd: 1930 – Soulton
2nd: 1942 – Phocion	2nd: 1934 – Farndale
2nd: 1943 – Counsel	2nd: 1944 – Lawrence
2nd: 1946 – On Target	3rd: 1927 – Son O'Mine
3rd: 1928 – Gothic	3rd: 1935 – Marabou
3rd: 1945 – Leonard	3rd: 1943 – Simmering
3rd: 1950 – Morse Code	

Seventeen horses won and placed in both the Melbourne and Caulfield cups. What an enviable but frustrating record for Lou Robertson.

Lou Robertson passed away in 1955 aged 81, always adamant that the best horse to pass through his hands was the brilliant import Gothic, who won the equivalent of seven Group 1 races.

New Zealand's loss, Australia's gain.

The sting

... gentlemen, it's payback time!

After Phar Lap's great win in the 1932 Agua Caliente Handicap, and the subsequent disbelief at his death some weeks later, the American public was asking if there were any more 'Wonders from Down Under'.

The Australian public were still incensed at the claims that the Yanks had murdered Phar Lap: 'They couldn't beat him, they had to kill him,' were some of the newspaper headlines. Maybe it was time for someone to get even with the Americans, by relieving them of some precious dollars.

In 1933, Australia had a pretty fair galloper in the shape of Winooka, a champion sprinter/miler who was raced by bookmakers Joe Matthews and Bill McDonald. Winooka had a very impressive string of victories in 1933, which included the VATC Futurity Stakes, the VRC Leonard Stakes, the AJC All Aged Stakes and the AJC Doncaster Handicap, run in Australian record time of 1.35.7 for the 1 mile (1600 metres). When one of Australia's biggest punters and two punting owner/bookmakers got together, something was brewing.

Back in the early 1930s, Australia had many renowned big-time punters, such as Eric Connolly, Andy Kerr and, of course, the one and only Rufe Naylor. Like all the big punters of that era, Naylor always had his ear and nose to the ground, and could sniff out any means possible to make a few extra quid. The story goes that Rufe Naylor convinced owner/bookmakers Joe Matthews and Bill McDonald that a horse of Winooka's ability may reap some very rich pickings in the United States if promoted the right way, via the power of the press. The idea was to get the Americans to promote a series of match races, one on one, with the winner receiving a handsome purse and the loser picking up some nice appearance money.

All concerned in Australia knew how good Winooka was, but they also needed a back-up plan. The idea was to take along a travelling companion for the champion, and the horse selected was Trevallion, who was quite a good performer and could handle himself in pretty good company. Trainer Mick Polson, a master conditioner of horses, was put in charge of getting both horses ready for their assault on the United States' best on offer.

As Winooka was the key to the promotion, nothing was mentioned about Trevallion, otherwise known as 'Plan B', just in case things went arse-up with the Wonder from Down Under.

The involvement of Rufe Naylor, one Australia's biggest punters of the 1920s and 1930s, in the promotion made it clear that there was an angle and that America should beware!

On arrival in the United States, the Aussie contingent was in awe of the huge crowds, photographers and press. They were all there to see the Wonder from Down Under and one could only imagine what was going on in the minds of Naylor, Mathews and McDonald. Undoubtedly American dollars!

The incredible turnout soon had the press clamouring for anything about Winooka, and it wasn't long before Rufe Naylor made his move. Before anyone could say 'Jack Robinson', America's best turf horse, Equipoise, was mentioned as the Aussie galloper's first opponent in a match race. However, this match race never eventuated and Winooka needed some early wins to bring him to his top. Two races in California and Seattle against some moderate opposition ended up being easy wins for the Aussie invader, with only the prize money being the target. It was too early for our punters to show their hand.

At his third start, the Aussie champ was set to race against a small field of horses on a track that he was not accustomed to. With heavy, relentless rain, it wasn't long before the dirt track became an absolute bog. Winooka was beaten well and truly out of sight. The news headlines might well have read 'The Blunder from Down Under'. Once back on dry tracks, he won at his next two starts. Unfortunately, at his following three starts, he encountered sleet, freezing temperatures and wet tracks, and ran according to his American wet track form. With that, it was up with the 'no go in the slow' sign.

Naylor, Mathews and McDonald had done their homework. Now was the time to bring in Plan B, the little-known Trevallion.

On the training track, Winooka was always a brilliant track galloper, unlike his travelling companion Trevallion. One morning the flying Aussie champ clocked 46 seconds for the 4 furlongs (800 metres), leaving his stable mate well and truly in his wake. However, being beaten by ten lengths still equated to Trevallion running his 4 furlongs in approximately 47.5 seconds. The Yanks weren't interested in the Aussie slow-coach track worker, and let him get under their guard.

Trevallion was entered in a selling plate race, now known as a claiming race. Being entered for the lowest claim, the horse received the lowest weight – right race, small claim, and bottom weight. Mr America was now going to get a lesson in how to set up a good old Aussie sting.

A select band of commissioners was organised, and just before post time, they hit the betting shops all over the United States, just like in the good old SP (see page 219 for a definition) days in Australia. There was no money on course for the horse – not one red cent as all monies were placed off course.

Trevallion bolted in at the very juicy odds of 15/1.

The bookmakers were not one bit happy. They were livid, and

why wouldn't they be? Within a few days, it was revealed that the Aussie sting had cost the bookies around US$300,000. The cry went out that they had been set up and that Winooka was only a front for Trevallion. It became obvious that the Americans had not checked the form of the winner, because he was definitely no slow coach in Australia.

'We were here with Winooka, but he did not show his best on dirt tracks'. Or was it 'We know what you did to Phar Lap, and this is payback'?

The Australian contingent, including Winooka, returned home, leaving Trevallion in the United States. It is believed that some months after his win, Trevallion was set for another claiming race. Unfortunately for Winooka, he never won another race, and was retired immediately after breaking down in the 1935 Doncaster Handicap.

Some years later, it was reported that Rufe Naylor once backed a greyhound in from 20/1 to 6/4. While collecting his winnings, someone commented, 'You'd never think it was the same dog that raced here a couple of weeks ago, Rufe,' to which he replied, 'It wasn't!'

He came, he saw, he conquered

... *Rising Fast – one of a kind!*

Some horses just stick in your mind. As a youngster, I can clearly remember listening to the races on the wireless on a Saturday afternoon with my dad. He hardly ever had a punt on the ponies, but when he did, it was down to the neighbourhood phone box to ring the local SP bookie. It was a little different in those days, with no TAB and no luxury of a home phone.

In the spring of 1954, at the ripe old age of eleven, I became completely fascinated with a horse from New Zealand, who seemed to be winning Saturday after Saturday in Melbourne. Rising Fast, the son of Alonzo, was foaled in 1949, and was purchased at the 1950 New Zealand National Sales for 325 guineas (approximately $700), by a gentleman named Leicester Spring. Rising Fast was a multiple winner in his home country, and was given close to top weight in the 1954 Caulfield and Melbourne Cups. The Australian handicappers were far too wary of the top Kiwi raiders, who year after year came to our shores and took our top prize money home.

Typical of all the great New Zealand stayers, he was a tough, seasoned five-year-old gelding when he made the sea voyage across the ditch to Australia. There was no such thing as flying thoroughbreds from country to country in those days; it was all by sea. The plan was to race the horse over here for a couple of months, pick up a little prize money, then get back on the boat and home to New Zealand. If he didn't do too badly, he would come back in 1955.

What an eventful trip it turned out to be, because at the 1954 Spring Carnival in Melbourne, Rising Fast won an incredible six Group 1 races, one Group 2, one Group 3, and one Listed race. In 1954, Rising Fast became the only horse in racing history to win the Melbourne Cup, the Caulfield Cup and the WS Cox Plate in the one season. He also won the Group 1 LKS Mackinnon Stakes on the Saturday prior to the Melbourne Cup. All this was in a two-and-a-half-week period. He carried top weight of 9 stone 5 lb (59.5 kg) in the Cup; it wasn't until 1969 that Rain Lover, in his second Melbourne Cup victory, carried more weight with 9 stone 7 lb (60.5 kg).

This great horse visited our shores in 1954, 1955 and 1956, and competed exclusively at our Spring Racing Carnival in Melbourne, apart from one stint at the Brisbane Winter Carnival.

In Group 1, 2 and 3 and Listed races at the Australian Spring Carnival over a three-year period, this wonderful racehorse had sixteen wins, eight seconds and one third. At his third attempt in the 1956 Melbourne Cup, Rising Fast was given top weight of 10 stone 2 lb (64.5 kg), and under that huge weight ran a very creditable fifth behind Evening Peal. During his career, he was trained by Ivan Tucker and later in Australia by Fred Hoysted, and was ridden in Australia by Bill Williamson and Jack Purtell. Rising Fast, bought as a yearling for 325 guineas ($700), had a total of 68 starts for 24 wins, 16.5 seconds and two thirds, for total prize money of £66,765 ($133,530), a king's ransom in the mid 1950s. Today's equivalent prize money value for his Australian victories alone equates to approximately $13 million.

In the 1955 Melbourne Cup, well into the straight, there was quite a bit of interference by the eventual winner Toparoa, ridden by Neville Sellwood. Rising Fast was jostled off stride at the 200-metre mark and subsequently ran second, with most believing that this interference cost him the race. The crowd fully expected his rider Bill Williamson to protest, but he didn't. After a stewards' inquiry, Toparoa's rider Neville Sellwood was suspended for two months.

Why was there no protest?

The owner, Leicester Spring, philosophically stated that it was a racing incident and the protest would not be lodged – a true gentleman of the day.

When Rising Fast retired, he was so popular with the Melbourne crowds that the Moonee Valley Racing Club honoured this great champion in a very unusual way. To the cheering of the crowd, and with a garland of roses around his neck, he strode up the straight as the band played a very fitting tune: 'The Maori Farewell'.

Rising Fast was inducted into the New Zealand Racing Hall of Fame and was bestowed the same honour into the Australian Racing Hall of Fame in 2002.

Rising Fast: he came, he saw, he conquered.

Bill Waterhouse versus the Babe

... no, not the pig in the movie!

Big Bill Waterhouse was always quoted as saying that having a duel with a big punter was like a duel to the death. Only one man could win and walk away. He said his strength lay in the fact that he never suffered from nerves and would try to get inside the head of a punter who was willing to challenge him.

Having never suffered from nerves, one would wonder whether the 100 cigarettes a day, every race day, had some sort of calming affect on him. He said that he only smoked heavily on race days; all other days he would only smoke around 80 cigarettes a day! Good to see that you could really cut back when you wanted to, Bill.

Bill took on the biggest there was at the time, in Frank Duval (The Hong Kong Tiger), Felipe Ysmael (often called The Babe and sometimes called The Filipino Fireball), Eddie 'The Fireman' Birchley, Peter Hunter (Huxley), Kerry Packer, Ray Hopkins, Freddie Angles, Harry Slamen (The Black Prince), Johnny Diamond, and not forgetting the enigmatic 'Hollywood' George Edser. At the end of the day, he came out with more than he went in with.

Here is the story about a duel he had with Felipe 'The Babe' Ysmael and the dire consequences that unfolded for one of them.

In an interview after publishing the book on his life, Bill was asked who was the biggest punter that bet with him, and what was the biggest bet that person ever had. He said that in the sixties, at the very height of the presence of these colourful characters, it was the stuff of nightmares when these leviathan punters walked onto the course towards the average bookie. Bill always held his nerve and that left him as the biggest satchel swinger in the world at that time. The largest bet he ever took from one man was from Felipe Ysmael, for $1 million. The horse won and he had no hesitation in paying up. Bill said he just went back to his hotel room and got on with things. 'The horse was a short-priced favourite and Filipe took about $500,000 out of my pocket, but you cannot alter an outcome like that.'

Bill says that he considered all these encounters as a 'duel to the death'. With two combatants facing each other, there is only one outcome; one will break the other. He always remembered Eric Connolly's words: 'Money lost, nothing lost; courage lost, everything lost'.

'On the day, you have to get inside their head and one day I did that to Felipe "The Babe" Ysmael, the Filipino Industrialist and friend of Ferdinand Marcos.'

On Melbourne Cup day, 1967, Bill had done his homework and in his opinion, Red Handed would beat the 4/1 equal favourite General Command. One of the things that Bill would also do was do the form on the bigger punters. Knowing that Red Handed was a favourite of Felipe's, he had that feeling that he would appear in the betting ring that day. He was ready for another duel. All of a sudden, Bill saw Babe out of the corner of his eye coming straight to his stand and he knew what was about to happen. He was ready for the bet from his adversary.

There are life-changing moments, and you have to back your judgement, take the courage of your convictions and see it through. Bill looked him straight in the eye and went for the knob beside Red Handed. This was a two-way street, and Felipe had done his homework too. With his confidence in his ability to back his judgement, he was riding high as well. Felipe thought that because Bill had spotted him, he knew which way he was going to bet, and that was to shorten the odds on Red Handed. However, in a surprise move, Bill turned to the board and lengthened the price of Red Handed from 4/1 out to 9/2.

He was offering better odds on Red Handed and you could see that 'The Babe' was starting to wonder why. 'What does Bill know that I don't know?' Bill knew he would be suspicious, and Felipe threw his judgement out the window! He did not break stride but walked up to Bill and placed $250,000 on General Command. Those last few strides that Felipe took before he placed his bet was the breaking point in this fascinating duel.

History books will show that Red Handed, ridden by Roy Higgins and trained by Bart Cummings, went on to win the Cup, with General Command coming in a disappointing sixth. That encounter had a tremendous effect on 'The Babe' and it signalled the end of his duels with Big Bill Waterhouse. On a downhill slide after that encounter, it was considered that this outcome wrecked his thinking, and especially his confidence.

Life went on for both men, but when Felipe 'The Babe' Ysmael died, he was penniless. Remember those haunting words from the great Eric Connolly: money lost, nothing lost; courage lost, everything lost. Bill just got inside Felipe's head, turned a few screws, and came out with both guns smouldering. A duel to the death!

Great work, Bill!

Claire Lindop

. . . a historic first for the ladies

To be the first at anything is a very special and unique achievement. It means that you have worked very hard at your craft and never given up in the face of adversity. Are you, or have you ever been, the first to do anything special, except beating your brothers and sisters around the backyard?

This young lady certainly believed in the saying 'The harder I work, the luckier I get'; she has earned her title as Australia's first lady jockey of the turf. Claire Lindop's first ride in a race was in May 1996, when she rode unplaced Arctic Mittens at Warrnambool. At her 20th ride in a race, Claire experienced her first win on a horse called Opinions Differ. The horse, trained by Jack Barling, won by two and a half lengths.

Claire became the first woman in South Australia to win a Jockey's Premiership, in Adelaide in 2005, when she beat all her rivals to come up with more wins in a given racing year than any other jockey in South Australia. In 2006, in front of a crowd of 30,000 cheering racegoers, she rode the six-year-old Exalted Time to an all the way victory in the then Group 1 Adelaide Cup. This gave Claire the honour of being the first Australian female jockey to win a Group 1 race in Australia.

Saturday 1 November 2008 dawned a beautiful sunny day in Melbourne for the running of the VRC Derby. Claire was riding the roughie Rebel Raider in the Group 1 classic, with all the punters' money going on to the well-deserved favourite Whobegotyou. Her mount was unwanted, even though both Claire and the trainer Leon Macdonald believed the only thing preventing Rebel Raider from being prominent in the race was his barrier draw of 15. During the running, Rebel Raider tracked Whobegotyou from the tail of the field, and when everyone thought that the favourite was home, Rebel Raider accelerated past Whobegotyou to go on and win by two and a half lengths.

Just to add some icing on the cake, Claire's mount started at the fairytale odds of around 50/1 – and thus Claire Lindop became the first Australian female jockey that sunny Saturday afternoon to win the Group 1 Victoria Derby in its 154-year history.

The fairytale dream of jockeys is to achieve a ride in the Melbourne Cup. It was a very special day for Claire on that first Tuesday in November in 2003. She was the first Australian female jockey to ride in our Melbourne Cup. As Claire was introduced to the crowd that day along with the other competing jockeys, the loudest and longest applause was for her – maybe it was her parents and their cheer squad in the stand, but whoever it was, it was well deserved for this 49 kg braveheart.

She was riding Debben, a horse with no form but with owners who just wanted the experience of having their horse run in the great race. Maybe it was the fact that Claire was making history that day, but the punters got behind her and backed Debben from 200/1 to 100/1. Unfortunately, he finished nineteenth behind Makybe Diva, but for Claire and others, that didn't matter. Simply to be in the race was a victory in itself, although she hastened to add that what she did that day, she did for herself, the owners and the stable. There was no thought of the feminist movement – just a jockey doing what she did best!

However, the best was still to come, the 'pièce de résistance' of her riding career. At Morphetville Racecourse on 8 October 2011, Claire Lindop landed the perfect punch to ride her 1000th winner and officially became the first Australian female jockey, and the first female jockey in the Southern Hemisphere, to do so. And the horse to give her 1000 winners said it all: its name was Perfect Punch.

Beverley Buckingham

... when the going gets tough, the tough get going!

We read many stories about people and how they rise out of the deepest, darkest calamitous events, never giving up when it all looks just too hard. This Captain Courageous confounded the experts. If the specialists said, 'You can't do this', then Bev Buckingham in her inimitable manner would say, 'Just watch me' – and she did!

Her story began in 1965 when she was born in Norfolk, England, the very year the Beatles released their movie *Help!*, and the year that saw a literary giant of the future, J K Rowling of *Harry Potter* fame, come into the world. It was a year that we lost a great fighter in the cause of freedom in Winston Churchill, but also reminded us of the lighter side of life with the passing of Stan Laurel of Laurel and Hardy comic fame. It was a year that shaped our future and showed us that some people are just destined to be what and who they are.

Bev's parents, Joan and Ted Buckingham, decided to try for a better life in a new country and emigrated to Tasmania, Australia, in 1967 when Bev was only two years old. Soon after the family's arrival, Ted started to train horses, so it was no coincidence that little Beverley would grow up with a natural affinity with the great thoroughbred. It wasn't long before she found herself doing chores around the stable complex, which then progressed to riding lessons and competing in pony club events.

The life of a jockey is not a glamorous one. There are the early mornings, every morning, looking after the horses, mucking out the stables, grooming the horses, and this goes on all day and even into the early evening. After the horses have finished their afternoon pick, some feed before retiring for the night, then the routine starts all over again early next morning. There is no rest, as the horses do not have time off for public holidays, Christmas, Easter – it is a difficult life and one that must give you great joy in order to continue for many years as good stable hands and jockeys do.

All Bev wanted to be was a jockey, and at the age of fourteen she was apprenticed to her father. This was the beginning of many new challenges. One has to understand that women at that time were unable to compete against male jockeys. They could work beside them and do all of the chores that a male did in a horse stable environment but they were not allowed to race against them. Were the men frightened that the fairer sex would show them up?

In the 1970s, the Lady Jockey's Association of Australia pushed for changes to be made. Fifteen races were set aside per season on the Victorian country racetracks, where female jockeys could contest on an even footing with their male counterparts. Serious lobbying continued and by 1979, women were granted permission to race as regular jockeys anywhere and everywhere in Tasmania.

In the early 1980s, Bev and her good friend Kim Dixon became part of racing history. They were among the first female jockeys to compete professionally against male riders.

It did not take Bev long to lead her first winner into the winner's stall. It happened at just her fourth ride in a race at Elwick in 1980. At the end of her first racing season she had ridden 22 winners, placing her ninth in the jockey's premiership. In the following season, at the tender age of seventeen, Beverley Buckingham became the first female jockey in the world to win a State Jockey's Premiership, booting home 63 winners to greet the judge.

By 1998, she had achieved many things that had been unthinkable a few years earlier. She had seen victory in the Devonport Cup, the Launceston Cup, the Queen's Cup, and the Hobart Cup on three occasions in 1986, 1996 and 1998. By winning the Queen's Cup, Bev received a somewhat special gift: a personal letter from Queen Elizabeth II, congratulating her for being the first female jockey in the world to win a race named in Her Majesty's honour.

Then came the fight of her life. In May 1998, Beverley was involved in a horrific race fall that threatened her very existence. You can only imagine the injuries that you can suffer when you fall from a horse in a race. You have the danger of injury caused by the hooves of the horses behind you. You also have to consider the weight and size of a horse, which is normally around 500 kg, compared with a jockey weighing about 50 kg. It is certainly a deadly combination.

Bev Buckingham fractured two vertebrae in her neck and specialists told her that she would not walk again, let alone ride her beloved horses. While lying in a hospital bed, unable to move, she must have found the time to go over in her mind her very significant achievements. That may have been the spark needed to keep the embers burning within her soul. She just needed one spark, any spark, to get her going again.

This courageous fighter just had to get up and go again, and so began a long road of rehabilitation. After spending months in a hospital, she returned to the family's property at Brigadoon, in Tasmania, to prove everyone wrong. Just imagine being told by specialist doctors that you would never walk again. That was their field of expertise, but they did not count on Bev's courage, determination and supportive family. After many weeks, she confounded them all. It wasn't a walk as we know it, but it was what Beverley called 'going for a walk'.

There was no stopping her now!

Just to have her last say on the whole life-changing event, Beverley Buckingham gave birth to a baby daughter, Tara, in 2000. She is now fulfilling her lifelong ambition in joining her dad as a racehorse trainer at Sienna Lodge.

Following is a list of some of Bev's remarkable achievements:

- Between 1980 and 1998 she rode 906 winners.
- In 1983 she won the apprentice's title and was ranked fourth overall on the jockey's table.
- In 1985 she won her first major cup, the Devonport Cup, on Exdirectory.
- In 1986 she won the Hobart Cup on Dark Intruder.
- In 1986 she won the Queen's Cup, receiving a personal letter from the Queen for doing so.
- In 1987 she won the Launceston Cup on Brave Trespasser.
- In 1987 she was the first woman to ride in the Caulfield Cup when she rode Brave Trespasser.
- She broke the 100 win barrier for the 1995/1996 season, riding 109 winners for the season and setting a new state record.
- In 1996 she won the Hobart Cup on Jam City.
- In the 1996/1997 season she won her third Tasmanian Premiership, with 64 winners.
- In 1998 she won the Hobart Cup on L'Espoin.
- In 2005, Beverley Buckingham was inducted into the inaugural Tasmanian Racing Hall of Fame.

Congratulations, Beverley, what a mighty effort!

Hoofnote: It was confirmed with the authors by Tasmanian racing journalist Greg Mansfield in October 2011 that Bev's 906 victories is correct, not 1000 as reported on many websites.

Winners or losers
... you be the judge

It is reasonable to assume that when you embark on horse ownership, you want a couple of wins, and a placing now and then to help pay the feed bill. There are some horses that we would regard as being unlucky not to get a win, while we have also seen champions who always find a way to greet the judge. Some say it's luck, some say that few horses have a will to win, and others say it is just chance in sorting out all of the things that can and do go wrong in the course of a race.

These are the unlucky stories of Leica Lover, Sometime, Tauto and Igloo.

Bart Cummings trained a very handy galloper in Leica Lover back in the 1970s, and if you were one of the owners (fortunately or unfortunately) who watched him go around in every race, you would have considered yourself very unlucky. He raced against the best of his era, and listed here are some of the placings that he so gloriously filled:

- AJC Derby: 2nd 1973
- Victoria Derby: 2nd 1973
- Western Australian Derby: 2nd 1973
- Canterbury Stakes: 2nd 1975
- Warwick Stakes: 2nd 1975
- Metropolitan Handicap: 3rd 1975
- Al Aged Stakes: 3rd 1976
- Chipping Norton Stakes: 2nd 1976
- Queen Elizabeth Stakes: 3rd 1976
- Doncaster Handicap: 2nd 1976
- Caulfield Cup: 2nd 1975

At the risk of repeating oneself, have a look at the record of the LJ Paterson-trained horse Sometime. He won a Caulfield Cup (1963) among some of his good wins, and was placed in the following:

- Caulfield Guineas: 2nd 1961
- Adelaide Cup: 2nd 1962, 2nd 1963

- Memsie Stakes: 2nd 1963
- Underwood Stakes: 2nd 1963
- WS Cox Plate: 3rd 1962
- Mackinnon Stakes: 2nd 1963

Let's not stop here; how about Tauto. Even though he won many good races, including a WS Cox Plate (1971), how different it could have been if he had done better than being placed in the following:

- Linlithglow Stakes: 2nd 1972, 2nd 1973
- William Reid Stakes: 3rd 1973, 2nd 1974
- Doncaster Handicap: 2nd 1971
- Newmarket Handicap: 2nd 1970, 3rd 1971, 2nd 1974
- Futurity Stakes: 2nd 1973, 3rd 1974
- Craven 'A' Stakes: 2nd 1970
- Lightning Stakes: 2nd 1971, 2nd 1972
- George Adams Handicap: 2nd 1971
- Goodwood Handicap: 2nd 1970

Just to round off this little quartet, how about Igloo. This magnificent horse was plagued throughout his short career by severe leg problems, always just falling short of championship status. In 1971, he had placings in the following races in a matter of weeks:

- Caulfield Cup (2nd)
- WS Cox Plate (2nd)
- CB Fisher Plate (3rd)
- Melbourne Cup (2nd)

How good could he have been if he had had four sound legs?

Edward Birchley – The Fireman!

… *the bookies' friend* – not

Stories of the big punter tackling the big bookmaker are those that touch and encourage the bravehearts of the punting fraternity. We somehow look upon these blokes as our mentors, and we look up to and respect them almost to a point of religious fervour. We just love to see the bookie hanging his head after a bad day; after all, he has been ripping us off for years and years. Just the thought that someone has come onto the scene who knows more than the bookies gives us that right to continue our journey in finding the truth or the trick on the form pages every Saturday morning, week after week, year after year. After all, they must know something that we don't, and they must have discovered the secret that allows them to continue to live that fabulous lifestyle we all envisage the professional punter enjoys.

Sorry to burst your bubble, but the truth is far from that perception.

Eddie Birchley spent seventeen years in the fire brigade, hence the nickname 'The Fireman'. Fire services don't pay enough to put aside a substantial cunning kick, and these big punters are very private men with humble beginnings. The road to success is a quiet one, but they know that the road could soon turn to a downhill run.

Up until a few years ago, Eddie, well into his 70s, lived on the Gold Coast and swam upwards of 5 kilometres every day. He spent a lot of time with the late Des Renford, the English Channel swimmer, and in his heyday he followed a strict fitness regime and swam 20 kilometres a day. However, in the late 1990s, he said, 'I was doing my normal marathon ocean swim when I was struck by a government survey boat, where I broke all of my ribs, and it left me with head and neck injuries. The propeller narrowly missed my head, otherwise I would have been a goner.'

As in all professions, there is a lot to learn if you're going to be successful, and Eddie applied himself in every aspect of the roles he played. If you are going to be the best at something, you have to meticulously do your homework on that subject, and if a gamble is involved, you have to be able to minimise your liabilities and risk to maximise your return. Eddie had thirteen professional fights as a boxer, winning them all. One of his boxing stable fighters journeyed south to fight the legendary fighter Tommy Burns, and came up trumps. Eddie found that you could win big money in boxing in those days, and with his mate beating Tommy Burns, he got 7/1.

He then used his knowledge in greyhound racing, and met with more success. A couple of dogs were very good to him; one was Archie's Wonder, the 1973/1974 Greyhound of the Year, and another was Top Simbi. He backed Top Simbi six starts in a row, with $50,000 on each of his starts; Top Simbi won those six races in a row, at the average price of around 2/1 on.

Up to this point, one of Eddie's biggest bets in harness racing was on the New Zealand champion Noodlum, which was a very short-priced favourite to win the 1975 Queensland Derby at Albion Park. He wagered $68,000 on him, and although Noodlum lost the start by at least 100 metres, so good was this pacer that he still managed to beat them home. If you wondered where the connections got the name of Noodlum from, New Zealand's prime minister at the time was a colourful politician by the name of 'Piggy' Muldoon, and if you arrange the letters of his surname from last to first, you come up with Noodlum.

Eddie's biggest ever punt on the gallopers was in Melbourne. He flew down with over $200,000 in cash tucked away in his suit pockets. You wouldn't even try that today for fear of a mugging or the like, but that day he walked the ring and backed the two-year-old Caboul at even money or less. Caboul brained them, so Eddie then did his lap of honour and collected the cash from his $208,000 wager from all of the bookies except two, as they could not pay up. You can see how much Eddie used to hurt them. On the punt, his average big bet was anywhere between $100,000 and $200,000.

He had a very simple philosophy, and this is where we can all take some advice. His bets were all on short-priced horses or the like, and he wasn't at the races every Saturday because the good bets do not appear week after week. You have to be patient; even if you are off the scene for quite some time, you must remain very patient. He also said, 'I will back a certainty at 2/1 on, 3/1 on or 4/1 on, as long as I know its right price is 100/1 on.'

His dashing presence in the ring was duly reported in the sports pages, but not all of his trips south ended in a pocketful. He said he never got tips, but did his own homework and backed only those that should win. At Rosehill in December 1974, Eddie dropped $105,000 on a two-year-old filly, Danish Dancer. The favourite got rolled. Two weeks later he lost another $130,000 on two of his should-wins. Eddie was finding out the hard way that 'should not be beaten' does not always mean 'could not be beaten'.

He was off the scene for a while, licking his wounds and who knows, maybe quietly building a bank again, and in 1975 on VRC Sires Produce day, into the ring walks Eddie 'The Fireman' Birchley. The crowd was buzzing and the bookies were starting to feel a little queasy. They quickly realised that the hot pot that day was the Bart Cummings–trained Blue Diamond winner, Lord Dudley. Eddie walked the ring and just kept on betting, and betting and betting. The bookies retreated to 10/1 on and realised that they could not wind the price down any further. Some bookies started writing the price on their board in pencil and some had Lord Dudley starting at 15/1 on because they could not, and did not, want to take another hit.

Lord Dudley, with Roy Higgins on board, never gave Eddie any cause for concern; he easily won the race. The Fireman struck a blow that day for every punter who had ever been caned by the bookmakers. The punting public revelled in the excitement as one man with a bucket full of cash and confidence to match tore the Flemington ring apart. They could not remember anyone else having a red hot go the same way Eddie did.

However, even the best of the best have off days that can continue for months and sometimes years. You know the feeling, when you feel pretty cocky but after a period of time Lady Luck just leaves you cold, and sometimes the harder you try to regain a lost fortune, the worse it gets. After a long series of losing bets, Eddie claimed that there was a system whereby signals were sent to the jockeys at the starting barriers by bookmakers to advise which horse Eddie had his money on. He also said that he would lift the lid on those responsible and name names. However, nothing ever came of these allegations.

When you are backing short-priced horses, you need to have a pretty good strike rate, because you have to outlay a substantial amount to win small. In other words, if a horse is 2/1 on, then you would have to wager $100,000 to win $50,000. There is not a lot of fat on the bone and if you had a series of losses, you would be out the back door in a real hurry. After a long series of outs, Eddie retreated from the public eye and led a much more subdued existence on the Gold Coast. Some people know when their time is up and rather than keep on chasing what they have lost, they call it quits. Eddie was wise with his winnings and went back to having a small punt and getting involved in a strict exercise regime – healthy body, healthy mind.

Over the years, Eddie has always said that he could not separate two horses as the best he had ever seen – champions Todman and Tulloch. Todman was a brilliant eight-length winner of the inaugural Golden Slipper Stakes, now the world's richest two-year-old race. Tulloch, on the other hand, could maintain his speed flat out for 1000 metres, when even the best can only sprint 600 metres at their optimum pace. In 1957 Tulloch laid claim to being the world's best racehorse. Eddie also stated that the Goondiwindi Grey, Gunsynd, was only a short head inferior to the two champions of the 1950s.

After some considerable thought about trainers, he said Neville Begg was the best he had ever seen, followed by Deagon trainer Jim Douglas. Jim was one of those horsemen who had the happy knack of getting crocks up and winning again, by swimming the horses at Nudgee Beach near Brisbane.

He had no doubt who the best jockeys were: George Moore and Mick Dittman. One thing he did say was that Mick had a far better disposition than George.

Eddie Birchley's philosophy of picking winners was simple. Do your homework, eliminate all the possible negatives, and be very, very patient. Even then, in The Fireman's own words: 'there is no such thing as a certainty'.

CHAPTER 2

The British Isles

The 'Olde' Toymakers

... and the story of the Flying Rocking Horse!

This story is about an outstanding young racehorse that had only seven starts and won all seven races in his two-year-old season, and whose legacy touched the hearts of many young children for decades after. 'A phenomenon' was one accolade handed down by the United Kingdom's National Horseracing Museum. He was inducted into the British Horseracing Hall of Fame and was named Britain's Two-Year-Old of the 20th Century, an amazing effort for such a young colt.

Who was this so-called equine phenomenon, winning all of his races with incredible ease? He was The Tetrarch, and it all happened in 1913.

A tendon injury ended his two-year-old campaign, and the following spring, the colt reinjured himself in training and never raced again. He died at the ripe old age of 24. However, it was that early period of his life where The Tetrarch really left his mark, or should we say spots. He did not win any awards in the good looks department because of his unusual colouring. Many archive photos show that he was quite a sight, with a grey coat marked with white dapples and a light grey mane and tail. Once the public saw what this incredible young horse could do in his early races, he was quickly dubbed the 'Spotted Wonder'. At stud, his brilliance continued and he became a very successful sire. Many grey horses racing today can trace their lineage back to this equine freak.

His childhood legacy begins after his retirement. Quite a few decades later, British craftsmen were responsible for making a very popular toy for young boys and girls. The toy was a rocking horse, and the most common colour combination was a grey coat, with white dapples and a light-grey mane and tail. Sound familiar?

Yes, The Tetrarch had made such a lasting impression on The Olde Toymakers that the Spotted Wonder also became known as 'The Flying Rocking Horse'.

John Singleton

... and a horse with no name

This is one of the most interesting pieces of trivia about the English Derby.

The 1797 English Derby was won by a horse that did not have a name. He was registered and raced as 'a colt by Fidget'.

John Singleton was the jockey, so what more can one say. A horse with no name ridden by a bloke who probably went by the nickname of 'Singo'. Could he have been a long-lost relative of the modern-day character of the Australian turf?

Eclipse won eighteen out of eighteen

... retired because no-one would race him!

Eclipse, the English Thoroughbred Champion, was born on 1 April 1764 at the Cranbourne Stud during an eclipse of the sun, hence his name. Eclipse was onsold after the death of his breeder for the princely sum of 75 guineas (approximately $160). The new owners were a notorious gambler, Dennis O'Kelly, and a brothel madam, Charlotte Hayes.

A lot of races in the early days would be run over 3 to 4 miles, and it is recorded that during those eighteen victories, he covered just over 63 miles. In other words, he ran an average 3.5 miles per race. Not forgetting that there was no thoroughbred transport in those early days, it is further recorded that he walked over 1400 miles to attend these race meetings all over England.

Eclipse did not start his racing career until he was five years old. He was very temperamental and to top it off, his running style was so unusual, many people just stood and laughed at him – until they saw what he did to the opposition. He won his next eighteen races straight, but it is how he won them that caused his owners to 'retire' him from racing early in his career.

Now here is the clincher. Eclipse was retired because it got to a stage where no bets were being laid on any of the other competing horses that raced against him. It was common knowledge that he never really worked up a sweat in any of his races, and he won each race by a staggering 100 to 200 yards. He was never whipped, spurred or urged forward – he just loped along and did everything easily. If we roughly calculate the length of a racehorse, we are saying that each race was won by a minimum of 50 to 100 lengths almost at a canter.

Eclipse went on to be a very successful and prolific sire of champions, and was responsible for nearly 400 winners. The Royal Veterinary College has determined that nearly 80 per cent of all modern thoroughbred racehorses have Eclipse in their pedigree. Not bad for a very average-looking horse that used to run with his head low to the ground, just like the world champ Kincsem. Unbelievable!

In 2011, a team of scientists from the Royal Veterinary College and Cambridge University gathered to do a DNA study of Eclipse, the stallion described as the greatest horse of all time. Unbeaten in his career, which lasted for only two years, 1769 and 1770, he was retired largely due to lack of competition.

Eclipse is only one of several champions of the turf who will have their DNA investigated. His whole skeleton and remains have been preserved by a museum. From previous examinations, his skeleton has already revealed that he was an unremarkable horse in stature, with average confirmation, normal leg bones, and standing only 15.2 hands high. The DNA test may show what made him an outstanding individual. Only time will tell.

Arkle

... they changed the rules to try and beat him!

He was a famous Irish thoroughbred, foaled in 1957 and dying in 1970. He was probably the greatest steeplechaser of all time. Arkle dominated this type of racing, so much so that they changed the rule book to try to bring him back to the field.

People have a misconception about steeplechasing, so here is a dictionary definition of the term:

> It is a horse race over a course equipped with obstacles to be jumped. For example, brush hedges, artificial hedges, ditches, water jumps etc.

Arkle was a gelding born in Ireland at Ballymacoll Stud, and went on to contest 35 races in his career for 27 wins, two seconds and three thirds. In his very first victory over jumps, there was a hint of his ability because he won by a breathtaking 20 lengths.

Here are some of his major wins:

- Cheltenham Gold Cup: 1964, 1965, 1966
- King George VI Chase: 1965
- Irish Grand National: 1964
- Hennessy Gold Cup: 1964, 1965
- Leopardstown Chase: 1964, 1965, 1966
- Whitbread Gold Cup: 1965
- Gallagher Gold Cup: 1965
- Punchestown Gold Cup: 1963
- Powers Gold Cup: 1963

His Timeform rating was a staggering 212, the highest ever given to a steeplechaser. How do we arrive at Timeform? It is achieved by a horse running against other horses using a scale of weight for distance beaten, over various race distances. In Imperial terms, the range can be 3 lb a length over 5 furlongs, 2 lb a length over one and a quarter miles, and 1 lb a length over 2 miles.

Arkle was ridden throughout his career by Pat Taafe and they are acknowledged as one of the greatest horse and rider combinations of all time to ever clear a steeplechase fence. What this equine athlete and brilliant jumper did was nothing short of amazing. Taafe's contribution to Arkle's success cannot be underestimated. They dominated National Hunt racing in the 1960s, and to this day when racing achievements are debated, there is only one winner: the team of Arkle and Pat Taafe.

Everything about this champion was special, including his way of jumping the fences. Whether it was taught, a habit, or just for style and comfort, he always crossed his front legs when jumping over an obstacle. Arkle went through his peak season of 1965/1966 unbeaten and would start favourite in all of his races. Even his price at 10/1 on was never any fancy odds and he would have no trouble winning by 20 lengths or so, such was his dominance.

The racing authorities in Ireland took unprecedented steps in the Irish Grand National to allow the allocation of a two weight system – one for Arkle and one for the rest of the field. Arkle won the 1964 race by a length, but he carried two and a half stone more than his rivals because of the new weight system devised by the authorities – to put that in perspective, it was an incredible 16 kg penalty, and that still didn't stop him.

The races he contested ranged from 2800 metres up to 5800 metres. He won the 1964 Irish Grand National carrying 65.5 kg and the 1964 and 1965 Hennessy Gold Cup carrying a staggering 69 kg in both races. In the 1965 Gallagher Gold Cup he conceded 7.5 kg to the other jumping champion Mill House, and broke the course record by a massive seventeen seconds.

In December 1966, Arkle was competing in the King George VI Chase at Kempton Park when he struck a guard rail, which resulted in a fractured pedal bone – he still completed the race and finished second, such were his championship qualities. After retirement, he was ridden as a hack by his owner, but unfortunately he died, which was brought about by advanced arthritis at the age when some jumpers are still competing – thirteen years.

At home in Ireland he was regarded as a true legend, and legends always have their own peculiar tales to enhance their reputation.

They say that he inherited super powers by imbibing in a couple of glasses of Guinness every day. We suspect that some humans would attest to that theory as well. Mail would be delivered to his 'retirement' home, simply addressed to 'Himself, Ireland' – and the letters always found their way.

Good on you, Arkle, one out of the box!

The Blue Riband event

... the difference in naming the Derby was a toss of a coin!

In England: 'They're away and running in the English Derby!'
In the United States: 'Annnnnnd awaaaaay theyyyy gooooo in the Kentucky Derby!'
In Ireland: 'They've jumped in the Irish Derby!'
In Australia: 'They're off and running in the VRC Derby!'

Only four countries, all with the same ending to that first sentence of the race broadcast ... 'Derby'. This classic Blue Riband event is for three-year-olds, and is recognised as the epitome of their racing career.

Many countries have their own equivalent of the time-honoured race, and some countries like the United States and Australia have multiple runnings of the Derby in different states. The Epsom Derby in England and the Irish Derby are run over approximately 12 furlongs (2400 metres), the Kentucky Derby in the United States over 10 furlongs (2000 metres), and the VRC Derby in Australia over 2500 metres, considered to be the longest Derby in the world.

First run in 1780, the Derby Stakes is now internationally known as the Epsom Derby or the English Derby. The Derby originated after the inaugural running of the Oaks Stakes in 1779, but history books tell us that it was nearly called something else. After the running of the Oaks that afternoon, a party was hosted by the 12th Earl of Derby, with the guest of honour being Sir Charles Bunbury. Amid the friendly banter that day, a suggestion was made that a coin be tossed between the Earl and Sir Charles, with the winner having the honour of a new Classic race named after him, to be run the following year.

It would appear that Sir Charles Bunbury, the Steward of the Jockey Club at the time, won the coin toss. However, being the guest of the Earl, he probably thought it honourable that he should politely offer back to the Earl the prize of naming the new classic race. With that, the Derby was born.

At the very first running of the 1780 Derby Stakes, the winner was Diomed, with the owner being none other than the gracious Sir Charles Bunbury. Unfortunately, it took seven years before the Earl of Derby won the coveted Derby Stakes in 1787 with his colt, Sir Peter Teazle.

But what if?

What if at that coin toss, Sir Charles had not been as gracious as he was portrayed, and had accepted the prize of naming in his honour that new Classic race scheduled to be run in 1780? Today, we just might be listening to the running of the English Bunbury, the Kentucky Bunbury, the Irish Bunbury and the VRC Bunbury. It just doesn't roll off the tongue, does it!

It seems we all owe a large vote of thanks to Sir Charles Bunbury for being a true gentleman way back in 1779.

Desert Orchid

... the white knight of steeplechasers

There is something very special about greys. I can remember my very first trip to the races as a youngster, and still clearly recall the lovely grey horse that took my eye. I can't remember whether he won or not but I can tell you his name was Tarwyn Blue, and from that day on I believed that greys were special and that they were born to win.

We had the great Gunsynd and of course the flying Schillaci, but the story that grabbed my eye most was about a steeplechaser on the other side of the world. He epitomised everything that you wanted in a horse and he just happened to be a white, ghostly grey that was consistent, courageous, determined, and never, ever gave up.

Foaled in 1979 at Goadby, Leicester, England; Desert Orchard, or Dessie as he was known to his thousands of followers, was by the sire Grey Mirage, with the grandsire being Double-U-Jay. His breeder was James Burridge and the owners were James, Midge and Richard Burridge, and Simon Bullimore. Trained throughout his career by David Elsworth of Wiltshire, Desert Orchard's record showed he had 70 starts for 34 wins, eleven seconds and eight thirds. He finished his racing career with total prize money of £654,066.

In 1983, his first race start proved to be a nightmare for the connections. It was a Novice Hurdle at Kempton Park and he fell at the last hurdle. It looked as though his career was over before it began as it took ages for Dessie to get to his feet, with everyone thinking the worst.

In the 1984/85 season he won just one race from eight starts, and in the last three runs over hurdles he was pulled up in both the Cheltenham Champion Hurdle and the Welsh Champion Hurdle, and finally he fell at Ascot. With that, the connections decided to try him as a steeplechaser, with amazing results. The rest is history. Desert Orchard had found his niche. After chalking up a series of four wins in a row at Sandown and then two at Ascot, the tongues were wagging about the big, bold white frontrunner. When you see photos of him at the jumps, he looks very special and you start to understand why he captured everyone's attention.

Returning to the scene of his first run and first fall, Desert Orchard took on the best in the 1986 King George VI Chase at Kempton Park, easily beating a star-studded field by fifteen lengths. His price that day reflected the company he was in because he started at 16/1, as most thought that the 3 miles (4800 metres) would be too much for a frontrunner. Not only did he show everyone that he could stay that day, but the spectators witnessed some of the most spectacular leaps ever seen from a steeplechaser. Dessie jumped his rivals into the ground.

As a nine-year-old he was about to tackle the Cheltenham Gold Cup, the one grand race that had eluded him. To win a Cup of this magnitude is one thing, to be trained to the minute for the opportunity is another, and considering the class of the opposition you then have to make sure that everything goes right on the day, especially being a steeplechaser.

Dessie showed an absolute dislike for a few things in his career.

First, he favoured the right-handed course, but the Cup is run over a left-handed course. Second, he detested the rain and heavy going, and third, he hated snowy conditions. As luck, or lack of luck, would have it, Desert Orchid struck the jackpot that day. It was a left-handed course, the rain and snow were falling relentlessly, the going was very heavy and of course he was a frontrunner. Toughest of all, the course distance was a very trying 3 miles and 2 furlongs (5.23 kilometres).

A crowd of over 58,000 people that day saw the Grey Ghost overhaul the mudlark Yahoo in the final stages of the race, and go on and win by one and a half lengths. Surrounded by thousands of fans, three cheers were called for as Desert Orchid was unsaddled.

A friend of ours, Peter Deacon, was there that day and witnessed the run. He told me, 'I really have never known a horse so brave. You could see that he just hated every step that he took in the going, but typically, he dug deep like all great champions do and would not hear of defeat – he was my hero and my favourite race of all time.'

The Cheltenham Gold Cup that year was rated by the readers of the *Racing Post* as the best horse race ever. He continued on with this form and at the age of ten years, he won the Irish Grand National at Fairyhouse carrying a staggering 12 stone (76.2 kg), winning by twelve lengths.

In his last season, and last start at Wincanton, Desert Orchid did a Don Bradman on us by being beaten in a race that is now named after him. After finishing third in the Peterborough Chase at Huntington Racecourse, he lined up in his final race, the 1991 King George at Kempton Park. Unfortunately he fell, but his legacy to jumps races lives on.

Desert Orchid's major wins were as follows:

- Tolworth Hurdle: 1984
- Kingwell Hurdle: 1984
- Hurst Park Novices' Chase: 1985
- King George VI Chase: 1986, 1988, 1989, 1990
- Gainsborough Chase: 1987, 1989, 1991
- Martell Cup: 1988
- Whitbread Gold Cup: 1988

- Tingle Creek Chase: 1988
- Victor Chandler Chase: 1989
- Cheltenham Gold Cup: 1989
- Racing Post Chase: 1990
- Irish Grand National: 1990

This racing legend died on 13 November 2006, and it was up to his former trainer to announce it to the world. Dessie died peacefully in his stable on that Monday; there was no trauma and he left this world in a dignified manner – it was time to go. His co-owner Midge Burridge said that the passing of this great horse would be felt deeply by fans all over the world.

Desert Orchid's ashes were buried in a private ceremony at Kempton Park near his statue, just a week prior to the running of the King George VI Chase.

What a horse!

Isinglass

... the lucky break that comes your way just once

This story has its beginnings back in the late 1880s in Great Britain, and it makes you wonder how often success and riches can miss us by a matter of a few seconds or just a few metres.

The mare Dead Lock, purchased for nineteen guineas by a Captain Mitchell, was sent to the stallion Isonomy. The resulting colt from this union was named Islington; he was foaled in 1888 and his dam, Dead Lock, was sold before he ever raced.

Islington started to show promise in his early starts on the racetrack, and as a consequence, the good captain started to regret selling the mare. He made several inquiries about Dead Lock's whereabouts, but the trail went cold when he discovered that she had been sold on a number of occasions. With that he stopped looking, and then the strangest thing happened.

Captain Mitchell carried on with his daily duties, often despairing about the whereabouts of the good mare Dead Lock, then one day he advertised Marvellous, his cart stallion, for sale. When a prospective buyer came to his yard to inspect the stallion, Captain Mitchell could not believe his eyes. Recognising the mare pulling the visitor's cart as the missing Dead Lock, he hastily did a deal with the stranger, who then left with the cart stallion. Captain Mitchell resumed ownership of his long lost mare Dead Lock.

Being very eager now that he had his mare back, he quickly arranged another union with the stallion Isonomy and in 1892, another colt was the result. He named this one Isinglass. It came as no surprise that the colt Isinglass had just as much talent as Islington, and showed just as much promise on the racetrack. From twelve starts over a couple of seasons, Isinglass won eleven and came second in the other. He became the Triple Crown Winner in 1893. His other race wins were as follows:

- 2000 Guineas, Newmarket
- The Derby, Epsom
- St Ledger, Doncaster
- Eclipse Stakes, Sandown
- Ascot Gold Cup, Ascot
- Jockey Club Stakes
- Princess of Wales's Stakes
- Newmarket Stakes

Isinglass became the only horse in history ever to win the Triple Crown, the Ascot Gold Cup and the Eclipse Stakes. His performance in races was characterised by his exceptional speed with his never-ending reserves of energy, doing only what was necessary to win a race. In the early 1890s, his prize money from his starts totalled an amazing £57,455.

Some things are just meant to happen!

The mighty Shergar

... the murder of a champion

It is inconceivable how humans can be cruel to animals, and it is inconceivable how humans can kill an animal for no other reason than to support a political ideal. There is no honour in a den of thieves and murderers.

This is the story of the great Shergar – a horse with untapped ability, and probably one of the most freakish animals ever to grace a racecourse.

Ireland is world renowned for its rich rolling stud land, and County Kildaire is no exception. This future champion was bred there by his owner Prince Karim Aga Khan IV. Aga (Agha) is a Turkish military title meaning 'noble' or 'lord', while Khan means 'commanding chief'. It therefore comes as no surprise that this precocious bay colt with the distinctive white blaze down his noble head had that look of noble courage and defiance right from his first steps.

Born in 1978 from a union of the sire Great Nephew and the talented dam in Sharmeen, his foray into the racing world was in 1981, when he had eight starts yielding six wins and one second. Envisage the great horses in the world of thoroughbred racing and imagine whether any of them have ever performed something like the following in the best company in the hot bed of international racing:

- Guardian Classic Trial, 1981: won by ten lengths
- Chester Vase, 1981: won by twelve lengths
- Epsom Derby, 1981: won by ten lengths
- Irish Derby, 1981: won by four lengths 'at a canter', according to the race caller!
- King George VI and Queen Elizabeth Stakes, 1981: won by four lengths

In 1981, Shergar was named European Horse of the Year.

The respected racing correspondent, Richard Baerlein, after watching the colt win his debut race by ten lengths, famously advised racegoers that at 8/1, Shergar was a challenge for men to act like men and back him in the Derby. In the Derby, he started odds-on favourite, and was ridden by nineteen-year-old jockey Walter Swinburn, whose recollections are as clear today as what they were in 1981. 'Just after the start, Shergar settled down to his own pace, as the leaders took off at at a million miles an hour. I put my hands down on his withers and let him travel at his own speed.'

Shergar pulled his way to the front early and went further ahead, so far in fact that John Matthias on the runner-up Glint of Gold thought he had won the race. 'I said to myself that I had just realised my life's ambition, then to my astonishment, I realised that there was another horse on the horizon.'

After the Epsom Derby, his next race was the Irish Derby, where he was ridden by Lester Piggott. The apparent ease with which Shergar beat the opposition in this race, winning by four lengths, caused racing commentator Peter O'Sullivan to exclaim that in his opinion, Shergar was out for an exercise gallop and was never extended. Shergar immediately became a national hero in Ireland.

His six wins in 1981 amounted to over £220,000 in prize money. Uppermost in the Aga Khan's thoughts was what he could do for the racing industry worldwide, so he made a very difficult decision to unselfishly send the great champion to stud that very same year, in October 1981. Everyone expected that he would be sent to a stud in America but the Aga Khan had other ideas – the great champion came home to commence his stud duties. Shergar was sent to Newbridge in Ireland, not far from where he was born.

A syndicate had been created for many more to enjoy the future stud performance of this wonderful animal. There were essentially 35 owners, with the Aga Khan keeping six shares – so in essence, there were 40 invested units at £250,000 per unit. This was a huge investment by any standards and his initial stud fee per serve ranged between £50,000 and £80,000.

It was after the first Shergar foal hit the ground that the most heinous and dastardly events unfolded. On 8 February 1983, the following events took place. At 8.30pm, a Ford Granada towing an empty horse box pulled off the main road to Dublin and into the Newbridge stud yard. At 8.40pm, armed gunmen knocked on the door of James Fitzgerald's home at the stud and three men dressed in Irish police uniforms entered the house and threatened James' family. James Fitzgerald, Shergar's stud groom, was escorted out to the stud building. Fitzgerald was then forced at gunpoint to aid in the loading of Shergar into the horse float. He later reported to investigators that there were six armed men involved.

Shergar was towed away. James Fitzgerald was forced into another vehicle and driven around blindfolded for three hours. He was then thrown from the car only a few miles from the stud. Before being thrown out, he was given a password, 'King Neptune', which would be used to authenticate the negotiations by the kidnappers. He was then told that he was dealing with the IRA.

The timing of the abduction seemed to be a piece of clever planning as well, because on this particular day, the largest registered horse sale was being held in the area, so there were horse floats on the move at all hours going in every direction.

What happened next was a case of inept reporting and police bungling. When Fitzgerald recovered from being thrown from the car, he called the stud farm first, probably to advise his family that he was okay. The farm in turn called Shergar's vet, who then called a racing associate; then that person called an Irish politician, and after eight long hours, the police were finally advised. One wonders why the stud farm never contacted the police immediately upon getting the call from Fitzgerald.

The abductors set about seeking a ransom and initially asked that they negotiate with a couple of racing journalists. Everyone involved in the investigation was advised, and so at 1.15am journalist Derek Thompson received a call from one of the thieves. Everyone had hope now that the process had started, with the police fully involved at every level. However, when officials asked about the trace on the telephone call to Derek Thompson, they were advised that all was in place but the officer who does the tracing goes off duty at midnight. It was 1.15am and so by this time, the officer in charge of phone traces was tucked up in bed.

The initial ransom demanded by the IRA was £2 million. The 35 owners agreed that they would negotiate with the kidnappers, but would not pay any ransom as this would just open the floodgates around the world for other copycats. The second demand went from £2 million down to £1000 per share, discounted after they found there were 40 shares, equalling £40,000 – a long way short of the

£2 million they had originally demanded. Obviously maths was not a strong point with this bunch!

Four days after Shergar was kidnapped, the thieves made their last call. The owners then issued a statement saying that it had been confirmed that it was the work of the IRA.

The next solid piece of information about the kidnapping came from an IRA supergrass who penned the book *Informer*. He stated that the money was going to be used to buy arms for their continued battle against their invaders – the British. He also stated that Kevin Mallon, a senior IRA official, was the ringleader. It was further reported that on 12 February, four days after Shergar was seized, the thieves felt it impossible to move the horse or free the animal from where it was being held, because of the heavy police surveillance on Kevin Mallon. The good Irish men and women were also on the lookout for the perpetrators. Worst of all, the kidnappers did not feel safe moving around, and with that Mallon sent two gunmen to dispose of the animal. The great Shergar was machine-gunned to death by two criminals representing Mallon and the IRA.

The informant said that the area was covered in blood. At the time of the attack, the brave and precocious Shergar stood his ground. With steely eyes and the courage of a lion, he took the best that they could throw at him. He did not fall, he did not slip to the floor in his own blood; he just looked his murderers in the eye and slowly sank to the floor. In terrible pain and in these shocking circumstances, this noble steed would not die quickly. The mighty Shergar was making a last stand.

A pit was allegedly dug somewhere in Ballinmore, County Leitrim, in an area that is also called Yellow River, and the remains of the great horse laid to rest.

In researching this story, I was able to speak to some of the wonderful Irish community, and I must say that they are beautiful people who live life to the full. Over a beer one day, a certain Paddy was quite outspoken and, I suppose, eloquent when we got talking about the death of the mighty Shergar. He told me the following, making his feelings crystal clear: 'He was our [the Irish] pride and joy, he was the common man's champion, he was the mighty Shergar, and the bloody IRA kidnapped him and the rotten bastards murdered him!'

When I asked Paddy how old he was and how he knew so much he just replied, 'I am a Paddy through and through and I am not too old to remember, because I was born at a very early age, in fact they tell me that I was fortunate enough to be born on my birthday.'

Punter's paradise

... backed from 280/1 to 8/1 and the horse wins!

The average punters turn up day after day and trust their judgement and the integrity of others involved with their bet, in the hope of getting a run for their money on their choice in the race. It is an attitude for the greater good of the industry, and if everyone would take that attitude, the officials wouldn't have to investigate anything that looks a little out of the ordinary.

Wherever there is money, unfortunately there will always be those after the fast and easy dollar to keep the establishment on its toes. Following is a story about one such incidence that attracted the attention of all and sundry in officialdom, but could just simply have been a betting plunge the news of which spread like wildfire. You be the judge.

It was August 2004 at the Nottingham Racecourse in England, where a maiden galloper by the name of Exponential was about

BEFORE AND AFTER A LOSING DAY AT THE RACES!

to have his second start in a race. Six weeks previously he had his very first start and finished last by seventeen lengths. Now, that does not give punters a whole lot of confidence. The runners in his second race were made up of quite an ordinary lot. The fields were published on the weekend, as this race meeting at Nottingham was down for a Monday. Exponential's price, after his inglorious start six weeks before, was an unbelievable 280/1. Well, that was until all betting shops opened for business on Monday morning; then they were hit.

His 280/1 price was snatched up until the price settled down to 100/1. This continued all though the morning and up until race time, when Exponential eventually started at 8/1. The bookies' alarms were going off big time! The race was off and running and was watched as closely as any football final. The payout was large, and some officials were trying to look for anything untoward in the race that would affect the outcome, considering the weight of money for one of the starters.

As it turned out, the race was run in a fair and normal manner and the winner by half a length was Exponential. His run was such a vast improvement on his first start that questions were being asked if it was the same horse. You never know ...

Weight's right and bets paid.

There were some extremely happy people, and on the other side of the ledger, some very sick bookmakers. An announcement was made immediately that the governing body of racing in the region would scrutinise Exponential's form reversal because of the way and the volume that the money was wagered, and they were suspicious that it could have been a very well organised attack on the betting shops. Rapid improvements in form are far from unknown in racing, after scandals involving the tipping by senior jockeys. The authorities were keen to be seen to be doing something regarding dramatic victories.

The Betting House of Ladbrokes said that it had taken a number of reasonable-sized bets to win at 100/1, and Coral Betting said it had several bets of £200 each way at the same odds. William Hill put its losses at £100,000. These were the only shops willing to offer up their losses, and it was estimated that Exponential's win that day cost the bookies in excess of £500,000.

Trainer Stuart Williams was called before the investigation and was able to satisfy all by saying that the horse had benefited greatly from its first run, and was able to train on and gain in stamina and confidence from its first effort six weeks previously. It must be said that all mandatory doping tests were done after Exponential's victory, and all came back clear. The ruling racing body played down suggestions that the situation was the result of a sting but, more likely, some people close to the horse, knowing of its improvement, had the confidence to have a decent bet. Along with that, the bets filtered down to the man on the street like wildfire, and we all know how that works.

The betting gods that day must have all been in alignment because on the surface, and there is no reason to disbelieve it, this was one punt that came off for everyone. After all, he only won by a half-length and that is not a lot for a certainty at any price.

Feeling jealous!

Red Rum

... the horse that made the Grand National his own!

Red Rum was foaled on 3 May 1965, his sire being Quorum and his dam Mared, and died on 18 October 1995. Born in Ireland and gelded early in his career, he became better known with the last of his trainers, Ginger McCain. There has always been a myth about his name, Red Rum, being 'murder' spelt backwards, but like all good myths, it is debunked; when you combine part of his sire's name and that of his damsire, Magic Red.

Having an incredible 100 starts for 24 wins, fifteen seconds and 23 thirds, his total earnings were £146,410. His record in the Grand National is unsurpassed and looks as though it will remain that way for many years to come, if not forever. He won it in successive years in 1973 and 1974 and again in 1977. Just to highlight his amazing talent, he came second in 1975 and 1976. This from a horse that was sold as a two-year-old in Ireland for a meagre 400 guineas.

History has a way of attaching coincidences to a legend, and in the first flat race Red Rum contested over 5 furlongs (1000 metres), he dead-heated for first. Ironically, the horse he dead-heated with was none other than Curlicue, the companion he was sold with in Ireland.

During his early racing, he was injury prone and consequently went from trainer to trainer. Finally, Liverpool car dealer Ginger McCain purchased him for his client Noel Le Mare and with that, Red Rum was famously trained on the sandy beaches at Southport, Merseyside. It was later discovered that Red Rum suffered from a debilitating incurable bone disease in his foot, and fortunately the sands and the water at Southport were just what the doctor ordered.

In his very first Grand National victory, he beat the Australian chaser Crisp (nicknamed the Black Kangaroo) in a race regarded as one of the greatest in the Grand National's history. After another defining victory the following year, he then came second in 1975 and some say basic jockey error was the difference. He came second again in 1976, but this time the winner Rag Trade was too good and there were no excuses. However, Red Rum did have to carry top weight of 12 stone (76.5 kilograms).

As a twelve-year-old in 1977, Red Rum was again entered in the great race with the record of two wins and two seconds from four starts, and he was already a massive idol of the public. His season by now was mapped out for him, to give him the best chance in the national.

For any great jumper in his prime to win this great race is a feat in itself, but most experts thought that the task was well and truly beyond Red Rum, at the age of twelve, to be attempting to win his third Grand National; many thought that his owner should just call it quits for this legend of the jumps. However, his trainer Ginger McCain knew that his champion chaser was in great shape with the help of the sand and water at Southport, and would give an excellent account of himself, even though he was still carrying top weight of 11 stone 8 lb (73.5 kg).

Rummie (as he was affectionately called by his adoring public) had no problems during the run and ran easily throughout the race, taking up the lead after Beecher, and kept surging ahead, winning the race by a remarkable 25 lengths. Even if he hadn't been before, he was now unquestionably a national hero at twelve years of age.

Red Rum and Ginger McCain went through their training routines exactly the same way in 1978 and 1979, with the intention in both years of running in the race that he had made his own. Unfortunately, just before each event, Rummie injured himself and would never contest the great race again. He led the field out in 1978 and continued to do so until the early 1990s, before passing away in 1995.

The memory of Red Rum is etched into the hearts and minds of many a racegoer in his country and all around the world, and his determination in the face of adversity is what makes his great achievements a piece of history. His statue can be found today at Aintree, where he was laid to rest on this great course in Liverpool with his head facing the winning post.

Red Rum's epitaph reads:

Respect this place,
this hallowed ground,
a legend here,
his rest has found,
his feet would fly,
our spirits soar,
he earned our love for evermore.

Thanks for the memories, Red Rum!

In defence of Lester Keith Piggott

... the greatest jockey in modern racing history

This is a story of comparison. You have the Fabergé egg, Wedgwood plates and the likes of Swarovski crystal as the crème de la crème of fine possessions, but when we talk of the very best of everything racing, our Mount Everest is the enigmatic Lester Piggott. Is he the greatest jockey to have worn the silks in the history of thoroughbred racing?

He was destined to live life in the saddle as his father and grandfather before him were champion horsemen in their own right, proof that the apple never falls far from the tree. Lester's father, Keith Piggott, was a successful National Hunt jockey and trainer who won the Champion Hunt in 1939, then went on to win the Grand National as a trainer in 1963 with Ayala. His grandfather, Ernie Piggott, rode three Grand National Winners in 1912, 1918 and 1919.

Lester was born in 1935 in England; he was popularly known as 'The Long Fellow', and lives in his English manor Florizel, named after another famous thoroughbred. He was considered to be the best of his generation, riding in excess of 5400 winners in 28 countries during his career. During his illustrious career, he was dogged by one bad decision, and unfortunately he is known more for that than his freakish ability.

It will come as no surprise to readers that with the pedigree that he had, Lester Piggott rode his first winner at twelve years of age in 1948. He rode his first Epsom Derby winner, Never Say Die, in 1954 at eighteen and went on to win another eight Derbies over the next 29 years. These winners included the greats such as Sir Ivor, Nijinsky and The Minstrel. He was quoted as saying that Nijinsky was the best horse he had ever ridden. He was known to be a difficult and temperamental animal and did his own thing even in training, where on occasions he would stand flatfooted and refuse to canter.

WHY DO THEY CALL IT THE SPORT OF KINGS PHILIP?

Lester Piggott was quite tall for his profession at 5 feet 8 inches (173 centimetres), hence the nickname of The Long Fellow. At a minimum of 8 stone (51 kg), he would have been slightly restricted in riding down in the weights, so his strike rate of rides to win was very good indeed. His career spanned from 1948 to his retirement from racing in 1995. During his riding career, he rode winners for 42 years (2184 weeks), which works out to be an incredible 2.5 wins per week, every week, over 42 years of racing.

There are not enough pages to list all of his achievements, so here for your enjoyment and perusal is a selection of some of Lester's achievements and highlights:

- nine Derbies
- three Prix de l'Arc de Triomphes
- eleven Championships, 1960, 1964–71 and 1981–82
- 30 Classic victories in England
- 25 century wins per season between 1955 and 1984
- wins in 27 countries outside England
- 465 Group race wins
- eight St Leger wins
- four 2000 Guineas wins
- six Oaks wins

There have been stories written of the rare ability of some individuals to understand a horse with contact, like the great Silent Tom Smith, who was recognised as the person who saw the unhappiness in the great Seabiscuit due to the way he was being handled. He bought that horse for Charles Howard and let him be himself, and the Biscuit went from being a horse that often didn't try his best to being one of the greatest horses in the history of racing in America.

We call these people Horse Whisperers. Lester Piggott was another one who was able to communicate with each horse he rode, so he knew exactly how to react to both good and bad habits of each horse he was riding under race conditions. Sometimes the changes were subtle and other times they appeared quite aggressive, but he knew how to get the very best out of each of them. Piggott could observe a horse finishing back in the field under another jockey's riding, but he would realise what it would take to get a better result from the mount if he ever had the opportunity to ride it. He just had that innate sixth sense where he could see what was required to reverse the form – almost getting into the brain of the animal. His calmness during a race was incredible. Whether riding in the Derby at Epsom or in a much lower class in a cold and windy mid-week race, he wore the same dour expression and there was no wonder he was also referred to as Old Stone Face.

In 1987 he was found guilty of tax irregularities, allegedly to the tune of £3 million. Lester, whose personal wealth at the time was estimated at £20 million, is said to have used different names to channel his earnings into secret bank accounts in the Cayman Islands, Singapore, Switzerland and the Bahamas. The general feeling among the community was that he was being made an example of and that the establishment was going to highlight what could happen to others if they were found not paying their fair share to the Tax Man. Lester Piggott copped a three-year prison sentence with a non-parole period of 12 months. Lester had been awarded an OBE (Order of the British Empire) in 1975, and after the court case and sentence, he was stripped of this award.

Lester served in excess of twelve months, and all of this had a profound effect upon the man. We lost Lester Piggott to racing for a period of five years. He resumed riding in 1990 and won the prestigious Breeders' Cup Mile in the United States, just days after his return. He won his last race in 1994 and the following year, he hung up his stirrups for the very last time.

Having had a huge influence on Mr and Mrs Public over the years, he had a great personal following and they would not hear of anything disrespectful being said about their hero. They simply would not allow this hiccup in his life to taint in any way his amazing talent and the great memories that were etched into their hearts.

Lester Piggott's record stands carved in the annals of racing history and it is easy to see why he is described as the greatest jockey in the history of horse racing. Lester, we salute you!

The Scottish conspiracy

... and how some people pay their way!

It was a peaceful August Bank Holiday in Scotland in 1974 when one of the biggest betting scandals of the area erupted, showing the honest day-to-day punter what people are capable of doing to earn their money.

Gay Future was trained by Anthony Collins, who was based in Scotland and had his steed nominated to run at the village of Cartmel, in Cumbria. Cartmel lies west of Grange-over-Sands near the River Eea, and is the last place on earth you would think that any sting or scandal of any proportion would take place.

There was a type of bet in the United Kingdom where you could couple a bet in a double with another horse. Punters would take the double with horse A to win at one course, and horse B to win at another course, but there was always an out if either horse was scratched. If that ever happened, all of the money would automatically be wagered on the horse left in the original double wager.

Anthony Collins had also entered two other horses besides Gay Future that day, namely Opera Cloak and Ankerwyke, in races at another course. A huge number of small bets were laid, with Gay Future being the first leg to win, and either Opera Cloak or Ankerwyke to win at the other course. The people involved believed that a number of smaller bets would go unnoticed over one large bet. Both Opera Cloak and Ankerwyke were then scratched from their races just before Gay Future's race and according to their rules of betting, their vast number of double bets suddenly became a single bet to win.

But still they had a way to go to keep everything under the radar.

It wasn't wash day, but out came the soap flakes. The flakes were rubbed into certain parts of Gay Future's body and legs, to make it look like he was sweating up very badly. When parading before the race, Gay Future gave the impression that he was having a bad case of the sweats, a sure way of distracting punters away from backing him. Anthony Collins knew it would keep the punters at bay and his price on course remained at a very healthy 10/1.

Gay Future felt no ill effects from the flakes and duly greeted the judge in first place. Thank goodness we have officials who have seen it all before, because immediately after the race, an investigation was held and tests were taken along with betting records on the race. All roads led back to Anthony Collins, Tony Murphy – an Irish building contractor – and the packet of soap flakes. The pair were convicted of conspiracy to defraud bookmakers, heavily fined and warned off racetracks.

The Stewards Investigative Team stated that without the appearance of sweating before the race, Gay Future would have started at much shorter odds, more than likely favourite.

What will you think when you see a horse sweating up now!

Nasrullah

... the Kingmaker

You never quite know what is around the corner in life. In racing it may just be that horse of yours that can pay the bills while you enjoy the ownership. It may be that champion you were fortunate enough to acquire that makes you rich beyond your wildest expectations. For most of us, you just never seem to get that Stakes winner and chase your tail paying the monthly account, always wishing and hoping the answer to your prayers is the next bet – but it never is. Your horse just doesn't seem to pay his way, but you hold your breath because you never know what is around that corner in this racing life.

There are no guarantees in breeding statistics. How many times have you seen those horses in the form guide that read of a top-shelf sire, but they could not run out of sight on a dark night? Not so with Nasrullah, quite rightly named the Kingmaker. Nasrullah was a British thoroughbred racehorse and a sire of champions. He had impeccable breeding, being by Nearco out of the regally bred Mumtaz Begum, thus making him a grandson of the flying grey The Tetrarch. Foaled in 1940 and bred in Ireland by the Aga Khan III, he was owned by Joseph McGrath of Brownstown Stud in County Kildare. During his racing career he was trained by Frank Butters and had a total of ten starts for just five wins, one second and two thirds, for total prize money of £4580. Following are the five wins of his career:

- Great Bradley Stakes
- Coventry Stakes
- Chatteris Stakes
- Caversham Stakes
- Champion Stakes

While these statistics may not fill you with great enthusiasm, he was always a horse that had the potential to pay his way. He was not in an elite group as far as his race record and prize money were concerned, and it seemed to be a mediocre result considering his breeding, as he was a good, but very temperamental, horse. Besides being temperamental, Nasrullah was also known for being lazy and very unpredictable, thus causing his trainer and work riders to have great difficulty motivating him during early-morning track work.

With all his bad traits it was finally decided to ship him off overseas to try his luck in the United States. Claiborne Farm in Paris, Kentucky was selected. This was a natural progression for him and for any entire that didn't light up the racetrack.

The Kingmaker, as he became affectionately known, rewrote the record books and became one of the most influential sires of the modern era. Reviewing the breeding of this great champion, even here in Australia, you find the influence of his line. Here are just a few of his sons: Bald Eagle, Jaipur, Red God, US Hall of Fame horse Bold Ruler, Noor, and of course Nashua. Nasrullah was also the grandsire of Mill Reef, Secretariat and the great filly Ruffian.

Nasrullah received several awards over the years: the United Kingdom Champion two-year-old Colt in 1942, Leading Sire in Great Britain and Ireland in 1951, and Leading Sire in North America in 1955, 1956, 1959, 1960 and 1962.

Nasrullah died on 26 May 1959 and was buried in the Row of Champions at Claiborne Farm.

This Kingmaker lives on!

Rubio

... the winner of the Grand National that fooled them all

The winner of the 1908 Grand National at Aintree was described as a plough horse and a trolley bus horse. The interesting fact is that they were half right in their description, but before Rubio was either of these, he was a very serious racehorse.

Bred in California, USA in 1898, he was sired by La Toquera out of the dam Star Ruby. As a yearling, he was sent to England and sold to James Haggin for 15 guineas. During his early and encouraging years on the racecourse, Rubio broke down so badly that he was sent for a two-year spell. After this long period of inactivity, his owner devised a method of recuperation that he hoped would restore some strength back into his legs. James Higgins offered him to the local transport authorities of Towchester to pull their trolley buses around the cobblestone streets. So began his first unorthodox steps back on the road to recovery.

At the age of ten he was thought to have recovered enough to nominate him for the 1908 Grand National Steeplechase at Aintree. The trolley bus horse from Towchester was not seriously considered in the betting, so it came as a surprise that at the glorious odds of 66/1 and ridden by Henry Bristoe, Rubio went on to beat his well-fancied stable mate in Mattie McGregor.

He returned in 1909 to have another crack at the race, but fell at the water jump and unfortunately aggravated the original serious injury he had suffered all of those years ago, and was immediately retired.

Always read your form!

Grand National trivia at Aintree

... more details on this great institution!

The Grand National is a world-famous national hunt horse race held at Aintree Racecourse, Liverpool, in the UK, and is scheduled to be run each year on a Saturday afternoon in early April. It is a handicap chase run over a distance of 4 miles and 856 yards (7.25 kilometres), during which there are 30 fences to be jumped.

Here are some interesting statistics:

Most successful horse with three wins:

Red Rum, in 1973, 1974 and 1977 (also finishing second in 1975 and 1976)

Leading jockey with five wins:

George Stevens, on Freetrader in 1856, Emblem in 1863, Emblematic in 1864 and The Colonel in 1869 and 1870

Leading trainers with four wins each:

- George Dockeray with Lottery in 1839, Jerry in 1840, Gaylad in 1842 and Miss Mowbray in 1852
- Fred Rimell with ESB in 1956, Nicolaus Silver in 1961, Gay Trip in 1970 and Rag Trade in 1976
- Ginger McCain with Red Rum in 1973, 1974 and 1977, and Amberleigh 2004

Leading owners with three wins each:

- James Machell with Disturbance in 1873, Reugny in 1874 and Regal in 1876
- Noel Le Mare with Red Rum in 1973, 1974 and 1977

Fastest winning time:

8.47.8 – Mr Frisk in 1990

Oldest winning horse:

Peter Simple, aged fifteen, in 1853

Youngest winning horse:

Alibiade in 1865, Regal in 1876, Austerlitz in 1877, Empress in 1880 and Lutteur III in 1909 – all aged five years

Oldest winning jockey:

Dick Saunders, aged 48, in 1982

Youngest winning jockey:
Bruce Hobbs, aged seventeen in 1938

Longest odds winner:
Tipperary Tim in 1928, Gregalach in 1929, Caughoo in 1947, Foinavon in 1967 and Mon Mome in 2009, all of which started at 100/1

Shortest odds winner:
Poethlyn in 1919 at 11/4

Largest field:
66 runners in 1929

Smallest field:
Ten runners in 1883

Most horses to finish:
23 in 1984

Fewest horses to finish:
Two in 1928

Most rides in the race:
Nineteen for Tom Oliver, 1839–59

Most rides without winning:
Fifteen starts for Jeff King, 1964–1980

... and there you have it!

CHAPTER 3
The United States

Ralph Neves the jockey
... dies on Thursday and rides on Friday!

This is a story of one of the great American jockeys of his time, who retired from riding in 1954 after having ridden in excess of 3770 winners. Ralph Neves was no slouch, but he very nearly missed out on enjoying the spoils of his rare racing talent when he died on that fateful day, Thursday 8 May 1936.

Born in 1916, he came of age in the middle of the greatest depression the United States had ever seen. Jobs were very hard to come by, and while general industry was suffering, a popular pastime was emerging that could generate something for the economy and allow the masses to forget their troubled lives for a short time. Horse racing became a popular expression of hope and at the same time created some work for the unskilled and the unemployed. This is where Ralph found his mark, initially as a rodeo rider and then making his way to the jockey's room to learn his craft. Along the way he had found work as a stunt double in the other burgeoning industry, motion pictures. His fiery temper and daredevil riding style soon earned him the nickname that stayed with him throughout his entire career: the Portuguese Pepperpot.

In 1934, at the age of eighteen, he made his way to the track, and this is where his story begins and nearly ends.

It is remarkable to think that within one year of commencing racing, Ralph became one of the leading jockeys on the west coast. We have the Melbourne Cup Carnival here in Australia, which is comprised of a number of meetings over a couple of weeks, and this was also the case at Bay Meadows back in May 1936, where on Thursday the 8th, the second-last day of their carnival, Ralph Neves took the mount on Fannikins. The prize for the most successful jockey of the carnival was US$500, as well as a gold watch to be presented to the winning jockey by none other than the legendary crooner Bing Crosby.

Ralph was running fifth on Fannikins behind a wall of horses. As they rounded the turn, a horse in front of him broke its leg and came crashing down, causing Ralph and his mount to fall. He was catapulted over his horse's neck as Fannikins propped to try and clear the toppling horse in front of him, only to lose its balance and come crashing down on top of Ralph. Officials got to the only jockey left on the ground, the unconscious Ralph Neves, quickly put him into the back of a pick-up truck that had been driven onto the course, and immediately took him to the first aid room. Remember, this is in 1936 and a lot of things that we take for granted at a racecourse today just weren't available in those very tough economic times.

While this story has been embellished over the years, the main facts remain indisputable, evidenced by the film of the race and the actual account as told by Bert Thompson, Ralph Neves' valet at the time. The on-field doctor and staff tried to revive the unconscious jockey, but he was pronounced dead in the first aid room. Imagine the stunned silence in the crowd as the on-course speakers made the shock announcement of Ralph's death, then asked respectfully for a minute's silence, which was acknowledged by all. His body was then transferred to the local hospital and the races resumed, albeit in a very somber mood. Ralph Neves' personal doctor made his way as quickly as he could to the hospital, only to find his patient toe-tagged and wearing the one boot, lying in the hospital's mortuary.

As a final act of desperation, Dr Horace Stevens injected a shot of adrenaline directly into the jockey's heart, knowing what a long shot it would be. Twenty minutes went by, and the story goes that Ralph sat bolt upright in the mortuary, realised where he was, and ran screaming from the hospital clutching his other boot. He managed to hail a taxi and went straight to the racetrack. Picture the scene as our unlikely hero, one shoe on and one shoe off, took the shortest route to the stewards' room – down the finishing straight. Officials chasing him, the crowd in utter disbelief, and all Ralph wanted to do was to finish his rides that day to stay in the running for the prize. Stewards managed to calm him down and, under the one condition that if he returned to the hospital for overnight observation, they would allow him to ride the following day, Friday the 9th, the last day of the carnival.

As the story goes, Ralph Neves did return to the track on Friday, and even though he only rode place-getters, he still managed to secure enough points to win the US$500 prize, as well as the gold watch presented by Bing Crosby.

This was the most amazing start to his career, and he rode many great horses in his lifetime, including one of the greatest American thoroughbreds of all time, Round Table. He was awarded the prestigious George Woolf Memorial Award in 1954 and was inducted into the National Racing Hall of Fame in 1960.

Ralph Neves' second death was reported on 7 July 1995. He was 79.

Bert Thompson, Ralph's valet over the years, made a commitment that day back in 1936 to work with others and bring about changes that would improve safety standards on all tracks in America. He was credited as the driving force for ambulances becoming a fixture at all race meetings and later, as the National Manager of The Jockeys' Guild, he worked with an inventor to create and produce safety helmets for jockeys. Bert was also partially responsible for the changes made to insurances for jockeys, and also hospital insurance in case it was needed.

Things happen for a reason in life, and from that amazing event, when Ralph died on the Thursday and then rode on the Friday, we can thank those in attendance that day for lifting the safety standards and conditions that jockeys enjoy on racetracks today.

Ruffian

... the brilliant filly that was her own worst enemy

During a lifetime, we come across special stories that make us sit and wonder, what if? This is one such story about an amazing filly.

Ruffian was foaled in 1972 at the famous Claiborne Farm in Kentucky, USA, a granddaughter of the great Native Dancer. She was a big and beautifully proportioned filly, and part-owner Barbara Janney reckoned she was a bit of a ruffian.

It is tradition that a trainer does not give too much information away to work riders, especially his private thoughts on how good a horse may be when legging up a rider for early-morning gallops. It is feared that if you do this, the racing gods may hear and strike down the horse's ability and subsequent expectations. On that first morning, Ruffian's experienced trainer was said to have remarked to the work rider, 'You're about to ride the fastest horse you have ever been on.' At Belmont Park that morning, everyone saw something special – an exceptional speedster with huge, powerful strides.

Ruffian had her first race start in May 1974 and won by fifteen lengths.

The Fashion Stakes was next, at Belmont, in a field where half of the contestants were unbeaten, and she won by seven lengths. This was followed by a win in the Astoria Stakes four weeks later, setting a new race record. She then ran in the Spinaway Stakes at Saratoga in August, beating a classy field, hard held, to win by thirteen lengths. Ruffian set a new race record in the Spinaway, the fastest time ever recorded by a two-year-old in the history of this track. For the uninitiated, this was the stuff that dreams were made of.

After the Spinaway, her handlers noticed she was exhibiting some unusual behaviour, so a vet was called. Subsequent precautionary x-rays showed the finest of cracks on the bone of her right ankle. The injury was treated and Ruffian was immediately sent out for a spell.

Everyone was satisfied with the progress of her injury during her recuperation, so she went back into training and was set for the Fillies Triple Crown, which consists of The Acorn, The Mother Goose and The Coaching Club American Oaks. Ruffian was now being openly compared to the great Secretariat and the legendary Man O'War – huge raps for such a young filly with a handful of starts.

In racing terms there is always great rivalry between the best colt and the best filly. Speculation was growing about whether we were going to see something similar to the 1930s match race between the legends Seabiscuit and War Admiral, where that race stopped a nation. The number-one colt at the time was Foolish Pleasure, the Kentucky Derby winner, which had won eleven out of his fourteen starts, while Ruffian had been just as impressive, winning all of her ten races by an average margin of seven lengths. It was inevitable that a match race had to be run to separate these two brilliant horses. The contest was set for 6 July 1975.

Just as they do with a World Championship heavyweight boxing title, there was a weigh-in. Ruffian tipped the scales at 510 kg, while Foolish Pleasure weighed in at only 481 kg, highlighting Ruffian's bulky conformation.

That Sunday afternoon, 50,000 people took to the track, with an estimated 13 million people watching the live telecast during a televised hour special called 'The Great Match Race'. The purse in 1975 was a staggering $225,000 to the winner and $125,000 to the loser. The race was to be run over 10 furlongs (2000 metres).

With Ruffian drawn on the inside and Foolish Pleasure on the outside, the start was a blur of pace as they scorched the ground, covering the first 2 furlongs in a touch over 22 seconds from a standing start. When they were on the other side of the track, it was almost impossible to see Foolish Pleasure as he was running on Ruffian's outside. He was completely obliterated by her massive frame as she was 7 centimetres taller than him as well. Slowly you could begin to see Foolish Pleasure's tail and rump appearing, as Ruffian was getting into stride and increasing her lead.

Then it happened ... *snap* – a sound like a dry twig breaking echoed over the track. Ruffian had taken a bad step, which resulted in a terrible injury. She began bumping into the colt and leaning in on him, but her instinct was to keep running. Both jockeys knew something was terribly wrong and Ruffian's rider tried with all of his might to pull her up. Finally she drifted to the middle of the track under a strangle hold, where she was brought to a bouncing halt. Her jockey jumped off and held her up until help arrived. She was in excruciating pain, her eyes wide and rolling – her determination to stay competitive and keep running had resulted in her pulverising her ankle and shredding the arteries, ligaments and tendons.

Foolish Pleasure was the invisible winner that day. The crowd of 50,000 watched the injured Ruffian, many with tears in their eyes. This was a sickening and heartbreaking sight. The one thing that made her great was also the one thing that had nearly killed her – her competitive spirit and her willingness to run.

There was no question what they had to do, and that was to save her for who she was – the brilliant Ruffian. A compressed air splint was attached and all attendants eased her into the horse ambulance, where she was immediately taken to the equine hospital close to the track. Doctors did their best to repair the damage and then fitted a boot enclosed in plaster to raise the heel and take pressure of the injured area.

While still laying on her side after the operation in the early hours of the following morning, Ruffian started to recover from the effects of the anaesthesia – she began to extend her legs, slowly at first, then building to a thrashing of all fours. She was trying to run, and who knows, still trying to beat the colt Foolish Pleasure in her confused state of mind. Attendants desperately tried to calm her down, but in her frenzied state, Ruffian stripped the plaster and special boot that had been made for her just hours before by dedicated vets. It did not take long before she had stripped open the wound.

Sometimes decisions are discussed, debated and considered, but her owner took it upon herself to immediately stop Ruffian's pain and anguish and asked the appropriate person present to have her euthanased immediately. It was a heart-breaking decision but the only humane one she could make.

The rare qualities that carried Ruffian through her races also carried her on to equine immortality. Ruffian was the first horse ever to be buried at any New York race club, and even today, flowers are placed on the stone that marks her final resting place. The story goes that she was buried in a position where her nose was pointing towards her favourite place … the winning post.

The life and death of Alydar

… the true story of a champion!

His life

Alydar was a chestnut colt foaled at Calumet Farm, Lexington, Kentucky on 23 March 1975. He was best known for being the horse to finish second to the great Affirmed in each of the three legs of the Triple Crown in 1978. Alydar was also remembered for the manner in which he died.

He had a total of 26 starts for fourteen wins, nine seconds and one third, for total prize money of nearly $1 million.

Here are some of Alydar's major race wins:

- Great American Stakes: 1977
- Champagne Stakes: 1977
- Tremont Stakes: 1977
- Flamingo Stakes: 1978
- Florida Derby: 1978
- Travers Stakes: 1978
- Arlington Classic Stakes: 1978
- Whitney Handicap: 1978
- Nassau County Handicap: 1979

Alydar's placings included the following:

- 2nd in the 1978 Kentucky Derby (first leg of the Triple Crown)
- 2nd in the 1978 Preakness (second leg of the Triple Crown)
- 2nd in the Belmont Stakes (third leg of the Triple Crown)

Alydar made his debut on a racetrack on 15 June 1977 in the Youthful Stakes at Belmont, finishing fifth behind a youngster called Affirmed. Alydar raced Affirmed on ten occasions throughout his career, winning three times. He was inducted into the National Museum Hall of Fame in 1989 and, during his stud career, was voted Leading Sire in North America in 1990.

What a great champion Affirmed was and how unlucky was Alydar to run into such a horse in his racing career. During preparation for the Brooklyn Handicap in 1979, Alydar fractured a sesamoid bone in his right hind foot, and on 24 July, he was retired to stud to stand at Calumet Farm in Lexington, Kentucky. Alydar went on to be a great sire of champions, while the champ Affirmed never enjoyed the same success during his stud career.

During the evening of 13 November 1990, Alydar, while in his stable, broke a bone in his right leg. He was supposed to have kicked his stable door. Surgery followed to set the bone by way of a surgical cast. The following morning, Alydar stumbled on the bad leg and fell, causing a second bone to shatter. The second injury was deemed to be unrepairable, so at roughly 8.30am on that fateful morning of 15 November 1990, Alydar was put to death by lethal injection.

Alydar's death

Prosecutors have never won an indictment against any individual in connection with the death of Alydar. Judge Sim Lake agreed that this case had strong overtones of circumstantial evidence that indicated the reason could have been for the collection of the insurance monies; however, all evidence was judged not to be able to be proven in a court of law 'beyond reasonable doubt'. You be the judge!

The cast includes:
JT Lundy: President and Head of Operations of Calumet Farms
Gary Matthews: Former Attorney and Chief Financial Officer of Calumet Farms
Alton Stone: Calumet Farms Groom
Frank Cihak: Vice-Chairman of the First City National Bank
Julia Tomala: Assistant US Attorney in Houston

To help you understand what is about to unfold, here is a brief history of Calumet Farm.

WM Wright acquired the land back in 1924. Following his death, his son Warren Wright Sr took over the business and developed it to become one of the most successful stud farms in thoroughbred racing history in America.

Warren Wright Sr died in 1950, and according to his will, his wife Lucille Parker Wright inherited the property.

Lucille Wright, the family matriarch, died in 1982 at the age of 93. Her granddaughter Lucille 'Cindy' Wright had married JT Lundy at the tender age of sixteen in 1962, and from the start the family matriarch viewed this union with great suspicion. Upon Lucille Wright's death, the terms of Warren Wright's Sr's will stipulated that it would all go to their son, William Wright Jr. However, he had tragically died in 1978, so the property went to his heir, Lucille 'Cindy' Wright, and of course her husband JT Lundy took over the operations of Calumet farm as president.

By 1983 Alydar's offspring would fetch an average $750,000 in the sales ring. In 1984 JT Lundy raised Alydar's stud fees from a healthy $40,000 per serve to a massive $250,000 per serve. He also started something that changed the landscape of thoroughbred breeding. Anyone with deep enough pockets could pay a fee of a couple of million dollars up front to Calumet Farm, and that would assure the purchaser of being able to send a mare to be serviced by Alydar, every year for the rest of his breeding career.

JT Lundy continued on his way with even more renovations to the farm, and he lived the high life, flying around in his $30,000 per month private jet and sponsoring the car of AJ Foyt, one of America's greatest IndyCar drivers. Around 1985 and 1986, JT Lundy took another mortgage out for $20 million and received another $15 million line of credit. Later in 1986, with the breeding industry in sharp decline, JT took out another extension of $10 million. In 1988, with the industry still in freefall, JT Lundy received another bank loan for a staggering $50 million from the farm's bankers, the First City Bancorporation of Houston, Texas.

The question was now being asked as to how Lundy could possibly get a loan from any bank in Texas, and who approved the deals. As it turned out, the person responsible for the deals was the powerful

Vice-Chairman of First City National Bank, a big man named Frank C Cihak.

It was hard to imagine that anything could shatter this cosy business relationship.

The news came out of Houston, Texas in 1990 that Frank C Cihak had resigned as Vice-Chairman of the First City National Bank. In the 29 months that Cihak had restructured First City, the bank's pool of bad loans had grown from zero to $433 million.

On 25 October 1990, the new Vice-Chairman contacted Calumet Farm executives and advised them that their loans were being restructured and they needed to come up with at least $15 million by 28 February 1991 – less than three weeks later, Alydar was dead.

In 1991, JT Lundy resigned and Calumet Farm was declared bankrupt.

Enter Julia Tomala of the US Attorney's Office in Houston. She assisted in investigating the failures of some 485 banks and 238 savings and loans institutions in Texas between 1986 and 1992. Tomala uncovered the complex schemes that Cihak had created using First City National Bank to cover secret fees and kickbacks. After Cihak's trial in 1993, he was sent to jail for twelve years and seven months. Subsequent investigations revealed other kickback schemes, so his sentence was increased to 22 years. Cihak had received payments of $1.1 million from Equine Capital Corporation (ECC) in Kentucky – Tomala found that even though the money was paid to Cihak by ECC, the ECC was actually run by Lundy and Associates.

Money had been channelled through to Cihak from JT Lundy and Chief Financial Officer of Calumet Farm, Gary Matthews, by a series of complicated manoeuvres, and there was no mention of repaying the amounts.

In 1996, Julia Tomala continued her investigation and found that Lundy and Matthews had needed to come up with their first installment of $15 million to First City National Bank in February 1991. Alarm bells rang when she uncovered the value of Alydar's death to Calumet Farm and the timing of the tragedy. Alydar had been insured for US$36.5 million. Was this the perfect time for a champion to die?

Julia Tomala's interviews with other people at the farm uncovered the fact that Alton Stone, the groom at the stallion barn, did not find Alydar in a distressed state with a broken leg as he had previously testified. It was another worker, Keed Highley, who had stumbled across the gruesome scene when he investigated distressing sounds coming from the barn.

It was theorised that a motor vehicle of some description had been driven into the stallion barn where Alydar was housed. One end of a rope was attached to his leg and the other end tied to the vehicle. The vehicle then drove off at speed, causing Alydar to fall to the floor and sustain a very bad break. This theory was backed up by a George Pratt, a Professor of Electrical Engineering and Computer Science at the Massachusetts Institute of Technology.

George Pratt found that to kick the door from its hinges, as Lundy's statement said, a horse would need to generate over 6000 pounds of force to hit the stall door in exactly the right place. By way of a comparison, a strong mature stallion could only manage around 2000 pounds with such a kick, given the same environment and the same circumstances.

After the jury returned into court to deliver its verdict in 1998, the many people in the gallery, including the dedicated investigative team, held their breath – they just wanted justice for Alydar, the most heavily insured thoroughbred in history. Alton Stone, the former Kentucky groom of Calumet Farm, was found guilty on two counts of lying to a federal grand jury. The first step towards justice had been won.

In the year 2000, two years after Alton Stone was found guilty of the charges laid against him, another jury handed down their judgement on the others. The charges included bribery and fraud relating to the death of Alydar. The ex-president of Calumet Farm, JT Lundy, was sentenced to four and a half years, while the one-time chief financial officer of the farm, Gary Matthews, received a sentence of 21 months. The prosecution had proven that Lundy and Matthews had paid a bribe of $1.1 million to First City National Bank in exchange for $65 million of unsecured loans during the late 1980s and early 1990s.

Frank Cihak, the boss of the First City National Bank at the time of the bribes, was sentenced to twelve years' jail in 1994. Frank and four of his associates were convicted of fraud and money laundering.

You be the judge.

Military, motors and a product of war

... such a small beginning, with a twist in the tale that you won't believe!

We would like to tell you a little yarn about a chance decision that changed many lives, and we are going to keep you in suspense for a couple of paragraphs so please don't read the end first. All of us make decisions that affect our lives, not knowing the full consequences of our actions or how they could develop in future years. Here is one such story.

There was a young man who was in the American military in the 1890s. He became ill and was discharged because of his illness. He found his way to San Francisco in 1903, not well prepared for his new life as he only had the princely sum of 21 cents in his pocket. As he had a mechanical background in the army, he gambled on his talent and opened a bicycle repair shop – these were the days of bicycle transport because those newfangled horseless carriages were still in their infancy. His reputation grew as he started to understand the 'workings' of these machines, and pretty soon his interest became a priority in his life. It wasn't long before disappointed owners of broken-down jalopies found their way to his door asking for advice. In a life-changing moment, he approached another very new and then insignificant motor vehicle builder, and asked if he could open up showrooms to sell their vehicles, but always in the back of his mind was the value-added business of repair.

This small vehicle builder took the opportunity of giving the young man the sole right of their vehicle sales in every western state of the United States. The young man in question, upon signing the deal, was reported to have said that this new business venture they were entering into spelt the death knell of the horse and carriage.

The young man in question was Charles Howard.

The fledgling motor vehicle builder was General Motors.

Charles Howard went on to own Seabiscuit, one of the greatest racehorses ever to grace the tracks of America.

Isn't it strange that Charles Howard is known more because of the horse that he owned and raced, than the influence he had in developing the car industry in America for the giant General Motors?

Belair Stud

... the home of champions and the family curse

As sure as night follows day, some people and circumstances, when brought together, are destined to explode.

This is the story of the great Belair Stud and its owners, and how it contributed to the history of thoroughbred champions in the United States. The Woodward family was shattered to pieces in the most terrible of circumstances, leaving a legacy of rumour, innuendo and tragedy.

The stud was founded by Sam Ogle, the Governor of Maryland in 1747 in what was called Colonial America. On a trip to England in 1740, two English-bred horses were presented to Sam Ogle by the Prince of Wales. The stallion Spark and the broodmare Queen Mab established the legacy of what was to later become Belair Stud. In 1898, the property was sold to a wealthy New York banker in James T Woodward, and upon his death, the stud was bequeathed to his nephew, William Woodward Sr. Under William Woodward Sr, the property was developed to be the centrepiece of the United States' stud and stable complexes. He was instrumental in bringing the great Sir Galahad III from France to America, and some of Belair Stud's famous achievers were the only father and son horses ever to win the US Triple Crown of thoroughbred racing, Gallant Fox and Omaha.

From 1923 to 1953, Belair Stud made its mark on American racing. Considering it was a stud first and a stable second, Belair's career record over 30 years was 631 wins, 568 seconds and third on 540 occasions.

Five of their horses were inducted into the National Museum of Racing and Hall of Fame, and under their legendary trainer, Sunny Jim Fitzsimmons, the stable won the following US Triple Crown races:

Kentucky Derby

Gallant Fox 1930
Omaha 1935
Johnstown 1939

Preakness Stakes

Gallant Fox 1930
Omaha 1935
Nashua 1955

Belmont Stakes

Gallant Fox 1930
Faireno 1932
Omaha 1935
Granville 1936
Johnstown 1939
Nashua 1955

Now, the tragedy of the Woodward family.

The players:

James T Woodward: bought Belair Stud in 1898
William Woodward Sr: his nephew
William Woodward Jr: Woodward Sr's son
Ann Eden Woodward: Woodward Jr's wife
James and William Woodward: the sons of Woodward Jr and Ann Woodward

Upon the death of James T Woodward, Belair Stud was left to his nephew William Woodward Sr. William was born into a wealthy family who made their fortune selling textiles to the Confederate

Government, and his father was the founder of the New York Cotton Exchange.

After finishing his law studies, William was admitted to the bar in 1901. He spent much of his early years in England with the political and economic elite and enjoyed the company of royalty at many fashionable events, including the great pastime of the royals, horse racing.

Returning to New York in 1903, he was made vice-president of the Hanover National Bank in New York City and married Elsie Ogden Cryder at Saratoga, New York on 24 October 1904. Their union produced a son, William Woodward Jr, and four daughters.

Over the years, horses bred at Belair won every major Stakes race in the US, including two Triple Crowns, as well as the Epsom Oaks, the St Leger Stakes and the 1000 Guineas. Their horses won many important races in Britain, and such were his achievements in thoroughbred racing on both continents that William Woodward Sr appeared on the front cover of the August issue of *Time* magazine in 1939. Nothing could stop his success … or could it?

William Woodward Sr died in 1953, aged 77, leaving his estate, including the Belair Stud, to his son William Woodward Jr. After graduating from Harvard University, William Jr fought in the navy in World War II, where he received a bravery medal as a consequence of his ship being torpedoed by the enemy. After leaving the navy, he became a director of the Hanover Bank. The woman who won his heart was an ex-showgirl and nightclub performer named Ann Eden Crowell; they married in March 1943. Young William Woodward's family was surprised at his selection to say the least, and what followed was a particularly turbulent marriage producing two sons. There were constant rumours of extramarital affairs and social climbing to an extent that caused the couple to fight often, publicly and privately.

After a dinner party for the Duchess of Windsor on 30 October 1955, William Woodward Jr and his wife returned home and retreated to their separate bedrooms. There had been rumours of prowlers in the area but both Ann and William each had shotguns at their disposal if needed. During the night, it is believed that Ann, on hearing a noise in the house, took her shotgun and fired at a prowler in the hallway leading to the living quarters, killing him instantly. Unfortunately she had shot her own husband, William Woodward Jr.

So controversial was the killing and the investigations surrounding the family that William's mother intervened using her influence and tried to prevent the scandal getting out of hand in the papers. In what *Life* magazine called 'The Shooting of the Century', the story followed the family wherever they went, and as a result of this, Ann was banished from high society and her two sons were sent to boarding school in Europe – 'out of sight, out of mind'.

The story of the Sport of Kings and the family of one of the wealthiest dynasties in the land was never far from every author's pen. A number of novels were written to expose the tangled web of truths and untruths that became the very essence of the Shooting of the Century.

Twenty years later, in 1975, Ann Woodward found out that the original publication of Truman Capote's novel about the killing of William Woodward Jr was finding its way back into the public eye in a well-known magazine of the time. The rumour and innuendo was far too much for Ann to bear and she committed suicide.

In a tragic end to the Belair empire and the dynasty of the Woodwards, their son James, after returning from Vietnam in 1976 and succumbing to heroin addiction, ended his own life. His brother, William, after being devastated by his recent divorce in 1999, also ended his own life.

They both jumped from multi-storey buildings to their death.

Pittsburgh Phil

... his pearls of wisdom picking winners!

George Smith was born in 1862 and passed away in 1905. To the racing fraternity he was known as the legendary 'Pittsburgh Phil', one of the world's most successful gamblers of all time. From a very young age he realised that horse racing and results were creating a distinctive pattern, and after a few short years he had devised '53 pearls of wisdom' to sort out the punter's age-old dilemma, 'Which horse will I back?'

So successful were his systems and subsequent gambling rewards that when he passed away from tuberculosis at the age of 43, he left an estate worth $3.25 million, which equates to a staggering $84 million today. His racing systems were first published in numerous newspapers and magazines in 1908. Here are just seven of those 'pearls':

1. A good jockey, a good horse, a good bet; a poor jockey, a good horse, a moderate bet; a good horse, a moderate jockey, a moderate bet.
2. Winners repeat frequently, while the defeated are apt to be defeated almost continuously.
3. Two-year-olds can give considerably more weight away to horses in their class, more than horses in the older division excepting in isolated cases.
4. It is well to back horses in winning form. A horse in winning condition generally repeats or runs into the money.
5. Watch all the horses racing closely. You may see something that will be of benefit later on.
6. When you feel yourself getting out of form, then take a rest and freshen up.
7. A man cannot divide his attention at the track between horses and women.

Makes good sense!

Secretariat

... was he the greatest horse of the modern era?

This is the classic case of losing the bet but coming up smelling like a rose.

Ogden Phipps owned the great stallion Bold Ruler but he did not enjoy success in the sales ring, and many said it was because he only sent his own mares to his stallion. All this changed one day when after a friendly toss of a coin, Penny Chenery, the owner of Meadow Stables, won the right to send some of her mares to Bold Ruler.

Rules governing the result after the first coin toss were simple. At a later date, when the progeny were on the ground, the winner of a second coin toss would have first choice of the foals and the loser would have to take what was left. The winner was Ogden and he chose the weanling filly out of the mare Hasty Matelda. Penny was then left with the two weanling colts and also took ownership of the unborn foal out of Somethingroyal.

On 30 March 1970, Somethingroyal gave birth to a bold chestnut colt. As a foal he was quite striking, with a star and narrow blaze down his head, and three white socks. The story goes that by the time this colt was a yearling, he was still unnamed. Meadow Stable's secretary Elizabeth Ham, who was responsible for applying to register names for their horses, was having a tough time getting a name accepted for this colt. Her first ten names were rejected, so in a desperate attempt to get something accepted, she decided to nominate the name Secretariat, which was a broad description of her previous employment.

The rest is history.

Before we look into his freakish wins, let us first acknowledge who he was and from whence he came. Meadow Stables owned him during his racing career. His trainer was Lucien Laurin and after 21 starts, he'd recorded sixteen wins, three seconds and one third. His total prize money was $1,316,808 – a staggering amount back in the early 1970s.

Secretariat's major wins were as follows:

- Sanford Stakes: 1972
- Hopeful Stakes: 1972
- Futurity Stakes: 1972
- Laurel Futurity: 1972
- Garden State Futurity: 1972
- Bay Shore Stakes: 1973
- Gotham Stakes: 1973
- Arlington Invitational: 1973

- Marlboro Cup: 1973
- Canadian International: 1973
- Kentucky Derby: 1973
- Preakness Stakes: 1973
- Belmont Stakes: 1973

It did not take Secretariat long to find his feet as a two-year-old, but it was his three Classic wins as a three-year-old (the Kentucky Derby, the Preakness Stakes and the Belmont Stakes) that people best remember. He became the first Triple Crown winner in 25 years and only the ninth in history to complete this historic feat.

The Kentucky Derby

Coming off a rare third in the lead-up to this race in the Wood Memorial, behind his stablemate Angle Light and the Santa Anita Derby winner Sham, the bookies still had a great opinion of Secretariat and had no hesitation in making him 3/2 favourite. Slow to start and dropping back to last place, he moved through the field, overtook the leader at the top of the straight and comprehensively beat Sham by two and a half lengths.

While winning a race of this importance was very special indeed, the quality of the win was reflected in two statistics. His overall time was 1.59.4, and it would be another 28 years before any horse in the Derby would cross the line in under two minutes.

When Secretariat's times were compared for each quarter-mile throughout the race, the results shocked all of the hardened clockers:

- First quarter-mile: 25.2 seconds
- Second quarter-mile: 24 seconds
- Third quarter-mile: 23.8 seconds
- Fourth quarter-mile: 23.4 seconds
- Final quarter-mile: 23 seconds flat

He continued to accelerate from the first quarter-mile and kept on running faster and faster throughout the entire distance. Ask any trainer how impossible that is to achieve, and you will understand how great his achievement was.

The Preakness Stakes

Secretariat was last away again in this race and made a bold move from last to first with 5 and a half furlongs to go. He was never headed and again won comfortably, beating Sham again by two and a half lengths.

The track's electronic timer had malfunctioned, so a hand-held time for the race was registered. This was quite controversial at the time, because it was accepted that he ran 1.53.4, which was a new track and race record. It took another fifteen years before Tank's Prospect (1985) joined Secretariat as a joint record holder.

The Belmont Stakes

And now, his most amazing win. The day of 9 June 1973 saw the running of the prestigious 12 furlong Belmont Stakes, the final leg of the Triple Crown, with only five starters. This elite group were the only ones left standing after Secretariat had shown his hand in the Derby and the Preakness. Sham was there again to give him a run for his money, but it would appear the race was Secretariat's for the taking as the bookies had him installed at 10/1 on. In other words, you had to put $10 on to win $1.

As expected, the field jumped and right from the start it appeared to be a race in two, with Secretariat and Sham going stride for stride over the opening distance. At the 6 furlong mark, Sham began to tire, but the mighty Secretariat didn't. He just kept on increasing his lead. The further the race went, the greater the distance between Secretariat and the rest of the field.

At the end of the mile and a half journey, Secretariat crossed the line an amazing 31 lengths to the second horse.

Imagine: 31 lengths!

This was the greatest margin of victory ever recorded, beating the previous Triple Crown winner, Count Fleet, who won by 25 lengths. Secretariat's time was also outstanding; he ran a flat 2:24 for the 1.5-mile distance, beating the previous record by two seconds. The time that day was regarded as the fastest in the world on a dirt or grass track. Around 68,000 people just could not believe their eyes that day. He certainly was something very special. Unbelievably, there were 5617 tote tickets never redeemed that day on course; obviously this great moment in time was not lost on the souvenir and memorabilia specialists.

Not long after his Triple Crown victory, Secretariat's owner signed a contract to syndicate the star that would not allow him to race after his three-year-old season. He was far too valuable in terms of breeding to the American thoroughbred industry. His final race was the Canadian International Stakes at Woodbine Racetrack in Toronto, Canada, and in typical fashion, he found a liking for running on grass. He easily won the race over the 1 5/8 mile distance by six and a half lengths.

While his early years at stud produced high-priced two-year-olds in the sales ring, their ability on the track in no way enhanced Secretariat's reputation as a stallion. Later in his stud career he produced some very good horses, including the 1986 Horse of the Year, Lady's Secret, and the 1988 Preakness and Belmont Stakes winner, Risen Star. There was also an Australian connection, as he sired the 1990 Melbourne Cup winner in Kingston Rule.

In 1989, Secretariat, suffering from a very painful and debilitating condition called laminitis, was humanely euthanased on 4 October at the age of nineteen. Secretariat was mourned by millions as the great champion that he was, and buried at Claiborne Farm in Paris, Kentucky. He was given the very rare honour of being buried whole. Normally they bury only the head, heart and hooves and the rest of the body is cremated. During the post-mortem, his heart was found to be the largest ever recorded for a racehorse – a staggering 22 pounds.

ESPN, one of the largest sporting networks in America, lists Secretariat as the 25th out of 100 in the list of the Greatest Athletes of the 20th century. He was the highest rated horse, with the other two legends of the turf being Man O'War in 84th position and Citation at 97th. Another top 100 list was created by the same network in 2005, listing the greatest sports performance by any individual athlete not necessarily human. Secretariat was the only horse on the list for his run in the Belmont Stakes – that incredible victory over his opposition by an amazing 31 lengths. For all of you basketball fans, he ran second only to Wilt Chamberlain's 100-point game, between the Philadelphia Warriors and the New York Knicks in March 1962. That night Wilt scored the highest-ever individual points in a season game, scoring 100 out the Phillies' score of 169 to 147 over the New York Knicks.

Finally, and incredibly, in May 2007 Secretariat was inducted into the Kentucky Athletic Hall of Fame, making it the very first time an animal received this honour.

Talk about winning on a losing bet!

From Darley to Lexington

... even blindness and a civil war could not deter him!

This story begins at the Smithsonian Institute, and it is important to understand the part that this institute plays in the history of the United States. You could say that it is the very heartbeat of a civilisation that protects everything that appears so culturally diverse to many, but nevertheless, everything that is the United States, was the United States, and made the United States the great country that its citizens are dedicated to upholding. In Washington alone, this world-famous institute has a number of museums, research facilities and, believe it or not, a zoo. It has over 130 million collected items catalogued. It publishes magazines about the Smithsonian's work, and also employs its own law-enforcement agency to protect all that is theirs. There are many other sites belonging to the Smithsonian Group scattered throughout the United States.

Not so long ago, the remains of the thoroughbred racehorse Lexington were gathering dust on the fourth floor of the Smithsonian Institution's National Museum of Natural History. Catalogue number 16020 was simply described as the 'Blind Hero of Woodburn'.

When foaled on 17 March 1850, he was classed as a bloody bay colt. His name was Darley; his sire was the great Boston. As a two-year-old, he grew to a very imposing 15 hands and 3 inches tall.

Darley easily won his first two races for Dr Warfield and his partner Burbridge Harry. Harry was once a slave and, being an African American, was unable to enter him in races in his name so the horse ran in Dr Warfield's name and colours.

He caught the eye of a Richard Ten Broeck, who was representing a syndicate, and soon after, Darley was sold for the sum of $2500. Upon handing over Darley's pedigree papers, Dr Warfield wrote on the pedigree sheet: 'The colt was bred by me, as was also his dam, which now I will forever own. Signed E Warfield.'

The syndicate changed his name from Darley to Lexington and sent him to Mississippi to train under JB Pryor. Lexington raced at the ages of three and four, and while he only competed seven times, many of the races were gruelling 4 mile events. He won six out of the seven starts and came second in the other.

Lecomte, also by Boston, was his main adversary in a few of those races. When Lexington won the Phoenix Hotel Handicap in 1875, it was his second match race with Lecomte, and this race at the time was regarded as one of the great match races of the century.

Unfortunately, his career was cut short and he was sent to stud because of his very poor eyesight. Incredibly, his sire, Boston, had also gone blind. Lexington stood for a time at Nantura Stock Farm before he was sold to a Robert A Alexander in 1858, to serve at the Alexander's Woodburn Stud at Spring Station, Kentucky. His sale price was US$15,000, at that time regarded as the highest sale amount ever paid for an American horse.

Because of his failing eyesight, he was called 'The Blind Hero of Woodburn'. Between 1861 and 1874, and then again in 1876 and 1878, Lexington became leading sire sixteen times in the United States. He sired three Preakness Stakes winners, Tom Ochiltree in 1875, Shirley in 1876 and the Duke of Magenta in 1878, which equalled the record of Broomstick, another great stallion.

During the American Civil War, horses were taken from Kentucky farms to serve as mounts in the bloody war. Lexington, at fifteen years old and blind, had to be ridden away and hidden to save him from such a cruel fate.

In 1955, The Blind Hero of Woodburn was inducted into the

National Museum of Racing and Hall of Fame. Lexington's dominance in the pedigree of American-bred thoroughbreds, and the fact that the British thoroughbred breeders considered him not a purebred, were large factors in the Jersey Act of 1913. This Act, enacted by the British Ruling body, would not recognise those thoroughbreds that could not be accurately traced back to the sires in their General Stud Book. Evidence has recently been unearthed that shows part of Lexington's pedigree goes back to an unnamed daughter of the great Eclipse, so we may see some further developments here.

The Belmont Lexington Stakes is run every year at Belmont Park in his honour, as is the Lexington Stakes at Keeneland Race Course.

John Solomon Rarey

... the first recorded Horse Whisperer

We quite often see or hear about people who have a way with animals. You have only got to take your dog to the vet to see the different reactions that your dog has to different people. Some have a real affinity for animals and it really does show. Horses are no different.

Take the single trainer with a team of about ten or fifteen racehorses. He or she has people on hand to assist with training and

WHAT'S HE THINK HE IS... A HORSE WHISPERER?

looking after the horses during the busy periods of the day. However, when you consider the single trainer and the time he or she spends with these animals, it once again becomes very apparent that some have a real connection with these giant thoroughbreds. Sometimes they call the connection horse whispering, where a person can tame the wild horse by getting inside their head and forming a trust or a bond.

John S Rarey was born in Ohio in 1827 and from an early age, he had a way with horses. He was able to train horses by the time he was twelve and over the ensuing years, people heard about his talent, especially with difficult horses. He built quite a reputation for being able to turn around the attitude of the most belligerent thoroughbreds.

At the age of 28, John staged an exhibition of his talent at the Ohio Stage Yards, where people were invited to come along and watch him demonstrate his unusual gift on two unruly horses that were chosen for him. He had no knowledge of either of the horses chosen, but astounded the crowd by taming one in 20 minutes and then the second in fifteen minutes. After spinning his magic for all to see, he was then invited to go overseas to demonstrate his rare gift.

The world is full of sceptics, because even though Rarey travelled widely through Europe demonstrating his gift, many accused him of using drugs on the animals. The truth was he was simply using a philosophy of kindness, firmness and patience.

Then along came Cruiser.

The Earl of Dorchester had bred a horse by Venison out of the mare Little Red Rover in 1852, and named it Cruiser. As a two-year-old, this sixteen-hand dark bay colt was regarded as the fastest horse in England, but unfortunately far too unruly to race because of his foul temper. The troublesome animal was vicious to say the least; he would go down on his knees and tear at the ground with his teeth. After killing two grooms during one frenzied attack, the stable hands developed a simple way of feeding him. There were always three grooms present: one to feed him, one to hold his chain and another one to stand there with a rifle at the ready just in case he went berserk and broke free. He certainly sounded like a very nasty piece of goods, and it was not unusual for Cruiser to kick the hell out of every square inch of his stall for what seemed like forever.

Kept in a solid brick stall with a huge oak door, he also wore an iron muzzle for three years, which restricted his ability to drink or eat normally. Cruiser was considered unbreakable; the Earl set the challenge, and John Solomon Rarey duly accepted.

Rarey was not a big man, approximately 5 feet 9 inches (175 centimetres) and weighing around 166 lb (76 kg). On arrival at the stall, he opened the large door and quietly stood in front of Cruiser. After a few moments of confusion, Cruiser screamed and lunged at Rarey, who was expecting it, and was able to dodge the charge. Then, amazingly, he approached the crazed horse, speaking in soft whispers. Onlookers, including the Earl, pleaded with Rarey not to do any more and escape the stall while he could, but all the time Rarey deliberately worked his way towards the horse, speaking in a low, calm voice.

Cruiser had calmed enough for Rarey to tie him to a sturdy rack on the wall, when all hell broke loose. The horse took objection to being restrained and put on one of the worst tantrums that the onlookers and the Earl had ever seen. He only stopped because he had nothing left to give, at which point Rarey would approach the defeated animal and attach small straps to one leg, all the while stroking and talking calmly to him. After a short time, he was able to ease Cruiser onto his side and he became quite calm.

Within three hours, and to everyone's amazement, Rarey was able to mount and ride him around as if there had been teamwork between them for years. The Earl was so taken with Rarey's talent and exhibition that he presented Cruiser as a gift to him and consequently, his international fame was assured. With his fame came the rewards that he so justly deserved, and on returning home to the United States, he built a house on the family's property and a special stall for his mate Cruiser.

In 1866, John Solomon Rarey died and was buried in the Groveport Cemetery. Strangely, within days of Rarey's death, Cruiser returned to his vicious and unruly behaviour.

The connection had gone and if nothing else, the story of John Solomon Rarey and Cruiser highlights the special talent some people have and why they call them 'horse whisperers'.

Leaping Plum

... not a horse like him anywhere in the world

Before we retrace this horse's history, let's try and get our head around what Leaping Plum achieved. Eight wins in the same race over nine years.

The Grasmick Handicap, run over 4 furlongs (800 metres), is definitely not in the same class as the Lightning Stakes or the Oakleigh Plate in Australia, but it is still a contest for horses irrespective of any injuries or illness, held at the same time every year. Affectionately called the Iron Horse, the grand old galloper Leaping Plum was fortunate enough to always save his best for this period of time every year.

Leaping Plum had a total of 66 starts for 29 wins, nine seconds and twelve thirds, for a total prize money value in 2003 of US$371,584. He was the son of Kentucky stallion Lightning Leap, a son of the great Nijinsky, and his home track was Fonner Park in Grand Island, Nebraska.

The Nebraska State Racing Commission has a policy that it is mandatory for horses to retire at the age of twelve. They have a special panel set aside to review horses approaching that milestone; it is their responsibility to have the horse's best interests at heart, as well as the fields that they may run against.

A spokesman for his owners said, 'We don't mean to be greedy racing him at his age, but as long as he is well, he just loves to run and compete, and we just love watching him.' Leaping Plum was reviewed when he was an eleven-year-old and again when he was twelve. The committee gave a verdict that he was allowed to run as a thirteen-year-old. As it turned out, he had one more race and collected a few hundred dollars for his effort, and then gracefully retired.

What an amazing feat!

Horse murders

... and the scandal that rocked the establishment

There was a period of time in the United States that involved insurance frauds related to the scandal of 'Horse Murders'. Many of the poor animals were expensive racehorses and showjumpers that were insured against death, accident and disease and were duly killed to collect insurance money.

Authorities still don't know exactly how many horses were killed between the mid-1970s and mid-1990s, but the FBI thought the number to be at least 50 and possibly as high as 100. As if these revelations were not bad enough, the millionaire candy heiress and animal lover Helen Brach also disappeared in 1977.

Law enforcement agents believe that she was murdered by the perpetrators of these crimes, because she found out their secrets and was threatening to report their shocking criminal activities to the authorities. She was 65 at the time of her disappearance and her body was never found. Continuing investigations involving her case led the FBI to uncover this insurance fraud in the 1990s. The scandal had been called 'one of the biggest and most gruesome stories in sport' and 'the biggest scandal in the history of equestrian sports'.

A total of 36 people were indicted in connection with the horse murders. The charges included insurance fraud, mail fraud, extortion, racketeering and animal cruelty. Of those 36 people, 35 were convicted. Of the 23 people indicted in July 1994 in Chicago connected to the horse murders, 20 of those charged pleaded guilty. Investigators were able to prosecute Richard Bailey for the disappearance and possible murder of Helen Brash, which investigators believed was linked to their investigation; he is now serving a life sentence in prison for soliciting her murder.

In some cases, horse-owners who were temporarily strapped for cash, and knowing that the animal was insured, would kill the horse without any remorse. This was in spite of the fact that many had a very promising career ahead of them. It also did not matter if some of the unfortunate animals happened to be prize-winning performers. This was the situation in the 1982 murder of the showjumper Henry the Hawk.

Henry the Hawk was a show horse that was owned and ridden by seventeen-year-old Lisa Druck, and because she was under-age, her father, James Druck, a Florida attorney, controlled her finances. Druck's legal practice mainly consisted of defending insurance companies against fraudulent claims. During the course of his work, he learnt one very important thing: if a horse was electrocuted in a certain way, it was extremely difficult for any veterinarian pathologist to find the actual cause of death as foul play. Colic was then deemed to be the cause of death.

Lisa Druck became a prize-winning equestrian. However, in a terrible twist on the father/daughter relationship, and unbeknown to Lisa, her father was involved in a cunning and cruel plot to electrocute horses, for the sole purpose of attaining insurance money. Following the death of her father in 1990, evidence taken from one Tommy Burns stated that Lisa's father had approached Burns to assist him in murdering a horse to collect the insurance. It is also believed that James Druck had devised a method of electrocuting horses and showed Burns how to do it. It would appear he was the brains behind it all but simply did not want blood on his hands.

Tommy Burns then proceeded with the plan and 'murdered' James Druck's daughter's horse, Henry the Hawk, for a reported US$150,000 insurance payout. With that start in a new career devised by James Druck, Burns spent the next ten years of his life perfecting and plying his dastardly craft.

James Druck collected the US$150,000 insurance policy for arranging the killing of his daughter's horse in 1982. The death of Henry the Hawk had such a profound affect on his daughter that sadly, she never competed again. In 1990 while under investigation by the FBI, Druck died of cancer in Tampa, Florida.

Tommy 'The Sandman' Burns travelled the circuits visiting stables offering his unusual talent. With horses insured for anywhere between $5000 and $40,000, his fee was 10 per cent of the insured amount, and unfortunately he found a few willing participants. Once an agreement and fee were negotiated, he would kill the horses for the owners, knowing full well that they would obtain their money from their insurance company. Why wouldn't they; he was simply the best. Burns defended his callous actions by saying it was quick and painless – to describe this method of electrocution as that, would be irresponsible to say the least. By informing on many other people, which lead to their being jailed, Burns struck a deal with the FBI, and with that, he was sentenced to only twelve months' jail. He spent the rest of his miserable life selling car parts.

Traveller

... history of a war horse

Confederate General Robert E Lee's most loved horse during the American Civil War went by the unusual name of Traveller.

Originally named Jeff Davis, he was foaled near Blue Sulphur Springs in Greenbrier County, Virginia. Weighing a sturdy 1100 lb (500 kg), Traveller was iron grey in colour with black points, a long mane and a flowing tail. His looks and conformation won him first prize at the Lewisburg and Virginia Fairs in 1859 and 1860.

In 1861, Robert E Lee ordered Captain Broun to purchase a good horse for his use during the war. The general took an immediate fancy to the horse, purchased for $175, and renamed him Traveller. Often referred to as 'his colt', he was a horse of great stamina and was very hard to upset. After the war, he accompanied the general to Washington College in Lexington, Virginia. Traveller lost many hairs from his tail to souvenir hunters, which were mostly taken by college students. Lee wrote to his daughter Mildred and said, 'The boys are plucking out his tail and he is presenting the appearance of a plucked chicken.'

During the funeral procession for the general in 1871, his faithful companion Traveller walked directly behind the casket with Lee's saddle and bridle draped in black. Later that year, Traveller succumbed to tetanus and as there was no cure for it at the time, he was euthanased so that the great horse would not suffer any further.

Traveller: a real war horse!

John 'Red' Pollard

... the story of Seabiscuit and the old suitcase

This is the story of one of the best-known jockeys in the history of horse racing in the United States. His association with the legendary Seabiscuit is etched into racing history.

It's a story of the jockey and the man.

The jockey

Red Pollard was the grandson of an Irish emigrant. His grandfather came to the United States in 1860 prepared to do it tough and forge a new life for the Pollards in the land of opportunity. Red's father spent many years in Illinois and migrated to Edmonton, Canada in 1898 to start a new venture with his brother Joseph, the Pollard Brickyard.

Red was born in 1909. There was a rich quality in their upbringing: their father's love of books, song and poetry. But the Depression years soon took their toll on the family business and the family found themselves dirt poor, desperately trying to keep their heads above water and their family together.

As a bit of a knockabout kid, at the age of fifteen, Red convinced his mother and father to let him pursue a career as a jockey. He was allowed to leave home in the company of a family friend, who would also act as his guardian.

As it turned out, he wasn't much of a family friend because Red was soon abandoned in a small town that was hosting a fair and carnival. He was left all alone with no benefits and having to use his head to find food and a safe place to sleep; just fifteen-year-old Red Pollard and his battered suitcase.

Red persisted with his racing, but the early days were not very lucrative so he supplemented what little income he was getting by fighting in preliminary boxing matches with the travelling carnival. His ring name was Cougar.

There are moments in time when the journey, irrespective of how hard it appears to be, brings you to a fork in the road and the split-second decision you make changes your life. Red was penniless when he found himself early one morning at a racetrack in Detroit. Now, like people attract like people. Red sidled up to a gentleman who was crusty in appearance and silent in nature, but who gave out warmth. This gentleman was Tom Smith. Tom had only recently been hired by another misfit in the racing game, Charles Howard, and together they had purchased a young colt that would change all of their lives.

For other owners, the young colt called Seabiscuit raced just about every other week as a two-year-old, having in excess of 20 starts as a youngster. He was racing in claim races with very little success. The story goes that Tom Smith saw in Seabiscuit's eyes a very unhappy horse, and Tom, being a so-called 'horse whisperer', bought the colt for Charles Howard for $7500. It is history now that this mighty animal, with Red in the saddle for most of his career, won in excess of $400,000. Red rode Seabiscuit on 30 occasions and won on eighteen of them. Together they had a great relationship as they entertained the racing public.

This was the chance meeting that changed their lives. Red was given a place to stay at Howard's stables and he and his battered suitcase began to make a change to his life with his new family.

Red was blind in one eye. This happened in his early days during a track gallop when a rock flew up and hit him on the skull, the impact of which affected that portion of the brain that controls vision. There were no skull caps in those days. He kept this injury from everyone as it may have ruined any chance of securing rides. Red was tall for a jockey at 5 feet 7 inches, and he also had weight issues to contend with. Back in the 1930s, there were two main ways of getting the weight off. The first was to don a rubber suit and be immersed in horse manure for extended periods of time. One would imagine that the warmth of the manure and the rubber suit acted as the very first green, or should I say brown, sauna.

The second method was extreme. If a jockey had to lose a lot of weight, desperation sought out 'special suppliers', where one could buy a tapeworm egg. The jockey would swallow the egg and after the hatching, the tapeworm would devour the contents of the jockey's stomach and all nutrients as well, and a substantial weight loss followed. Afterwards, the person would go through extreme measures to eliminate the worm from their body, in some cases being admitted to hospital for an operation to remove the tapeworm. Desperate measures in desperate times.

The lack of nutrients in the body also had the side affect of making jockeys' bones very brittle. In 1938, Red suffered a terrible fall when riding and he suffered a crushed chest, broken ribs and a broken arm. After his recovery he went back to the only thing he knew, but soon after he suffered a compound fracture of his leg from a runaway horse on the track. During that recovery at Charles Howard's ranch, he met and married his private duty nurse, Agnes Conlon. So then there were three: Red, Agnes and his battered suitcase.

It was just prior to the Match Race of the Century against War Admiral that Red was injured by that runaway horse and was unable to ride him on that memorable day. The ride went to his very good friend George 'The Iceman' Woolf, and the rest was history – the Biscuit made the Admiral more of a Rear Admiral than a War Admiral.

Soon after this, Seabiscuit ruptured a suspensory ligament and he found himself recuperating with Red at the Howard Ranch. The racing public thought that they would never see them together again. They did make it back to the racecourse, and had pretty dismal showings on their first two comeback races. The racing public were starting to vent their anger on the broken-down jockey who was riding their champion. They believed that Red was keeping Seabiscuit back.

On their third start back, they tackled the one prize that had eluded them for years, the Santa Anita Handicap. The Biscuit, ridden by Red Pollard, won that day and took home the US$100,000 purse – a huge amount in 1940. Red had to wear a metal plate on his fragile leg, otherwise there was a chance of it buckling and breaking. He was reported to have said after the win, 'Between us today, we had only four good legs.'

Seabiscuit retired that day and Red Pollard never rode for Charles Howard again.

Red tried to enlist in the forces for World War II but was rejected by all branches. In 1945 he suffered another serious fall and was bedridden for some time. After getting the okay from the doctors again, he went back to riding until 1955, when this enigmatic horseman retired at the good jockey age of 45. From then until 1981, Red tried his hand at training, and teaching young riders. He had a stint in the Racecourse Post Office and finally, and humbly, he worked as a valet in the jockey's room, shining other jockeys' boots.

Red died in a nursing home in 1981, and his dear wife Agnes died two weeks later from cancer. They were survived by two children.

The life and times of John Red Pollard. His journey was difficult, but you don't realise the life that a man lives outside of his profession, and the legacy he leaves.

The man and the old battered suitcase

His father and grandfather before him left a fortune to Red – and one that he spent wisely. His treasure lay in his battered suitcase. Books, books and more books; volumes of Shakespeare, Omar Khayyám and many others. His love of poetry and the written word transcended the hard and sometimes disappointing and bitter life that he experienced.

When asked by his children in their later years about how well known and famous he was during career, they said Red would say: 'Fame is a food that dead men eat. I have no stomach for such meat.'

Omar Khayyám was one of Red's favourite poets. He was born in Persia in 1048 and died in 1131. Taken from of Omar Khayyám's *Rubaiyat* (a collection of four-line stanzas), we think this best describes Red, his nature, his struggle and the important things that made him the man he was:

> I need a jug of wine and a book of poetry
> Half a loaf for a bite to eat,
> Then you and I, seated in a deserted spot,
> Will have more wealth than a Sultan's realm.

Never judge a book by its cover.

Silky Sullivan: heart attack material

... some said he was just a running fool!

Silky Sullivan was a horse with a personality and a unique way of showing off his prodigious talent. A brass plaque on top of his final resting place holds a long tribute left by one of his fans, and one stanza of that tribute says it all:

> ... Out of the gate like a bullet of red,
> Dropping behind as the rest sped ahead,
> Loping along as the clubhouse fans cheer,
> Leisurely stalking the field in first gear.

Silky Sullivan was a chestnut red colt foaled in 1955, the son of Sullivan out of the dam Lady N Silk, and was regarded as the best finisher racing has ever seen because of his unique style. This brought praise and comment whenever he contested a race.

His record shows that he started on 27 occasions for twelve wins, one second and five thirds, for prize money of just over US$157,000 in the 1950s, which would equate to a considerable amount today. The punting public gave him the nicknames Mr Heart Attack and the California Comet, because if you backed him, you had your heart in your mouth watching him decide when it was time to chase the field down, and believe me, he decided.

Hall of Fame jockey Willie Shoemaker often rode 'Silky' and said that on one occasion he galloped along in a race at his own pace until the field was 41 lengths in front of him. When he decided to go, he still won by three lengths. To make things a little more interesting, these were not long races, with all under 10 furlongs (2000 metres) and some as short as 5.5 furlongs (1100 metres); he would finish the race like a whirlwind.

Willie Shoemaker was quoted once about Silky Sullivan:

> You can't do a thing with him. You just have to allow him to run his own race, at his own speed, in his own style. You just sit there and wait hoping you won't have to wait too long, because when he really

> decided to chase the other horses down, you had to be alert or he might leave you behind – and then you hung on for your dear life.

He was bred by Californian dentists Dr Riley Roberts and his wife Nell Roberts. Silky's dam Lady N Silk was a non-winner in four starts and she was rescued from the Santa Anita track in 1951 before she was to be destroyed, due to a serious injury to her left foot. His sire, Sullivan, did not have a great record as he raced mostly as a sprinter in his early days in Ireland, winning only once. When he came to California, he had won five of eight races. Strange how some legends have their beginning.

Jack Lynaugh was responsible for all of the young horses at Three Rings Ranch in Beaumont, California, where Silky was sent to be prepared for the upcoming Yearling Sales. Jack could remember him clearly:

> He was all personality, more than any other horse I have ever handled and I have handled thousands since 1932. I have always been crazy about him. When the other yearlings were let out of the paddock, Silky would just hang back and wait until they were half way across the 28 acre pasture, and then he would take off after them. He always wound up on top – just like the races he contested later in his career.

Silky Sullivan was sold in 1956 to Phil Klipstein and Tom Ross for US$10,700, and then sent to Devonshire Downs in San Fernando to be trained by Reggie Cornell. The first race he contested was a 5.5 furlong (1100 metre) maiden dash at Hollywood Racetrack in May 1957.

Reggie Cornell remembers: 'He came out of the gate in a trance and I thought to myself, well here's one for the glue factory. Then all of a sudden it was like he was stung by a bee. Until he made that big move, I thought I would be looking for a job.'

Jockey George Taniguchi said:

> He jumped with the field but it was like he was being sucked back and I thought to myself, oh my God, what is he doing? He was

> already 15 to 20 lengths behind the other horses. I let him go like that until the three furlong mark before I gave him a tap on the shoulder, then he changed gears. I never ever thought we would catch the others up because we were so far back over a short race. I never rode anything like that before – we were flying.

And the Silky Sullivan legend was born.

They began to document his achievements, not the times that he ran, or the number of wins that he had, but his unique place in the history books was determined by how many lengths' start he would give the rest of the field before he decided to fly.

On 7 December 1957, he was entered into the $25,000 Golden Gate Futurity over 1 mile (1600 metres). After walking out of the gates and giving his opponents a 27 length start, he went on to win the race in typical fashion. Hall of Fame jockey Manuel Ycaza said after the race:

> When I asked him to run, he responded and ran like the wind. You knew then that he was something special. It takes a lot of speed when you are 20 lengths behind the field, just to challenge and be so competitive right to the end of the race. You have to be greased lightning.

Early the next year, on 30 January 1958, he contested a race that ultimately confounded two of the best jockeys around, making them sit up and take notice of his amazing speed and talent. In the field were two very good horses in Circle Lea, ridden by Ray York, and The Shoe, ridden by Willie Shoemaker. These two horses staged a duel in a tearaway performance and appeared to have the race between them, with the main bunch of the field lengths behind. Silky Sullivan brought up the rear and people had every reason to believe that he was being pulled up, such was the distance he was behind the bunched field.

The two leaders went hammer and tongs down the straight and across the line, giving nothing else a chance – or so they thought. When the tote board flashed a photo, York, riding Circle Lea, was sure that he had edged out Shoemaker. 'I beat you this time Willie,' said York.

'You sure did, Ray, but you didn't beat that sucker on the outside,' was the reply.

Sure enough, they were so absorbed with their own battle that they didn't notice Silky Sullivan running, or should we say flying, down the outside until it was all over. Silky had done the impossible again, and when Ray and Willie had the benefit of watching a replay later, they just shook their heads, got up from their chairs with a look of astonishment and a smile from ear to ear, and walked out of the room.

It didn't always go to plan, because a few weeks later he ran in the $67,000 California Breeders Champion Stakes and failed to run down the eventual winner by a neck, after giving him and the rest of the field a 40 length start. The rider of the winner, Old Pueblo, the great Eddie Arcaro, said of Silky Sullivan that day, 'He's just a running fool. He runs the last 200 metres like the wind. You feel like you are standing still when he comes up alongside.'

Just to prove a point, in Silky's next race in a 6.5 furlong (1300 metre) race on 25 February 1958, he came from 41 lengths last, to win running away. He didn't do it to show off; it was just the way he ran. This prompted CBS to use a split screen concept when televising his races, to show the general field in one panel and Silky in a second panel. They all knew that he would be on his own out the back and a normal screen would not capture his position in the field. So when you see the split screen concept being used today, you can think back with fond memories to Silky Sullivan.

Mr Heart Attack retired at the end of his four-year-old season. He was sent birthday cards and Christmas cards by the adoring public for the rest of his life. On 18 November 1977, at the age of 22, Silky Sullivan died peacefully in his sleep. He was buried at the course at the Golden Gate Fields, right near the Tote Board. He was considered to be one of the greatest finishers of all time, and that one stanza on his plaque says it all.

A Kentucky Derby winner and Martin Luther King Jr

... a twist in a very controversial tale

There are two major players in this 'untold' story. One is a remarkable thoroughbred racehorse admired by a nation, and the other a great man of peace admired by the world.

Dancer's Image was an American thoroughbred racehorse, born in 1965 and bred at Ryemeadow Farms at Rye, New Hampshire, in north-eastern USA. Owned by Peter Fuller and trained by Lou Cavalaris Jr, the grey colt was sired by the great Native Dancer and his career record was 24 starts for twelve wins, five seconds and one third, resulting in prize money totalling at that time of US$236,636.

His unusual place in history is that he was first across the line in the 1968 Kentucky Derby by a clear one and a half lengths in front of the second horse. Unfortunately the records show that the race was awarded to the favoutite Forward Pass, with Dancer's Image relegated to last place.

As a two-year-old, he won a number of Stakes races in Ontario, Canada, which showed that he had a very promising career ahead of him. As long as they could keep him on the straight and narrow, he would have an even more lucrative stud career.

Here are Dancer's Image's major wins:

- Clarendon Stakes: 1967
- Grey Stakes: 1967
- Vandal Stakes: 1967
- Maryland Futurity Stakes: 1967
- Wood Memorial Stakes: 1968
- Kentucky Derby: 1968 – (first past the post but relegated to last)

During his career, the brilliant three-year-old always had trouble with his ankles, which needed treatment on a regular basis. On the Sunday prior to the Kentucky Derby, his handlers noticed that the ankles were again becoming an issue. A veterinarian was called and he subsequently administered a painkilling substance that would also assist in reducing the inflamed joints. It was legal in many parts of the United States and was quite a common practice. The substance was still on the banned list at Churchill Downs, the home of the Kentucky Derby, but the medication had time to dissipate from the horse's system as there were still six days to go before the running of the Derby.

Phenylbutazone is described as a non-steroidal anti-inflammatory drug and is probably one of the most common medications used in horse racing today in the United States. Just to give a comparison, thirteen of the sixteen runners in the 1986 Kentucky Derby (won by Ferdinand) competed in the race while on this painkiller. However, we are talking about the 1960s.

In his lead-up to the Kentucky Derby and Triple Crown Series in 1968, Dancer's Image won the Wood Memorial Stakes, which was a Grade 1 race, but still remained second favourite to Florida Derby and Blue Grass Stakes winner, Forward Pass. Dancer's Image stamped his quality in thoroughbred racing by winning the 1968 Kentucky Derby, defeating the favourite Forward Pass, and as is the case in all racing, samples were taken from the horses after the running and sent away for laboratory testing.

Some time later, it was announced that Dancer's Image had tested positive to the prohibited drug phenylbutazone and was subsequently relegated to last, with the new winner for the record books being Forward Pass. The owner, Peter Fuller, and connections of Dancer's Image were devastated. Fuller and the horse's handlers believed that someone had given their colt another dose of the drug after the safe cut-off time for detection and then was instrumental in filing an appeal for his disqualification.

The Kentucky State Racing Commission was advised but the distribution of the purse was released to Calumet Farm's Forward Pass. The owner of Dancer's Image did not take this lying down; he took legal action and in December 1970, over two years after the event, a Kentucky court awarded first place prize money to go to the owner, Peter Fuller. An appeal was filed and a further eighteen months later, in April 1972, the decision was overturned in the highest court in Kentucky, and the original disqualification stood.

The story of the 1968 Kentucky Derby was featured in just about every sporting editorial throughout the United States and overseas. Controversy and innuendo still surround the decision today, so much so that as recently as 2008, the Churchill Downs Media Guide for the Derby still showed Dancer's Image as the official winner in their illustrated chart. The *New York Times* is quoted as describing the race and the outcome as 'the most controversial decision in the history of the Triple Crown'.

Dancer's Image ran in the second leg of Triple Crown in 1968, the Preakness Stakes, after the debacle of the Derby, and was again beaten by Forward Pass, this time into third spot. Unfortunately, in this race he was relegated to last again for interference in the running with a horse called Martins Jig. Unfortunately his ankle problems persisted and on retirement he was sent to stand at studs in Ireland, France and finally Japan, where the little grey warrior passed away at the grand old age of 27 on 26 December 1992. His immediate progeny gave us great champions in Godswalk, the flying mare Absaretch, the prolific producer Lady Rushen and many others.

Now the link to Martin Luther King Jnr ...

Just to refresh your memory on the great man, he was born in 1929 and died in April 1968, the month before the running of the Kentucky Derby. Dr King was the leader of the American Civil Rights movement, and as such had millions of followers collectively trying to break down the walls of segregation and racism. Unfortunately, King had many enemies, none more so at that time than in the southern states of America, where African Americans were treated as second-class citizens. How can we forget those freedom marches and the subsequent violence in the southern states during this period?

In 1964, Martin Luther King Jr made history by becoming the youngest person to receive the Nobel Peace Prize for his work to end racial segregation and racial discrimination. He raised public consciousness to this cause and also established himself as one of the great orators in US history.

And here is the talking point.

Forty years after the disqualification of Dancer's Image in the 1968 Kentucky Derby, owner Peter Fuller still believes he was a victim of prejudice. He was well known as a wealthy Civil Rights sympathiser from Boston and believed he offended the Kentucky racing administrators by donating a $62,000 purse won by Dancer's Image to Coretta Scott King, the wife of Martin Luther King Jr. This act of generosity was made two days after King's murder, and just a few weeks before the 1968 Kentucky Derby.

What do you think?

The great American 'Battleship'

... and a feat that has never been equalled!

It is well recognised that steeplechasing is probably the most difficult and punishing form of horse racing that has ever been devised. Not only are the horses and their riders asked to travel over long race distances, some as long as 7 kilometres, but in doing so, they have to jump as many as 30 fences along the way. Fences can be made of timber, rock, plastic and steel, with the much friendlier versions today made of a synthetic brush. These fences can be up to 52 inches (over 1.3 metres) high, so is it any wonder that over the years we have seen many horses meeting their demise in the midst of one of these events?

The most recognised of these steeplechase races are on opposite sides of the world. The great English Grand National held at Aintree, near Liverpool, England, is a race steeped in tradition and folklore with echoes of the adoring public cheering on the great Red Rum, and his unforgettable contribution to the history of this great race. Run over a staggering 4 miles 856 yards, which is the metric equivalent of 7.242 kilometres, it comprises two circuits, with the first fourteen fences jumped twice and a further two fences in the finishing straight combining to total a staggering 30 fences and ditches. It is a handicap race open to horses aged six years and over, and prize money as at 2011 was in excess of £500,000.

The Breeder's Cup Grand National Steeplechase, now known as the American Grand National, is held at Moorlands Farms Racecourse, Far Hills, New Jersey, United States. With a total of fourteen fences and run over 2 miles 1100 yards, the metric equivalent of 4.22 kilometres, it is the oldest and one of the most important steeplechasing events held outside Europe. In more recent years, the race was brought back from obscurity due to the deeds of the multiple winner McDynamo, which won it five times in a row from 2003 to 2007.

Then along came Battleship ...

Foaled in America in 1927, Battleship was the son of the great American champion Man O'War. Standing just over 15 hands tall, he epitomised the saying, 'It's not the size of the dog in the fight, but the size of the fight in the dog.' What a courageous horse he must have been. Chestnut in colour, he raced as an entire throughout his long career.

In 1931, after a reasonable career in flat racing, Battleship was sold at the age of four to Marion DuPont Scott of the prominent wealthy DuPont family of chemical manufacturing fame, for US$12,000. The intent was to have him trained in steeplechase racing and at the age of seven, he won the American Grand National, which at that time was the most prestigious steeplechase race in the United States.

After bowing a tendon in 1935, he was sent to England for treatment. His new English trainer was Reginald Hobbs, and after a significant lay-off, Battleship returned to jumps races in 1936, but won only once from five starts. Further improvement followed in 1937, and he won five of his thirteen starts.

In 1938, the eleven-year-old became the first American-bred horse to win England's Grand National at Aintree. In a string of firsts that day, he was ridden by the youngest Grand National winning jockey, Bruce Hobbs, the trainer's seventeen-year-old son. What a great sight it must have been, a 6 feet 3 inch (1.9 metres) young jockey astride a compact 15-hand champion chaser. As at 2011, Battleship remains one of the smallest entires to have won Grand National races on opposite sides of the Atlantic Ocean.

In fact, since he was so short and muscular, the British nicknamed him 'the American Pony'.

A remarkable horse, with a remarkable achievement – a real Battleship!

Julie Krone

... the 'pocket rocket', one of the tiniest but best American jockeys

Born on 24 July 1963 in Benton Harbor, Michigan, Julie Krone went on to ride over 3158 winners. She was inducted into the Michigan Sports Hall of Fame in 2002. On the strength of it, these statistics sound very impressive, but behind the scenes and from very unusual and humble beginnings, her chosen path was fraught with obstacles that would have denied a future for the average person chasing the dream.

Julie was far from average; her autobiography, *Riding for My Life*, and the feature film of her life, *The Boys Club*, highlight her special qualities and her determination to achieve what she set out to achieve.

How difficult it was for female riders to be recognised in those early days. Kathy Kusner went to court in 1968 to become a jockey in the United States. Around that time, Penny Ann Early was shown the back door when she tried to get a mount at the home of the Kentucky Derby, Churchill Downs, and in 1969, discrimination was at its worst when the trailer home of jockey Barbara Jo Rubin was stoned in a bid to frighten her away from her dream.

As a young child, Julie and her brother had an upbringing that could have been best described as bohemian. They had the run of

A BIG HORSE HE SAID... BUT THIS IS RIDICULOUS!

their small property and as a two-year-old, Julie bonded very quickly with the family's horses. Her father was an artist and photographer while her mother was a riding instructor, so her upbringing was one of freedom and appreciation of expression and one that stood her in good stead for what lay before her.

Great horse people all seem to have that ability to communicate with these magnificent animals and Julie, with her unusual upbringing, had a love for these great steeds; she was able to sooth the savage beast, so to speak, and get the best out of the horses that she rode.

Standing 4 feet 10 inches tall (147 centimetres) and weighing 100 lb (45 kg), she was much shorter and lighter than her counterparts and was a Captain Courageous. After completing her sophomore year at school, Julie made her way to Churchill Downs with her mum and a forged birth certificate. She just wanted to be a jockey and her mum backed her 100 per cent. Together they knocked on many doors, and finally Julie was given a chance at her dream by trainer Jerry Pace. Their introduction was what movies are made of, and showed what determination and focus she had at such a young age.

Jerry Pace, trainer: 'So, you want to be a jockey?'

Julie Krone: 'No, I'm *gonna* be a jockey!'

So her life as a jockey began, and just five weeks after this introduction, Julie rode her first winner. Her tiny frame and child-like appearance hid the strength that she possessed. Maryland trainer Ben Perkins Jr told the *New York Times* in 1981 about when he was introduced to Julie for the very first time. He said, 'This tiny, child-like figure had a handshake like a vice and she brought me to my knees.'

There were times during her career when she lived on the edge, experimenting with drugs and fast cars; however, it was the horrific race falls that put an end to her career and left her pondering about life after horses.

Her life was also one that was littered with firsts. It was at Maryland where Julie was the first woman to win a title at a major racetrack. Just to prove this was no fluke, she went on to win riding championships at no less than five other tracks: Belmont Park,

Gulfstream Park, Monmouth Park, Meadowlands and Atlantic City Race Course. Julie was the first woman to ride in the Kentucky Derby and one of only a handful of riders to win six races in the one day. In 1993, riding the 13/1 shot Colonial Affair, she became the first woman to win a Triple Crown event, the Belmont Stakes.

After a couple of serious race falls, there were many months of recovery and soul searching. On 18 April 1999, after three winning rides and two seconds, Julie Krone quietly got off her mount after the last race and said, 'I won't be riding any more.'

Her record shows that she was the winner of many of the United States' classic races, and while her admirers were disappointed not to see her wearing the silks again, Julie knew that her time had come to an end – maybe her nerve and confidence played a part in her decision that day, but it certainly was the right decision.

There are many things said about Julie's illustrious career and her fight for the acceptance of female jockeys, but there are two statements, one from her employers and one from herself, that clearly indicate the riding skills and the determination that she had.

From the trainers: 'Julie would get on a horse that we would call wild, and they would just melt in her hands – they would just relax and do stuff they had never done before.'

From Julie: 'I want my life to be a lesson for every kid out there, and if the stable gate is closed, climb over the fence.'

One very special lady.

McDynamo

... the McDynamite of the American Grand National

With the blue blood of Ribot, Nashua and Northern Dancer running through his veins, it was no wonder that Michael Moran parted with US$82,000 in 1998 at the Keeneland Yearling Sales to buy this young thoroughbred. His pedigree was top shelf and a successful racing career on the flat was almost assured.

However, fate has a way of dealing a hand that sometimes comes as a great surprise to all. McDynamo matured and grew to be absolutely nothing like his pedigree suggested. He was an average-looking brown horse that did very average things, and it wasn't until 2002 as a three-year-old that he had four starts for one win. Just as things looked a little brighter, he had a lengthy period on the sidelines after an operation on his hind ankle, before having five starts the following year for another single win.

The dreams all began to unravel for Michael Moran so rather unexpectedly, he changed tack and sent McDynamo to Senna Hendricks in the hope that his determined little underachiever would fare a little better over the jumps. The horse proved to be a willing student under Senna, who rode him in most of his track work. For a so-called average horse, he possessed a fierce determination and attitude that had to be kept under control if he was to go on and compete successfully over the jumps.

Compete he did. In a remarkable period beginning in 2003, McDynamo won the most revered steeplechase race in the United States, the Breeders' Cup Grand National, five years in a row, completing this amazing feat in 2007 as a ten-year-old. Few racehorses have managed to win the same race a number of times, but his record stands testimony to his sheer determination, his strength and endurance, and the nurturing of his trainer, Senna Hendricks.

It wasn't as if they were easy races to compete in, because to prove his championship qualities, in 2007 he was one of 42 other horses and was the oldest of them all, but still managed to win this prestigious event.

Here are his greatest wins:

- three Eclipse Awards: 2003, 2005, 2006
- five Breeders' Cup Grand National Steeplechases: 2003, 2004, 2005, 2006, 2007
- three Colonial Cups: 2003, 2005, 2006

McDynamo was dubbed 'The King of Far Hills' by his racing fans as he won an astounding seven wins from seven starts at the New Jersey course.

The parting word on McDynamo belongs to his trainer Senna Hendricks, as she best describes his growth over the years:

> He's got grey hair now and he's a lot quieter. As a four-year-old I was trying to rein him in and keep him under control. At ten, my job was to try and perk him up. Has he lost his desire? I don't think so. He's gotten more mature and he now understands his job. When he was four it was let me at 'em, every fence, every step of the way. Now he knows the race is 2 miles 1100 yards.

What a dynamic McDynamo.

From slavery to the Prince of Pigskin!

... a story of the two great African American jockeys

This is the story of Willie Simms and Alonzo 'Lonnie' Clayton, the part they played in the wake of the American Civil War, and the African Americans' march to equality and recognition in the United States. But first, let us consider the timing and the circumstances.

In 1860, the United States had 3,953,760 registered African American slaves and 488,070 registered free African Americans. The American Civil War began in 1861, and this marked the beginning of the end of slavery in the US. After the start of the Civil War, the figure was changed to zero slaves and 4,880,009 free African Americans, with the total general population at that time in America being 38,558,371.

Freedom for a great many African Americans never really eventuated until many years later. To assume that their journey during this period was one of free people is very much a misinterpretation of the facts, because their struggle for equality was a continuous journey that lasted for many, many years.

Willie Simms was born on 16 January 1870 near Augusta, Georgia, in the United States. He began his racing career at the age of seventeen and just seven years later, in 1894, he won the United States riding title of Champion Jockey by Wins, including back-to-back Belmont Stakes. Willie was one of those rare horsemen that looked as one with the thoroughbred he was riding, and was credited as being one of the pioneers of the short-stirrup riding crouch in the United States that is synonymous with the great jockeys of the world today.

In 1895 he rode in England and has the rare distinction of being the first American jockey to win on an American horse in that country. Returning to the US the following year, he continued to win many classic races, including more legs of the US Triple Crown. Willie remains the only African American jockey to win all the American Classic races (the Kentucky Derby, the Preakness Stakes and the Belmont Stakes).

Retiring from the saddle in 1901, he finished with over 1100 wins. On 26 February 1927, he passed away at the young age of 57, and it's a clear indication of the prejudice during that time that this great American jockey is not spoken about as one of their greatest champions of all time.

Here is a sampling of Willie Simms' Classic wins:

- Kentucky Derby: 1896, 1898 (US Triple Crown)
- Preakness Stakes: 1898 (US Triple Crown)
- Belmont Stakes: 1893, 1894 (US Triple Crown)
- Spinaway Stakes: 1891
- Champion Stakes: 1892

Of course, he won many more races than this list shows. Willy was inducted into the United States Racing Hall of Fame in 1977.

Alonzo 'Lonnie' Clayton was born just six years after Willy, in 1876, and unfortunately died on 17 March 1917 at the age of 41 years. He was described as one of the great riders of the New York racing circuit all through the 1890s, and today still holds the record of being the youngest jockey ever to win the Kentucky Derby in its 136-year history up to 2011. Not a bad distinction for a fifteen-year-old who was born one of nine children in Kansas City, Missouri. At the age of ten, Lonnie's family moved to North Rock, Arkansas, where he attended school, and to help support his family's meagre income, he worked at the local hotel as a shoeshine boy.

Leaving home at the tender age of twelve, Lonnie gained

experience around racehorses, working as a stable hand and exercise rider, and in 1890, at the grand old age of fourteen, he began his professional racing career at the Clifton Race Track in New Jersey. Such was his talent for riding horses that he enjoyed immediate success and followed up by riding the 1892 Kentucky Derby winner Azra, at the age of fifteen. In 1895, at nineteen, he won an amazing 144 races and finished in the money 60 per cent of the time.

Lonnie Clayton's riding success allowed him to acquire some property in Little Rock and the family home he built was described as the 'finest house on the North Side'. Unfortunately, after a few years, because he was denied the right to earn a living doing what he did best, he was forced to sell his home and investment property. Today his residence is known as Engelberger House, and in 1990, it was listed on the National Register of Historic Places.

The tragedy, and it's not such an uncommon story, is that Alonzo 'Lonnie' Clayton lived his last few years in California working as a hotel bellhop. He died of chronic pulmonary tuberculosis in 1917. However, what cannot be erased is his amazing racing record; here are just a few of his achievements:

- Kentucky Derby: 1892
- Kentucky Oaks: 1894, 1895
- Champagne Stakes: 1891
- Travers Stakes: 1892
- Arkansas Derby: 1895
- Jermone Handicap: 1891
- Clark Handicap: 1892, 1897
- Monmouth Handicap: 1893

In 1893, he won the Leading Rider Award at Churchill Downs.

Willie and Lonnie, true champions for their cause!

CHAPTER 4
Around the World

Introducing Kincsem: 54 starts, 54 wins
... she was the best of all time!

These facts are irrefutable. The following historical data show there is no doubt that this Hungarian champion thoroughbred was the best of the best.

Kincsem was a chestnut filly born in Hungary in 1874 and her record has stood the test of time; in nearly 140 years of racing and compiling records, no-one has beaten her. She had 54 starts in her career for an amazing 54 wins. You can scan all statistics recorded in thoroughbred racing, and you will never find anything quite like her.

While her sire Cambuscan had his beginning in England, being owned by Queen Victoria, he eventually found his way to the courts of Hungary where he stood at the national Stud and gave to the world of racing this mighty mare. Kincsem, the Queen of the Turf of her time, certainly didn't look the part. She was quite the ugly duckling to look at, very lean, and would always have her head drooped so low that one thought she had something wrong with her neck and was unable to keep her head upright. She enjoyed a privileged upbringing in a large estate and would run wild through the fields with other horses of her own age.

On one early occasion, Kincsem went missing from her home and was found days later in the company of a band of gypsies. When her Hungarian owner confronted the gypsies they said, as they would, that they had found her cantering along the road. But the owner wasn't convinced so he asked them point blank why they had taken her and not another of the well muscled and better-looking horses. The answer came from the head of the travelling gypsies, that 'it may be so but she is fleet of foot and is a champion'.

Racing throughout Europe, she won all ten races she contested as a two-year-old and the seventeen races she contested as a three-year-old, and so on, and finally, after five years of racing and the opposition not wanting to compete against her, the mighty Hungarian mare was retired.

Here are just a few of Kincsem's great wins:

- Hungarian Two Thousand Guineas: 1877
- Hungarian One Thousand Guineas: 1877
- Hungarian Oaks: 1877
- Hungarian Autumn Oaks: 1877, 1878, 1879
- Hungarian St Leger: 1877
- Austrian Derby: 1877
- Austrian Kaiserpreis: 1877
- Grosser Preis von Hanover: 1877
- Grosser Preis von Baden: 1877, 1878, 1879
- Staatspreis Eister Classe: 1878
- Goodwood Cup: 1878
- Grand Prix de Deauville: 1878

Suffering a common colic attack in 1887, she died, but not before she was able to foal exceptional racehorses that only added to the memory of the great champion she was. Here are a few of them:

- Budagyongyw: won the German Derby
- Ollyan Nincs: won the Hungarian St Leger
- Kincsor: second in the Austrian Derby
- Kincs: an influential broodmare as her daughter
- Napfeny: a Classic Stakes winner

There is no doubt that those who study the mighty thoroughbred historically simply regard Kincsem as the best of the best.

Muhamed

... the horse that could solve mathematical equations!

There was a horse in the nineteenth century that could solve mathematical problems. His name was Muhamed.

I don't profess to know what a cube root is, so for those of you like myself who would like to understand, here is a dictionary explanation: 'a number that produces a specified number when it is multiplied by itself twice. The cube root of 8 is 2'. Hope that is clear for everyone!

It was late in the nineteenth century that the claims of Muhamed's intelligence started to surface. His owner Karl Krall was known to have told all and sundry that his charge could solve maths problems, namely cube roots. The claims did not stop at maths, as Muhamed was also reported to have an interest in music as well. Karl had developed a relationship with his horse whereby the answers to maths questions would be tapped out by his hooves: one hoof pawing at the floor would represent units of ten, and the other hoof following the same motion would be the signal for single units. Muhamed was not the only gifted equine in the stable; the story goes that Karl had a stable full of smart horses, but Muhamed was clearly the best. The stable lads who worked at this farm had the feeling that they could communicate with the wonder horse as well.

After much conjecture, the day came when Muhamed was to be tested by academics and skeptics in his own environment. Numbers were written on the wall of the stable and everyone watched with great anticipation as Muhamed tapped out the answer. They were amazed at his accuracy but as his owner pointed out, even human savants were able to complete complicated tasks and they were not thought of as geniuses in any way at that time.

Several attempts by the skeptics to disprove his ability came to nothing, so to everyone in attendance he was a freak. On the other hand, maybe, just maybe, they hadn't noticed a trick between master and his horse to debunk the entire theory. The academics were amazed at what they saw and could only deduce that there was a relationship between the pair that in some way transferred brainwaves from master to horse.

Unfortunately for Muhamed, he was taken to serve in World War I and was never seen again.

Just imagine a horse like that in today's environment, mingling with other horses before being put into the barrier stalls at the start of a race.

Maybe the conversation would go something like this: 'Okay, I want everyone to go flat out and approaching the turn, just pull back until I get to the lead and then chase me down the straight to the finishing line without going past me. Pass it on as I don't want any stuff-ups and I especially do not want any interference from those little men up top!'

Lammtarra – from chocolates to boiled lollies

... the kingmaker who ended up a heartbreaker

Lammtarra, regally bred and regally owned, enjoyed a racing career that was probably as good as it could possibly get. His racing record stood at only four starts for four wins, but they weren't ordinary races; they were the Epsom Derby, the King George VI & Queen Elizabeth Stakes, and what is regarded as the most prestigious race in the world, the Prix de l'Arc de Triomphe in 1995. His only start as a two-year-old saw him take out the Washington Singer Stakes. His sire was the great Nijinsky and he was owned by Saeed bin Maktoum Al Maktoum, whose father actually bred Lammtarra at his stud farm in Kentucky.

After winning his first race as a two-year-old, Lammtarra became seriously ill with Marie's disease and was off the scene for about ten months before he had his second race start, in the Epsom Derby. As the field rounded Tattenham Corner in the Derby, with Lammtarra way back near the tail of the field, there was no hint as to what was about to eventuate. With only 400 metres left to travel, Lammtarra took the challenge and chased the leaders to win running away by a length. He had spent so long away from the track with such a serious condition that those close to him had their doubts as to whether he could mount a challenge first up over the Derby distance. But the champ was back and fulfilling all of his promise, and he broke the track record as well.

The other two classic races followed as a three-year-old; he showed no mercy to his opposition when he won the King George VI & Queen Elizabeth Stakes and then 'the Arc'.

His connections must have believed in Federico Tesio's theory that lightly raced stallions are the most successful at stud. He was immediately retired and sent to the breeding barn at Dalham Hall Stud at Newmarket. With his unbeaten record in winning the classic races of 1995, his stud fee rose to dizzy heights. Four career starts for four wins.

In 1996 Japanese breeders paid US$30 million for his services, with the initial stud fee starting at around US$100,000. To the utter disappointment of his investors, he met with limited success. His stud fee was discounted to around US$10,000, so when the opportunity arose, his original breeder bought him back from the stud in Japan. He thought that with a little more maturity, his chances for success would be enhanced just on the strength of his own breeding.

Jockeys who had ridden him remarked that he was possibly the best horse they had ever had the pleasure of riding; however, this was one case where the talent never transferred to the breeding barn.

A very sad twist in the tale

Lammtara's first educator and trainer was a gifted young horseman by the name of Alex Scott. His success as a trainer was well noted by his peers for the way he handled horses and prepared them for their racing career. He won many classic races right from the beginning, so the industry was certainly taking notice of him. Success breeds success; he was offered the young colt by the great sire Nijinsky to train for the Sheik.

Scott saw so much potential in Lammtarra; he instantly recognised that the colt was an ideal Derby prospect and he would train him, good luck permitting, to win the English Derby within two years.

Acting on what he had seen so far from the unraced colt, and with the courage of his convictions, he placed a bet of £1000 there and then at a betting shop, at odds of 33/1, for Lammtarra to win the English Derby later in his career – unbelievable!

In a tragedy befitting a modern-day opera, Alex Scott was shot and killed at the age of 34 by a disgruntled employee in his very own stables in September 1994. Lammtarra went to another trainer and in 1995 he did win the English Derby; his owner made a very emotional acceptance speech for all of those who knew the story. There weren't too many dry eyes in the house that day. The betting shop that held Alex's original wager put the icing on the cake for Alex's wife, Julia, when a full eighteen months after Alex's bet on Lammtarra to win the Derby, they presented her with a cheque for £33,000.

Fanfreluche

... another victim of kidnapping

What do Fanfreluche and Shergar have in common? While kidnapping is a very serious crime and does happen in the world of human drama, it is an extremely rare occurrence in the animal world. These were two thoroughbred champions that were subject to kidnapping events, with the outcome of each poles apart.

Fanfreluche was a dark bay filly foaled in 1967 in Canada, apparently named after a popular identity in a children's program on TV. Sired by the great Northern Dancer from the dam Ciboulette, she had 21 career starts for eleven wins, six seconds and two thirds. At the end of her racing career in 1970, the three-year-old filly had amassed prize money of US$238,688.

Successfully racing as a two- and three-year-old in Canada and the United States, Fanfreluche won the Sovereign Award for Canadian Horse of the Year, and the Eclipse Award for Outstanding Three-Year-Old Filly. After finishing racing as a three-year-old, she was sold to prominent American identity Bertram R Firestone of the Firestone tyre empire. Fanfreluche's major Classic wins included the following:

- Princess Elizabeth Stakes: 1969
- Natalma Stakes: 1969

- Manitoba Derby: 1970
- Alabama Stakes: 1970
- Benson & Hedges Invitational Handicap: 1970
- Quebec Derby: 1970

She also won the following industry awards:

- United States Co-Champion Three-Year-old Filly: 1970
- Canadian Horse of the Year: 1970
- Sovereign Award for Outstanding Broodmare: 1978
- Canadian Racing Hall of Fame: 1971

With such an enviable record on the track, this beautifully bred mare soon gained the attention of all of the major breeders and they were lining up to have her covered by the very best stallions standing throughout the world. One of her early unions was with the mighty Secretariat, arguably the best horse of the modern era and one that would guarantee a record price in the sales ring for the foal, as well as creating a talent pool that would be the envy of every other breeder in the world.

One night in June 1977, while in foal to Secretariat, Fanfreluche just disappeared. All the security was in place at Claiborne Farm, but one of their security patrollers had a lapse in judgement when he assumed the head count in a particular paddock. It was discovered at first light that their star mare was missing. That would be the last thing you would expect – the security patrollers would have expected a veterinary issue with so many mares ready to give birth.

When the morning head count was completed a second time, their worst fears were realised. On closer inspection, it was discovered that part of the fence had been dismantled. Only one thing could have happened: Fanfreluche, in foal to Secretariat, had been kidnapped. The authorities were immediately informed.

One may wonder what advantage there would be for anyone to kidnap a racehorse, especially one in foal; it didn't take long for all to realise that after the foal was born and with careful falsification of documents and some willing participants, they could have a talented young horse. Obviously there would be no reference to Fanfreluche or Secretariat on the identity and breeding registration papers, but they just may have one that could race like the wind. A huge reward was immediately posted for Fanfreluche's safe return.

This sort of crime could not be acted out without the knowledge of at least a couple of undesirables. When more than one person knows a secret, then it isn't a secret anymore and it wasn't long before the state police were looking for one William McCandless. He was well known for all the wrong reasons in the racing fraternity, and finally after a few months the authorities received a tip-off that led them to a small farm in southern Kentucky, where they found the mare Fanfreluche being cared for by a local farmer who had found her having a feed on the side of the road nearby. He was quickly cleared of any involvement and was rewarded for his kindness in looking after an abandoned mare in foal.

The perpetrator must have heard on the grapevine about those who were looking for him, so he decided to quit his plan and let the mare go. Later, back at Claiborne, Fanfreluche gave birth to a Secretariat colt and it was named Sain Et Sauf. A loose translation of the name from French to English is simply 'safe and sound'.

When McCandless was found a few years later, he was already serving time for other offences. He was subsequently charged with the kidnapping of Franfreluche, and was sentenced to three more years in jail.

While Fanfreluche continued producing world-class foals from the very best of sires, Mr McCandless on the other hand continued on his merry way by conceiving all sorts of dodgy practices within the racing game, the most well known and despised of which was his trick in not allowing a horse to run to its full potential.

You couldn't say he developed the art of sponging, but he perfected it around that time. Sponging is the practice of inserting the appropriate-sized sponge up both nostrils of a horse about to race. Its purpose was to block part of the air passage of the animal and not allow a full intake of air as it was running. Hence a horse would finish well down the order in the contested field and look as though it had a bad day as it was labouring for breath. When you consider that people who take bets could be more interested in a well-performed horse not being able to win, that creates a gold mine for the shifty bookie and the unsuspecting punter. All the money would end up in the bookie's bag, and of course a commission would find its way into the pocket of William Michael McCandless.

Not much more can be told about this gentleman, because after many years of indiscretions he was once more wanted by the authorities, but he did a runner and was never heard of again – good riddance.

The IRA must have read this story because a few years after this kidnapping, in 1983, the Irish champion Shergar was kidnapped; unfortunately for him, he was never found and never heard of again.

What a ride …

A very clever Hans

… a horse is a horse is a horse of course – isn't it?

Here is another one to confound the critics. Once more there seems to be something in the water in Germany, because hot on the heels of the intelligent horse Muhamed, along comes a very clever Hans. Hans was also able to show the sceptics that a four-legged animal may have a lot more intelligence than we give it credit for. Hans was an extremely good trotting horse bred for racing. Hans and his owner became famous as a pair that could display communication and calculations for all to see.

In the early 1900s there was a lot of interest shown in animal intelligence compared to human intelligence by one Charles Darwin. His theories were astounding for that time and he and others started to talk about the theory of evolution.

Hans' owner Wilhelm von Osten was a very unique and one could say strange individual. Although quite learned, he had found his forte, much to the amazement of people around him, by communicating with his horses. Wilhelm held no fear about showing the rare talent of his horse to anyone who was willing to watch. His very clever Hans would perform to the public, displaying his ability to understand mathematical questions and, more importantly, to offer the right answers to the questions. Hans also enjoyed dabbling with musical notes.

In his open public displays, the common thread with Muhamed's performance was not so much how Wilhelm asked the question, but how Hans was able to give him the answer. The questions were always written on a board, and when Hans had deduced the answer, he would then paw at the floor with his hooves to tap out numbers that would represent tens or units and thus answer the question. Wilhelm and Hans travelled throughout Europe giving performances of their rare talents. Their story was so well known at the time that a feature article on them was published in the *New York Times*.

There was so much public interest in Hans' achievements in company with Wilhelm that in 1904 the Education Board appointed a group of learned men to investigate the claims of exceptional intelligence and to report their findings after the investigation. A leading academic, Carl Stumpf, headed the group that was known as the Hans Commission, and their findings stated that there were no tricks used in Hans' performance.

It really does raise more questions than it answers, doesn't it?

Von Osten died in 1909, and as if by fate, instructions had been given to executors of his estate that Hans would then be transferred in ownership to Karl Krall. Karl was the gentleman responsible for the horse Muhamed, which had the ability to solve complex maths problems using the same 'units and tens' method that Hans had used.

Horses of yesteryear

... these may jog your memories of times long gone!

Cast your mind back to when these names were mentioned in the old school history books, or memories that may be jolted from the early motion pictures that kept thousands of enthusiastic youngsters occupied in the stalls at the long-gone 'picture shows'. These names may take you back to more innocent times, happier times, or times that are better left alone!

Black Bess – the highwayman Dick Turpin's horse
Brown Beauty – Paul Revere borrowed her for his famous ride
Buttermilk – Dale Evans' horse
Champion – Gene Autrey's horse
Diablo – the Cisco Kid's horse
Incitatus – Roman emperor Caligula's favourite horse
Muhamed – the German horse capable of solving cube roots
Red Fox – a horse of Jesse James
Rocinante – Don Quixote's horse
Sampson – the tallest horse in the world, 21 and a half hands high
Scout – Tonto's horse
Silver – the Lone Ranger's horse
Thunder – Red Ryder's horse
Tony – actor Tom Mix's horse
Tornado – El Zorro's horse
Trigger – Roy Rogers' palomino
Topper – Hopalong Cassidy's horse

Do you remember any of them?

Federico Tesio

... in pursuit of excellence

It's a very special accolade when you are regarded as the best of the best in your particular chosen field, especially when it involves the worldwide thoroughbred racing industry. You would regard it as the pinnacle of your life's achievement to have your theories stand the test of time, and become a standard by which horse breeders today measure their success, no matter which side of the fence you are sitting on.

Federico Tesio changed the landscape of breeding and his theories have become such a science that there would not be a stud anywhere in the world that does not practise to a certain degree what he preached all those years ago. He has proven over time that the union of a heavily raced mare mated with a heavily raced sire, both of which were regarded as exceptional horses, would not produce an offspring that would match their ability. This theory is illustrated in today's modern breeding because when you have outstanding colts and great mares, they are retired early so that they can be introduced to the breeding barn in a very healthy and fit state. Connections normally do not wait until their opportunity rises for retirement because the horses are feeling the stress of a lot of racing.

Federico began life in Turin, Italy in 1869, and after passing his university exams he went on to serve in the Italian Army. Upon leaving the forces, he tried his luck in politics. However, in 1898, Federico Tesio with his wife Lydia had a sea change, or I should say a lake change, and bought a small farm on the edge of Lake Maggiore in Italy, where they began their life's work in changing the landscape of breeding thoroughbreds.

At their Dormello Stud, they kept what could only be described as ordinary broodmares, and no stallions. However, the mares had been very carefully chosen using a complex method of selection working back through many generations. In a careful study of the sires that were on offer, Federico and Lydia would delve deep into the horses' ancestry, going back quite a few generations of the complete family tree, and based on this knowledge they selected the stallions to cover their mares. It is interesting to note that none of the sires selected were what you would call fashionable.

Probably the most notable of the champions that they had bred on their property were Ribot, Donatello, Nearco and Cavaliere d'Arpino. They were all undefeated in their respective racing careers, except for Donatello, which had nine starts for eight wins and one second. Federico always stated that he felt it was very poor judgement by the rider who lost that race for Donatello, as the horse was asked to do too much too late in the race to be able to greet the judges in first place.

Nearco and Ribot contested 30 Classic and Group races between them and were undefeated in all of them. Federico Tesio's super-horse, Ribot, was an unraced two-year-old when Tesio unfortunately passed away, so he never got to see what most people regard as one of the most brilliant horses the world has ever seen.

Just to highlight the dominance of Federico and Lydia's theories on breeding, they together bred 22 Italian Derby winners, while they were involved in the ownership and training of sixteen of them. One of the greatest trainers on Australian turf is the inimitable Bart Cummings. His record at the end of 2011 was twelve Melbourne Cup winners, training them all and owning just a few. Just imagine if we could say that Bart had trained 22 winners of the Melbourne Cup, and that while he trained them all, he was the owner or part-owner of 16 of them – and he bred all of them. It is amazing when you consider that achievement.

Nearco was the leading sire in Ireland and Great Britain for a number of years, and also took the title of leading broodmare sire later in his career. His major wins were as follows:

- Gran Criterium: 1937
- Derby Italiano: 1938
- Italian 2000 Guineas: 1938
- Gran Premio de Milano: 1938
- Gran Premio d'Italia: 1938
- Gran Prix de Paris: 1938

These were great classic races, attracting the best there was to compete, and as previously stated, he remained undefeated right through his entire career.

Because of the political unrest in Europe in 1938, it was decided to extricate him from such an unpredictable environment, and so Nearco was sold to the Beech Horse Stud in Newmarket, England to continue his blossoming stud career. The foundation sires of his great empire were his three sons, Nearctic, Nasrullah and Royal Charger, which continued on the great work begun by their sire.

This family tree was responsible for giving the thoroughbred world such horses as Secretariat, regarded as one of the greatest racehorses ever to set foot on a racetrack. That line was also responsible for Seattle Slew, Ballymoss, the ill-fated Shergar, Mr Prospector, Nijinsky (the winner of the Triple Crown races in England), Invasor, the Aussie champ Better Loosen Up, and of course the sire of Secretariat, Bold Ruler. Simply the best of the best.

It was customary for Federico to make notes in his stud book whenever foals were born and finding their feet so he could judge their strengths. When Ribot was born and making his way around the paddock, Federico could find nothing encouraging to write about this unremarkable weanling, so the entry beside his name was left blank. He probably felt that if you could not say anything positive about a product of their program, then don't say anything at all.

When Ribot was put into training as a two-year-old, even though his size was described as medium, one outstanding feature had developed for him. Special girth straps had to be made because his chest was so robust there was nothing at the stud that would fit him. Federico Tesio's wife Lydia raced him after Tesio died.

Some of Ribot's major classic wins were as follows:

- Gran Criterium: 1954
- Gran Premio del Jockey Club: 1955
- Prix de I'Arc de Triomphe: 1955 and 1956
- Gran Premio de Milano: 1956
- King George VI & Queen Elizabeth Stakes: 1956

It was not just the fact that he won all of the sixteen classic and group races that he contested that was so amazing; it was the way he won them – every race was won with great ease, and some seemingly done in nothing more than a training gallop, with the jockey never having to wield the 'persuader'.

In 1959, it was decided to lease this great stallion to American interests for five years so that they could enjoy his genes on the other side of the world. The lease price for the five years was in excess of US$1.25 million – and this was in the late 1950s. However, he never returned home, and because he developed an unpredictable temper and disposition, no insurance company would cover him for his return to Newmarket. A deal was done and with that he spent the rest of his life in Kentucky.

His progeny won many classic races all over the world, including the Irish Derby, the English St Leger, the King George VI & Queen

Elizabeth Stakes, the Eclipse Stakes and the Prix de l'Arc de Triomphe, as well as all legs of the American Triple Crown, the Kentucky Derby, the Preakness Stakes and the Belmont Stakes.

His list of greatness just goes on and on, and the bloodlines that they created still dominate the breeding statistics all over the world. There is no doubt that the patience and understanding of the mild-mannered Federico, with his wife Lydia, played a significant part in what is described in industry terms as the most enviable legacy that we are able to enjoy today. Such is the reputation of this team that a number of races named after Federico and Lydia are contested every year all around the world. From humble beginnings in Turin, he always knew that he needed to make that change to breeding thoroughbreds, changing the way we look at the industry.

Their input was unmistakable and the very best we can do is to say, sincerely and simply, thank you, Federico and Lydia Tesio.

Sea Bird – Timeform's No. 1

... now here is the very best of the best!

Foaled in France in 1962, the Etienne Pollet–trained chestnut son of Dan Cupid was bred and owned by wealthy business owner Jean Ternynck. Sea Bird had eight starts for seven wins and one second, and became famous for his amazing wins in Europe's elite classic races, the Epsom Derby and the Prix de l'Arc de Triomphe.

Sea Bird's major wins were as follows:

- Criterium de Maisons-Laffitte: 1964
- Prix Greffulhe: 1965
- Prix Lupin: 1965
- Grand Prix de Saint-Cloud: 1965
- Epsom Derby: 1965
- Prix de l'Arc de Triomphe: 1965

Sea Bird's only defeat was not because Grey Dawn was a superior horse, but was attributed to his jockey unnecessarily holding him back until it was far too late to make up so many lengths on the leader. He was a champion but not a magician on four legs! Having said that, Grey Dawn trained on to become a very good performer in his own right with 22 starts for eight wins, four seconds and one third. Grey Dawn ended up having a Timeform Rating of 121.

Sea Bird had everyone talking about his championship qualities as a three-year-old, not only for the quality of the Classics that he was successful in, but also for the way he did it. He started his three-year-old season with an effortless three-length win in the Prix Greffulhe, followed by a six-length romp over the great Diatome in the Prix Lupin. In Europe and France, these Classic races are regarded as the absolute elite. It was time for his connections to take him across the channel to challenge all comers in the Epsom Derby. Starting at 7/4 favourite, he easily defeated Meadow Court, winning by two lengths. Reports by journalists the following day all commented on how great he was winning the English Classic. He gave nothing else a chance in the race and won very easily.

Following on from this race, the second-placegetter Meadow Court went on to win the Irish Derby and the King George VI & Queen Elizabeth Stakes. In Sea Bird's absence, Meadow Court would have been crowned one of the all-time greats!

The best of Sea Bird was still waiting back in Europe. He had a lead-up race in the Grand Prix de Saint-Cloud, winning easily by over two lengths. Then came the main event, the Prix de l'Arc de Triomphe. The contenders in what is regarded as one of the most elite races in the world read as a who's who of racing. The field consisted of Sea Bird, his old adversary Meadow Court, as well as the Preakness Stakes winner, the French Derby winner and the Russian Derby winner as well. This was certainly a gathering of the greatest and most talented group of horses of the era.

Starting at the odds of 6/5, he annihilated the opposition, and although he raced erratically in the straight, jockey Pat Glennon just patted him down the neck over the last 100 metres of the race and he still managed to win by an incredible six lengths. Nothing else was given a chance as he treated his elite opposition with contempt. A newspaper article read: 'In the running of the Arc of 1965, Sea Bird crushed the strongest international field ever assembled while the victory defines true championship qualities – the more you relive the details of this racing exhibition, the superlatives just don't seem to be enough.'

Following his final race, Sea Bird was leased to the Darby Dan Farm in Kentucky for a period of five years for a staggering US$1.35 million. He did not leave his greatness on the track; his outstanding qualities followed him to the breeding barn as well. Among his progeny were Allez France, the 1974 Prix de l'Arc de Triomphe winning mare (with a Timeform rating of 136); Little Current, winner of the 1974 Preakness Stakes and Belmont Stakes; Sea Pigeon, winner of the Champion Hurdle; and Gyr, runner-up to the Triple Crown winner Nijinsky in the 1970 Epsom Derby.

Sea Bird sired many champions and whenever his progeny entered the sale ring, there were always very high expectations and very high prices paid – for example, Miss Oceana, which was sold for a record US$7 million.

Undoubtedly a master on the track and in the breeding barn, there is no wonder that Sea Bird earned his Timeform rating of 145 and will go down in history as the greatest in the modern era.

Sea Bird – you never ever know what is around the corner!

Prix de l'Arc de Triomphe

... a walk of freedom led us to France's jewel in the crown

The year was 1919, the scene was the Champs Élysées; it was the time of the great victory march by the Allies down the magnificent avenue in Paris and under its great centerpiece, the Arc de Triomphe. This was a symbol of France and freedom, marking the end of the Great War – the war to end all wars.

Famous for being the most expensive piece of real estate on our planet today, the Champs Élysées measures nearly 2 kilometres long and is 70 metres wide. The great Arc represents an important part of history in France, and also lends its name to one of the most renowned races in the world today – the Prix de l'Arc de Triomphe.

The creation of this race goes back to the wake of World War I. In

1920, a committee meeting was held to try to complement further the great races that had been established in France, by taking a minor event and elevating it to Championship status, officially naming it the Prix de l'Arc de Triomphe.

Unlike some of the great races in France where nominations were very restrictive, this race was opened up to all international thoroughbreds (with the exception of geldings) on a basic weight for age system. Three-year-olds would carry 56 kg and four-year-olds and older would carry 59.5 kg. There was also an allowance of 1.5 kg for all fillies and mares.

The great race is run at Longchamp Racecourse in Paris, and is run over 2400 metres on a right-handed track. It is popularly referred to as the 'Arc' and is regarded as one of the most prestigious races in the world, carrying prize money in the millions of dollars. Many of its winners are subsequently regarded as champions, and its roll of honour features such acclaimed horses as Ribot, Sea Bird (the highest-rated Timeform horse in thoroughbred history), Dancing Brave and Sea the Stars. Although prize money for the Arc does not compare with some of the world's richest races, it is still regarded as one of the most prestigious.

The funding of the Arc was by way of a lottery until the 1980s, after which the race was funded by major sponsors. The current sponsor is the Qatar Racing and Equestrian Club (QREC), which has the rights up until 2012. The race was cancelled because of the war in 1939 and 1940 and was run at another racecourse in France in 1943 and 1944.

The first running of the Arc in this format was on Sunday 3 October 1920. The inaugural winner was a three-year-old colt named Comrade, owned by Evremond de Saint-Alary, and the winner's purse was a staggering 150,000 francs. The total prize money for the 2011 Prix de L'Arc de Triomphe was €2.3 million, with the winner Danedream earning approximately €1.2 million.

Following are some statistics from the great race:

Most successful horses (each with two wins)

- Ksar: 1921, 1922
- Motrico: 1930, 1932
- Corrida: 1936, 1937
- Tantieme: 1950, 1951
- Ribot: 1955, 1956
- Alleged: 1977, 1978

Leading jockeys (each with four wins)

- Jacques Doyasbere: Djebel 1942, Ardan 1944, Tantieme 1950 and 1951
- Freddy Head: Bon Mot 1966, San San 1972, Ivanjica 1976, Three Troikas 1979
- Yves Saint-Martin: Sassafras 1970, Allez France 1974, Akiyda 1982, Sagace 1984
- Pat Eddery: Detroit 1980, Rainbow Quest 1985, Dancing Brave 1986, Trempolino 1987

Leading trainer (seven winners)

- Andre Fabre: Trempolino 1987, Subotica 1992, Carnegie 1994, Peintre Celebre 1997, Sagamix 1998, Hurricane Run 2005, Rail Link 2006

Leading owner (six winners)

- Marcel Boussac: Corrida 1936 and 1937, Dejebel 1942, Ardan 1944, Caracalla 1946, Coronation 1949

Fastest winning time

- 2.24.49: Danedream (three-year-old-filly), 2011

Widest winning margin

- Six lengths: Ribot 1956, Sea Bird 1965, Sakhee 2001

Oldest winning horse

- Motrico, 1932 (seven-years-old)

Leading sire of Arc winners

- Bruleur: three winners – Ksar, 1921, 1922; Priori, 1925; Samos, 1935

Most runners in the race

- 30: in 1967 (current maximum is 20)

Fewest runners

- Seven: in 1941

Number of times fillies and mares have won

Eighteen occasions:

- Pearl Cap: 1931
- Samos: 1935
- Corrida: 1936 and 1937
- Nikellora: 1945
- Coronation: 1949
- La Sorellina: 1953
- San San: 1972
- Allez France: 1974
- Ivanjica: 1976
- Three Troikas: 1979
- Detroit: 1980
- Gold River: 1981
- Akiyda: 1982
- All Along: 1983
- Urban Sea: 1993
- Zarkava: 2008
- Danedream: 2011

Countries in which the winners were bred

- France: 44 wins
- Ireland: 17 wins
- United States: 14 wins
- Great Britain: 7 wins
- Italy: 6 wins

Here are a few more tidbits about the history of the Arc:

- Cadum finished in first place in 1925, but was relegated to second after a stewards' inquiry.
- The 1947 winner Le Paillon was one very versatile racehorse. He was also runner-up in that year's Champion Hurdle.
- Midnight Sun dead-heated for first in 1959, but after a stewards' inquiry was relegated to second place.
- Sagace finished first in 1984. He also finished first in 1985, but he too was relegated to second after another stewards' inquiry.
- The only woman to have trained an Arc winner is Criquette Head-Maarek, who trained Three Troikas to victory in 1979.
- The third-placegetter in 2006 was Deep Impact. He was later disqualified after testing positive to a banned substance.

This is one of the great races on the international scene. It was a race born out of conflict, but nevertheless, is a race for great champions.

Grey Way

... affectionately known as the Washdyke Wonder

This bloke had a bit to live up to because he came from the same area in New Zealand as the mighty Phar Lap. Born in Washdyke, New Zealand in 1970, his sire was Grey William and his dam Waybrook. Grey Way went on to be admired for his tenacity and longevity on the racecourse, and proved to be a true blue Iron Horse.

The aptly named Grey Way raced as a gelding, and although grey in colour in his early years, he turned white midway through his career. Even though he started racing as a two-year-old, remarkably he was still winning races right up until retirement as a ten-year-old. This Iron Horse had an incredible 164 starts for 51 wins, 27 seconds and 21 thirds. The total prize money back then amounted to NZ$253,020. The most incredible thing to understand out of those statistics is that he consistently had around 20 starts per year from his beginning as a two-year-old until he retired as a ten-year-old, and anyone who has been involved in racing would be the first to put their hands up and say, what a great achievement!

Winning at distances from 1200 metres to 1600 metres and everything in between, Grey Way did have some limited success over longer journeys. Awarded the title of Horse of the Year in 1973, his claim to fame was that he invariably defeated nearly every champion running around in New Zealand during his reign.

At one stage, he broke the Australasian record for 1400 metres carrying 60.5 kg. Having an intense dislike for heavy or rain-affected tracks, he surprised his connections by winning the 1974 Chirnside Stakes on a soft track. Apparently soft tracks in Australia aren't really the same as soft tracks in New Zealand.

He didn't slow down as he got older, because he ran consistently and won right throughout his career. As a ten-year-old he won race numbers 50 and 51 before knocking his leg at Trentham, which forced him into retirement. His coat ended up snow white towards the end of his racing career, which certainly accentuated his movement through the field as he made his winning way to the line once again.

What a wonder!

Sir Tristram 1971–1997

... the courage of conviction and the greatest gamble of all

This is a story of one man's courage of his convictions. You may have heard this saying through your life, but do we truly understand or appreciate the calculated gamble associated with it?

There was a young stud master from the Cambridge Stud in New Zealand in 1975 who travelled to the most famous training establishments in England, Ireland and France in search of a stallion to fill his needs at their fledgling stud back in the Land of the Long White Cloud. He had a budget of around NZ$200,000 to invest in the future of their stud, but after an exhausting few weeks, he was unable to unearth what he was looking for. This young stud master, Patrick Hogan, believed in himself; he was after a horse with particular strengths. He must have seen hundreds of potential stallions during this time and it would have been easy to accept one with most of the credentials he was after, but he believed so much in his endeavour that he eventually went back to New Zealand empty-handed.

The NZ$200,000 he had to spend was not his alone; it was a shared investment by a number of stakeholders, prepared to part with their hard-earned money hoping to strike it rich with a stallion that would be the success they had all dreamed of. Call it fate, luck or chance, but soon after he arrived home he received a letter in the mail that contained a pedigree, and he knew immediately that this horse was exactly what he was looking for.

The pedigree was of a stallion called Sir Tristram. He was by the champion English three-year-old Sir Ivor, from the Royal Charger sire line. His dam Isolt carried impeccable bloodlines – a real blue blood in racing terms. His race record was not at all spectacular; he had run nineteen times for only two wins in France. Sir Tristram had been sent to Churchill Downs by his owner to run in the 1974 Kentucky Derby, and he could only manage eleventh place.

Patrick Hogan commissioned Britain Bloodstock Agency to inspect the horse and send their report to him. Things were getting serious. The report was not very flattering, and in the back of everyone's mind was the fact that Sir Tristram's sire, Sir Ivor, was proving to be 'a dud at stud'. Patrick Hogan must have had some worrying times with some of the investors when all of these facts were placed before them.

As Patrick Hogan was reading the report, he remembered the words of his father, who was a very good judge of horse flesh: 'No horse is perfect. Accept a few faults behind the saddle, but don't accept too many faults at the front end.' After he had read the detailed report on the horse, particularly the front and rear end, he then noted the Bloodstock Agent's remarks, and weighed all of the points against his father's words. Patrick Hogan knew his journey had come to its conclusion. This horse was what he was looking for, although it did not please of a number of the investors.

Courage of conviction and backing your judgement – real character building, no doubt.

After the decision to purchase was made, Sir Tristram was about to encounter one more problem. His journey to the stud in New

Zealand was nearly over before it had begun. A blaze broke out at the quarantine station and in all of the panic trying to get the horses away from the fire, he crossed paths with a mare that duly let fly and kicked him in what could only be described as a very private place. His 'jewels' were subject to much scrutiny by his handlers and everyone associated with his care, and they all held their breath in anticipation waiting for 'everything' to be found 'in good order'. However, the racing gods were on his side that night, and as they say in the classics, the rest is history. As his namesake, the thirteenth Knight of the Round Table, did, this Sir Tristram began to reshape history and to leave a legacy that is equalled by very few.

Paddy, as he was affectionately called, had developed a reputation for being an extremely difficult horse to handle, although not a trait that any of his offspring have carried. His handlers had to wear protective gear, which remains on display for all to see at Cambridge Stud. Sir Tristram's stud fee started at NZ$35,000 and just before his death, he was asking and getting NZ$200,000 for his service.

This big stallion set high standards and reinvented the New Zealand thoroughbred industry by setting new benchmarks in racing and breeding. He produced 1272 foals, 10 per cent of which went on to be Stakes winners, including an incredible 45 Group 1 winners. He began with the talented Sovereign Red in his first crop, and ended with the last of his three Melbourne Cup winners in Brew in the year 2000. His offspring took over $50 million in stake prize money, seventeen official Australasian Sire Premierships, and nine Broodmare Sire titles.

We should salute Sir Patrick Hogan, as we are forever in his debt. He stuck to his original plan and the courage of his convictions, even though there were great doubts surrounding the decision he made. Back then, we had no way of knowing that this man and his newly acquired stallion would have such an impact on the breeding stock in Australasia, which would leave a legacy to the thoroughbred world that is second to none on the world stage.

Here are just a few of his offspring:

- Sovereign Red: VRC Derby, Caulfield Guineas, Doomben 10,000, Underwood Stakes
- Gurners Lane: Caulfield Cup, Melbourne Cup
- Grosvenor: VRC Derby, VRC Sires Produce, Caulfield Guineas
- Dr Grace: AJC Derby, Underwood Stakes, Chipping Norton Stakes, Tancred Stakes
- Maurauding: Golden Slipper
- Riverina Charm: Canterbury, Rosehill and VATC 1000 Guineas, Air New Zealand Stakes
- Empire Rose: Mackinnon Stakes, Melbourne Cup
- Brew: The Dalgety, Melbourne Cup

Sir Tristram's daughters have also proven to be extremely valuable in their own right, producing over 3400 foals to race, which included over 200 Stakes winners of such quality as Ethereal, Saintly, Viscount, Triscay and Bint Marscay.

If you consider Sir Tristram's son, Zabeel, and his record at stud, then you will understand that this apple did not fall far from the tree. Zabeel's record was nineteen starts for seven wins and five placings; his wins included such races as the MRVC Stakes, the Australian Guineas and the Craiglee Stakes. Zabeel commenced his stud duties at Cambridge Stud in 1991. As of February 2010, he had had sired 1153 runners, of which 791 have won, and they included winners of 126 Stakes winners and 31 Group 1 races. His progeny has already earned in excess of AUD$140 million. He has been Champion Australian Sire twice and Champion New Zealand Sire (combined Australia and New Zealand earnings) an amazing thirteen times. Remember, Zabeel only commenced his stud duties in 1991.

In 1998, Zabeel became the first sire to have progeny earn in excess of $10 million in the one year. His own progeny read just like his dad, the ultimate who's who of the racing elite; Octagonal, Might and Power, Jezabeel, Sky Heights, Efficient, Maldivian, Don Eduardo and so on.

In 1997, Sir Tristram, at the age of 26, broke his shoulder and had to be euthanased. In ancient times, great warriors were buried on their horses in the upright position – forever ready to ride into battle. Sir Patrick Hogan loved Sir Tristram to such an extent that he had him buried standing up to honour him. It took many men that day to maintain Sir Tristram's body in the upright position so the earth could be packed around and under him.

His head faces the rolling pastures of Cambridge Stud, and his legacy is one that changed the landscape of breeding in Australasia and set standards so high that it is no wonder that our Australasian-bred horses are admired greatly and are in wide demand on the world stage.

Good on you, Paddy and Sir Patrick.

The Happy Valley mystery

... and the criminals continue to test the limits!

Happy Valley Racecourse is one of two racecourses in Hong Kong, the other being Shai Tin. Located in Happy Valley on Hong Kong Island, it proved so popular with the early British people in the region that it blossomed after its humble beginnings in 1845.

To assist with the development, the government of the day forbade rice growing by the villages in the local area. The first race was run in 1846, and as time went by, horse racing became very popular among the residents. The racecourse flourished and expanded for many years and it was a tragedy for all concerned when it was burnt to the ground in 1918, causing the death of hundreds of people.

WHAT AM I SUPPOSED TO DO WITH THIS?

After many years lying dormant, the racing facilities were rebuilt in 1995 and became known as one of the great showpieces of modern thoroughbred racing in the world.

Racing at Happy Valley has become a major attraction for local and overseas visitors, enticing large crowds to watch the spectacle. It is much more than a racetrack and has become a spectacular area, comprising multi-storey buildings and stables that support the local industry and consequently the local economy. In 2007, the track had 5000 permanent and 20,000 part-time staff.

While a race day supervisor was doing his cursory rounds of the track at the end of March 2007, he noticed a slight change in the turf under the starting gates at a particular starting position. It didn't look that different but was more of a difference of texture rather than a difference of colour in the turf.

On closer inspection of the suspect area, he found a narrow strip, the length of the barrier stalls, directly under where the horses would be placed before the starting gates opened for the race to get underway. The supervisor prised up a portion of what was a green-coloured tape very similar in colour to the turf at the track. Under the tape he noticed a kind of mechanism and he immediately advised his superior, and the racetrack officials called in the Bomb Squad.

The device was found to contain what looked like electronic controls fitted with tiny liquid-filled needle-type objects that could be fired into the underbelly of a selected horse or horses when they were loaded into the barrier stalls just prior to the start. The theory was that the trigger of compressed air would enable the needles to fire.

Officials were notified of the breach in their security, and the Bomb Squad took the device away for analysis. To this day the type of substance in the needle-type objects has not been released to the public and we would assume that the less the public knows of the chemicals involved, the safer racing will be.

A Race Committee meeting was hastily convened to discuss security at the track and the possibility of the device having been deployed in the past. It would have been impossible to trace any beaten favourites or horses that acted erratically during the course of a race. The mechanism and a description of the firing trigger, along with some samples of the mixture, were sent to other major racetracks throughout the world. All came back with the same comment: 'This is a brand-new device, the likes of it we have never seen before.'

Although the track had security cameras, the trench was dug in a blind spot and could not be detected by the cameras. With the track surrounded by apartment towers and the residents objecting to floodlights on site, video cameras were quite useless at night. The most efficient security measure was to have patrols walking the racetrack at night.

It is a misconception that you have to pick a winner to be able to succeed in the racing game, because for a vast number of people who are heavily involved in holding a book on a race, it can be just as important picking a loser.

Here we go again!

Hambletonian

... the cornerstone of history in American pacing

This horse had such an unremarkable beginning that it is hard to fathom the influence he ended up having on American harness racing. Not much to look at, Hambletonian carried the bloodlines of Messenger, the English thoroughbred sire that carried the bloodlines of the three foundation sires in England.

Thanks to the ancestry of Hambletonian, the American horse world was about to change. He became the standardbred foundation sire, with 99 per cent of all registered trotters and pacers now able to trace their bloodlines back to him.

A great-grandson of the imported sire Messenger and sired by Abdullah, Hambletonian was born in May 1849 in Sugar Loaf, New York. He was owned by Jonas Seeley. William Rysdyk was a worker at the Seeley complex and soon became so attached to the colt and its mother that he just had a feeling the colt would someday be worth something. One day he asked Jonas Seeley if he could purchase them and surprisingly, Seeley agreed. With that, William

Rysdyk paid up the $125 that was asked and took his prize possessions home.

The description of the mare and foal at foot at the time was not very encouraging at all: 'The mare looked like a hunched cripple with an ugly cat foal at foot.' Just to complete the history of the family's good looks, it was also noted that his sire Abdullah was 'ugly in body and temperament and so much so, that he was sold to a fish peddler for $5'.

At the age of six months, Hambletonian made his first public appearance at the nearby county fair and made such an impression at this early age that horsemen started to take notice of him. The ugly duckling had become the swan.

Another Abdullah colt, Abdullah Chief, was looming as a competitor in the local stallion honours. The owner of Abdullah Chief had nothing but contempt for Hambletonian and claimed that he would never be a trotter, only a show horse. To settle their differences, both Hambletonian and Abdullah Chief were hitched to wagons at Long Island in 1852 to see which horse would prove the best. Hambletonian easily defeated Abdullah Chief in two match races. Harness racing in the United States was the clear winner and this 'ugly cat foal at foot' was sent to stud for a fee of US$500. His reputation quickly grew as a sire of speed and his owner's judgement was vindicated. Although making a modest fortune from performance at stud, he was the recognised sire of over 1300 foals.

William Rysdyk died in 1870 and Hambletonian died on 27 March 1876, at the grand old age of 27. Both were buried in Chester, New York. Seventeen years after Hambletonian's death, a granite monument was placed over his grave on Hambletonian Avenue.

Bloodlines of this champion were so dominant that basically all other family lines became extinct in the United States. Hambletonian had four sons and they became the foundation sires for nearly all American trotters and pacers today.

The Hambletonian Stakes is a prestigious American harness race named in the horse's honour, as he was known as the father of American trotters. The race is held annually for three-year-old trotting standardbreds, and the 'Little Brown Jug' is regarded as the United States' most prestigious race for pacers. Currently held at Meadowlands Racetrack every August, the Hambletonian is the most important event in the United States Trotting Triple Crown.

Not bad for a haunched crippled mare and an ugly cat foal at foot, was it?

Big Bum

... the story of Bret Hanover

A superstar of harness racing, and possibly the best there ever was. Affectionately known as Big Bum, the outstanding American standardbred Bret Hanover, a bay stallion bred at Hanover Shoe Farm, was foaled in the United States in 1962. His sire was the great Adios, with his dam Brenna Hanover and damsire Tar Heel – hence his name.

One of nine pacers to win the Triple Crown of harness racing for pacers, in all probability Bret Hanover's championship and superstar status lies in the fact that he had 68 starts for 62 wins, five seconds and one third, never being out of the place in his whole illustrious career. At the end of his four-year-old season in 1996, the champion was retired with earnings of a staggering US$922,616 in prize money.

Bret Hanover became the only horse to win Harness Horse of the Year in three consecutive years: 1964, 1965 and 1966. Trained and driven by Frank Ervin, Bret Hanover was undefeated in his debut season as a two-year-old, winning all 24 races he contested, and would continue to remain undefeated for his first 35 starts. In his second season he had 24 starts for 21 wins, which included a world record (1.55 over a mile) and Horse of the Year honours again.

He never dropped his intensity in his four-year-old season, his last before retirement. He had 20 starts for 17 wins and was placed in the other three. A remarkable statistic was that there were only three horses that could get close to him in his whole career. The only horses that beat him into his six placings were the legendary Cardigan Bay, Adios Vic and True Duane. He had some memorable duels with the great New Zealand pacer Cardigan Bay, the two most memorable being the Pace of the Century, in which Cardigan Bay defeated Bret Hanover, and the return race at Yonkers Raceway, titled the Revenge Pace, in which Bret Hanover turned the tables on his great rival. Cardigan Bay was the first million-dollar prize money harness pacer, so he was in very elite company even though at that time Bret Hanover retired as the richest and fastest standardbred ever.

Bret Hanover was sold to Castleton Farm in Lexington, Kentucky, for a record $1 million, and went on to be a very influential sire of winners that amassed more than US$64 million in prize money. He is remembered as being one of the better broodmare sires in harness racing history. Upon his death on 21 November 1992, a statue of Bret Hanover was created; it stands over his original gravesite. His grave was later moved to the Lexington Kentucky Horse Park.

... now, the Big Bum thing.

Every great champion has his own little foible and Bret Hanover's was that whenever he won, which was quite regularly, Frank Ervin would get out of the driver's seat and, in front of the crowd in the home straight, Bret Hanover would cross his legs and bow to the crowd, sticking his big bum skyward. All watching his antics would go absolutely crazy with applause.

What a sight that would have been!

CHAPTER 5
Bits & Bridles

Weight's right!

... the story of Jim 'Grafter' Kingsley

The dictionary defines 'graft' as 'a criminal's special branch of practice – profit by corrupt means'. Jim's nickname 'Grafter' was somewhat, shall we say, appropriate.

Where there is money, there are always the opportunists who believe they have the right to take more of their share by any means possible and indulge in skullduggery at any level, at anyone's expense, as long as they benefit. Jim 'Grafter' Kingsley epitomised this type of racecourse rogue, whose every waking moment was dedicated to any plan that would earn him an extra quid or two the easiest way possible.

The theory in horse racing is that the fields are evened up as much as possible, with different weight allocated for the jockeys to carry according to the performance and class of the horse. When a winning jockey comes back to the scales after a race win, he must weigh in at exactly the same weight he was allocated and registered for at the official pre-race weigh-in. Besides the luck of the draw with the barrier position, the weight a racehorse has to carry is one of the main factors that can affect a horse's performance, or at least Jim 'Grafter' Kingsley thought as much.

On a sunny Saturday afternoon in April 1903 at the Newcastle racecourse, a very well backed winner called Gentleman Jim was being led back to the enclosure after winning the main race on the card.

Gentleman Jim was owned by none other than Jim 'Grafter' Kingsley.

As Kingsley was making his way to the jockey's official post-race weigh-in for correct weight, he was momentarily delayed by a very irate bookie. The bookie took issue with Gentleman Jim's win and had his suspicions about the large payout that Kingsley would be collecting from him on the punt on his own horse.

Wherever Grafter Jim was, his mere presence caused a very uneasy feeling in those who took any of his bets. No-one could prove anything, but most knew he certainly was a grafter and there was always an angle where he was concerned. He took flight from the bookie as soon as he could and quickly made his way to the stewards and the scales. All present were scratching their heads when Jim arrived, as Gentleman Jim's jockey weighed in 29 lb (13.5 kg) light – a weight difference that would certainly affect an outcome in any race. It would be like a horse carrying a heavy weight up against a well-credentialled performer carrying a postage stamp.

Kingsley, being the gruff and outspoken man that he was, requested firmly that his jockey weigh in again and he stomped his foot to accentuate his demand. Surprise, surprise; this time the jockey weighed in 100 per cent.

'Weight's right' was the call by the stewards, and all bets were paid on course.

Some racing officials still had an uneasy feeling that day about what had happened, so after the course was closed for the day, they resumed their inspection of the scales just to make sure that they were working correctly. They weighed a couple of the stewards present only to see time and time again that their weights were correct. On closer inspection at the back of the scales, they found a thin wire leading from inside the base of the official scales to a small hole in the floor. When they examined outside of the scales room, they noticed that the floor sounded hollow.

A few floorboards were lifted, and they found a small underground compartment that led all the way, via a tunnel, to an escape hatch at the back of the building about 10 metres away. Someone could enter and exit and no-one would be the wiser.

When inspecting the small chamber under the scales, the stewards, to their amazement, found food scraps, empty soft-drink bottles, lolly wrappers and a 29 lb weight. After some deep and meaningful discussions, they realised the ploy was that a small boy would be in the hole biding his time until he received a signal, which appeared now to be the stomp of someone's foot beside the scale. The boy would then attach the 29 lb weight to the wire as the jockey went on the scales and, abracadabra, the right weight was recorded.

The jockey could be a light weight, but with the help of the 29 lb weight impacting on the scales, his weight was a false reading – much heavier than he actually was, and the correct weight he was supposed to be in the race.

Yes, the stewards all remembered Jim 'Grafter' Kingsley and his petulant stomp on the floor beside the scales for that all-important second chance weigh-in. *Sprung!*

He was subsequently banned for life.

The was a young gun called Jim,
Whose sole purpose on the course was to win,
With a shovel to dig,
In a small hole his boy hid,
But alas all Jim got was the sin-bin.

Alan W.

Now please consider this: a tunnel was discovered under the scales following the running of the Melbourne Cup in 1901 at Flemington, just two years before the Gentleman Jim fiasco at Newcastle. Police found weights, as well as food and blankets – sounds familiar, doesn't it?

The 7/4 favourite Revenue won the Cup and the runner-up was San Fran. San Fran was down to carry 9 stone 7 lb (60.5 kg) according to the race book, a whopping 25 lb (11.5 kg) more weight than Revenue, and he was beaten by only half a length.

Maybe something went wrong on the day. Maybe Jim was doing his apprenticeship. Who knows!

The curse of the Doorman

... that never held water!

The scene: Eagle Farm racecourse, Brisbane
The time: Labour Day holiday, a Monday in the early 1980s
The players: Frank Pearson, Norm Collins, and yours truly, Barry Wood

For the purpose of the story, the two horses involved in the latter part of this tale will be called Silver and Rainbow.

At 11.30am on that one day in my life that I will never forget, I picked up Frank and headed to Eagle Farm racecourse in Brisbane, a drive of about 30 minutes. My mate was dressed in his best punting gear: black Stubbies shorts, white T-shirt, packet of ciggies in his breast pocket, pair of 'Chinese riding boots' (rubber thongs), wallet, and the ever-reliable racing form guide.

It just happened to be coincidental that on that very same day, one of our other mates, Norm, was also going to the races. In the early 1980s, anyone with the Christian name of Norm often had an extra moniker attached due to the popularity of an infamous character of the time that the media had dubbed 'Norman the Doorman'. Such was the case with our mate Norm.

Frank and I paid our way through the turnstiles, and the conversation went something like this:

Frank: 'Christ, a man's f***ing jinxed.'

Me: 'What do you mean?'

'Have a look who's up ahead of us.'

'Who?'

'Norman the Doorman.'

'Christ, he's a mate of ours, Frank, how can you be bloody jinxed?'

'I know he is one of our mates, but today he is going to f***ing jinx me, I just know it!'

'Rubbish,' was all I could say.

Greetings were made all round and the first thing on the agenda was a malt sandwich. On the way to the races, Frank had told me he had the first two races covered with his standout selections. Ten minutes before the first race, the Doorman piped up and told us which horses he was backing. Unbeknown to Norm, they just happened to be the same two horses that Frank had selected as his standouts, and with that, the Doorman was off to place his first bet.

'Christ, I told you he would f***ing jinx me.'

'How can he jinx you, he just happens to like the same horses as you do.'

'I know, but the man's a jinx. I'm going to have to back something else. Christ, why didn't he stay home today?'

Frank's original standout selections in the first two races duly won and just before Norm arrived back at the bar, Frank let fly. 'I told you the Doorman is a bloody jinx.'

The Doorman sauntered back to the bar and said, 'I had a good collect on those first two winners. How did you go, Frankie?' Needless to say, Frank must have been going through a slow boil so I thought that discretion was the better part of valour and decided to keep my mouth shut. After surviving the Doorman's gloating and Frank's long count to ten, Norm was off once more to terrorise the bookies.

Up until now, Frank was having a shocker on the punt because of his unwillingness to follow his original selections after the Doorman had mentioned his tips in the same sentence. 'I had to get a sling from one of my penciller mates because I am skint,' he said when Norm was out of earshot.

The afternoon dragged on with no result for Frank, and 20 minutes before the last race, the two of us decided to head off, leaving Norm to keep backing his winners at the track. Just before we left, and again out of earshot of the Doorman, Frank said, 'Stop at the Hamilton Hotel on the way home, will you, I want to back Silver in the next and I am going to ring Lennie [his SP bookie] because he'll set me. I think the only danger in the race is Rainbow.'

That was okay because the Hammo was only five minutes away.

Just as we were about to leave, up pipes the Doorman: 'I'm staying for the last, fellas. What do you like in it, Frankie?'

Without a doubt, I reckon I knew what was coming next from Frank, probably a tip on a 50/1 shot. However, before he could respond, the Doorman quickly continued the conversation. 'I've had a pretty good day, so I am going to have a good go at Silver in the last.' Our Norman the Doorman was off in a cloud of dust.

For Frank, I think that was the straw that broke the camel's back. 'Christ! I told you the man's a f***ing jinx. Let's get to the Hammo quickly before they jump in the last. I'll have to rethink now what I will back. Why the bloody hell did he have to turn up today?'

We got to the pub, and I ordered two beers while Frank appraised the situation. 'Christ, I can't back Silver now because that bastard has jinxed me and he is due for a loss. I'm going to have a good go at that other horse, Rainbow. I told you the man is a bloody jinx.'

At that point, there was definitely no comment from me.

We sat in silence and listened to the race broadcast from the public bar. It resulted in a photo finish between Rainbow and, you guessed it, Silver. I could see the blood drain from Frank's face as the race caller announced Silver as the winner by a short half-head.

Frank was now a distinct shade of grey, and this was definitely the time to pull up stumps and head off home. That was one of the longest drives I have ever encountered and the only conversation on the 30-minute trip went something like this: 'I told you that bastard was a f***ing jinx. It was all his fault. Why didn't he bloody well stay home?'

Did the story end there? No, it certainly did not.

The Doorman's jinx continues ...

Back in the 1980s, Frank and I would meet every Friday after work at the local footy club and have a few cleansing ales. He had made up some lost ground with a big win on the Wednesday following 'black' Monday, so all debts had been paid with a little left over.

'I told you the Doorman was a bloody jinx and you won't believe what happened after you dropped me off home Monday arvo,' he said.

Now Frank could tell the funniest of stories and not crack a smile.

'After you dropped me off, the wife and kids weren't home, so I got into the grog feeling sorry for myself and started thinking about that bastard who f***ing jinxed me at the races last monday. I know that he is one of my best mates, but he jinxed me, I'm sure of it.'

The conversation continued without him missing a beat. 'I got pretty pissed and was so depressed that I decided enough was enough, and I was going to end it all. So I filled up the kitchen sink with water, took the thongs off my dirty feet, got up on the sink and put my feet in the water. I got hold of the breadknife, grabbed the jug cord, cut the end off, bared the wires and held them in the sink between my toes and then leant over to plug it into the wall socket and turn the bastard on. I'd really had enough.'

'So, what happened?'

'You are not going to believe this but I cut the wrong bloody end off the jug cord. Christ, a man's bloody unlucky.'

I just sat back on the barstool and thought ... a man's bloody unlucky ... what next? To this day, more than 35 years later, we still have a laugh about it. Was he fair dinkum? Only he knows.

I don't think Frank and I went to the races together after that – too bloody dangerous. We just might run into the Doorman.

What's in a name, as Aussie humour rises to great heights

... just below the waist

One of the greatest joys of owning a racehorse is the endless pursuit of selecting the right racing name. Some say that the name makes the horse; others say that the horse makes the name. However, some names selected lead us to ask, what the hell does that mean and how the bloody hell do you pronounce it?

There was a horse that raced around the provincial circuit of western New South Wales during the Depression years of the 1930s. Times were extremely tough back then and many trainers walked their horses from meeting to meeting just to win a few quid. Any win was a win. This particular horse raced under a very unusual name. His name was Elohesra. It was not derived from a foreign language, but simply good old 'arsehole' spelt backwards.

You can bet that his name was selected late one night after too many bottles of the amber fluid were consumed ... love that Aussie humour.

Anything is possible

... especially after a nuclear holocaust

In December 1959, the American film company United Artists released a film about a nuclear holocaust set in the future of 1964, about how life on Earth had been exterminated, with only Australia spared. Filmed in Melbourne, Australia, the movie was *On the Beach*, starring the great American actors Fred Astaire, Gregory Peck and Ava Gardner.

Both Fred Astaire and Gregory Peck loved to have a bit of a punt on the horses. On a sudden urge, one of the actors told their manager to go to the thoroughbred sales in Melbourne and buy them a horse so they could at least have a distraction away from filming. Once the horse had been purchased, it was time to think about what to name it. When the manager asked what they wanted to call it, the answer came back, 'Oh, just call it anything' ... and he did!

Their horse was registered and raced as 'Anything'. Trained by Angus Armanasco, he turned out to be a very capable galloper, winning many races in and around Melbourne, including the 1962 Ballarat Cup. The horse raced in the partnership of Fred Astaire and Gregory Peck until the day he was retired.

So there you have it; Anything can win at the races, and he did.

Speaking of Fred Astaire, there was a horse foaled in 1981 by the stallion Be Friendly out of the mare Floor Show. Its name ... Fred Astaire. What else!

F***KEN oath!

... more great Aussie humour

This one just might emphasise the Aussie attitude towards the establishment. Every time we can sneak one past the racing authorities, it is almost like a win for the workers.

Any red-blooded punter studying the form guide on race day would have to look twice, blink, clean his glasses and look again if he saw horses running with the name Bloody Hell and Bloody Oath. During the years between 2002 and 2008, two unusually named horses were running around the provincial racing circuit of Victoria, competing with limited success. One was by Kenvain, and the other by Kenny's Best Pal.

Their names ... Kenelle and Kenoath.

A typical race day conversation somewhere in Australia might go something like this.

'***kenelle, did you see the run by the horse that ran fourth?'

'***kenoath, what an absolute ripper.'

It seems a very polite way of expressing yourself, without using one of the great English four-letter words of our time. In this case a definite winner for Australian slanguage.

Some pearls of wisdom and wit

... and those gems that enhance the folklore

- 'Money lost, nothing lost; courage lost, everything lost' – Eric Connelly, one of Australia's leviathan punters of the 1930s
- 'Mr Cummings, you have far too many flies in your stable ...' 'Well, how many flies am I supposed to have?' – discussion between Bart Cummings and a Health Department representative
- 'I do make a habit of winning and it's a good habit to get into' – Bart Cummings when interviewed by the media
- 'She's a pretty little thing, and she rides well too' – Bart Cummings' interview with a TV journalist after Michelle Payne's 2009 Group 1 winning ride on Toorak Handicap winner, the Bart Cummings trained Allez Wonder.

- 'We're all entitled to a bad decade' – former Australian Rugby Union prop Stan Pilecki
- 'A friend is one you don't even need to ask for help' – Dato Tan Chin Nam. Nam was the man who stood with Bart Cummings when the pricing collapsed on all yearling purchases in the 1980s and Bart had everything to lose, and very nearly did.
- 'Is it easy to train a smart horse? ... Easier, it's pretty hard to train a dill' – Bart Cummings when interviewed by 4BC's Greg Carey
- 'Do you think you should get a second opinion?' – Bart Cummings' discussion with Darren Beadman when told by the jockey that he was quitting racing to become a minister of religion
- 'What did you get up to after Viewed won the Caulfield Cup?' ... 'That's personal' – Bart Cummings when interviewed by the media the morning after
- 'You can't buy experience, you've got to earn it ... I've earnt a fair bit, and it's starting to work' – 82-year-old Bart Cummings when interviewed by the media at 'Breakfast with the Stars' on the Tuesday before the 2009 WS Cox Plate
- 'Why did you decide to run the three-year-old So You Think in the Cox Plate?' ... 'We needed the money' – Bart Cummings when interviewed by the media after So You Think took out the 2009 Cox Plate
- 'There are a lot of people that have died today who have never died before' – Keith Thomas Wood on the philosophy of living
- 'You can lead a horse to drink, but you can't make him water' – former Queensland Premier Sir Joh Bjelke-Petersen when interviewed by the media
- 'It teaches discipline' – when Dato Tan Chin Nam, a successful Malaysian businessman with a passion for horseracing, was asked by the media why he played chess
- 'Always make new friends but never forget old friends. Not only because the more friends you have, the happier you are, but also the fewer enemies you have' – Dato Tan Chin Nam's philosophy on friendship has never changed
- 'Mr Cummings, I would like you to buy me a horse and train it for me' – More than likely a phone call discussion between Dato

Tan Chin Nam and legendary trainer Bart Cummings way back in the early 1970s. Bart Cummings has now trained over 260 winners for the Dato

Stand and deliver

... the bushrangers' catchcry!

In the early days of the Australian colonies, bushrangers robbed many a bank and stagecoach and their only means of escape was on some not-so-fast stock horses. Because of the speed and clumsiness of both horse and rider, some of the outlaws were captured in a very short time.

What was the answer? Simple, just steal a thoroughbred!

Dr John Dunmore Lang, a noted historian of early racing, recorded that the bushranger Ben Hall stole the brilliant racehorse Troubador and the outstanding brood mare Sappho on six occasions.

Nothing like getting on a horse worthy enough to be a Melbourne Cup contender, a quick stand and deliver, and away before the hapless constabulary could say, 'Gee, I should back that thing next start.'

A pair of pyjamas

... and having shares in a hospital

'Have you got all your riding gear, Darl?'

'Yeah, just checking it now.'

'I've also packed a nice pair of pyjamas in a brown paper bag so you can put them with your riding gear.'

'Yeah, okay, hope I don't need them though. Christ, me luck's gotta change soon.'

This just may have been the conversation between knockabout Adelaide jockey Les Boots and his good wife on the morning of every race program that included jumps races. Was Les Boots the unluckiest jumps jockey that the world has ever seen?

Les Boots' unlucky moments

- He had 39 rides and fell off 41 times. In one race, after falling, he caught the horse, remounted, only to fall off again.
- On one occasion when Les fell at the first fence, he broke his leg. He then fell out of the ambulance on the way back to the casualty room. Then while the ambulance bearers were carrying him across the lawn, he fell off the stretcher.
- During his illustrious career, Les broke nearly every bone in his body.
- He rode for eighteen years, and reckons he spent around twelve of those in hospital.
- Poor old Les' wife barred him from taking their young kids on the merry-go-round at the local showground after he fell off three times.
- It was alleged that the nurses at the Adelaide General Hospital always checked the daily race papers, not to have a bet, but to see if Les had a ride that afternoon, so as to prepare a bed in advance.
- Irrespective of the form, the bookies always posted 100/1 for any of the horses to be ridden by Les.
- In a hilarious interview with legendary race caller Bert Bryant in the late 1980s, Les said that the South Australian Jockey Club considered barring him from riding because he was putting too big a strain on the then Worker's Compensation Fund.

However, the best was still to come.

One very foggy afternoon at Victoria Park Racecourse, Les fell at the first jump and completely winded himself. While lying on the track waiting for the ambulance to arrive, he could hear a voice through the fog saying, 'I think we'll have to shoot him.' The poor bugger panicked, jumped up, and beat the ambulance back to the jockeys' room, where he was sedated and told, 'No, Les, they were only talking about the horse.'

Poor old Les must have come home on many occasions looking like a bloke who had gone 'a round or two for a pound a two', but at least he was always prepared with his pyjamas in the brown paper bag.

The Birdsville races

... the real deal!

There cannot be anything more iconic than the Aussie race day held at Birdsville every year. It is an institution that highlights everything Australian in a real party environment. They are unashamedly there for the duration of the carnival to see old mates, have a terrific time, and yes, to watch the races as well.

From the onlooker's perspective, it is like watching an episode of *Survivor*, where the props are nothing more than a pub, a few horses, and an endless supply of the amber fluid.

The newly formed township of Birdsville held their first meeting over three days: the 20th, 21st and 22nd of September 1882. Birdsville is situated on the Diamantina River approximately 8 miles (13 kilometres) north of the South Australian border. The meeting was attended in the main by nearly 150 station owners, managers, stockmen and other employees attached to the outback stations. The weather was typical outback and the nominations for the various races were adequate, with the finishes to most of the races close and exciting. Nearly £200 was raised by public subscription, which spoke loads for the prosperous conditions of the district at that time.

All bets were settled at Mr Tucker's Hotel, after which a meeting was held in Burt & Co. Iron Store, where the Border Jockey Club was formed with a total of 42 members. The next meeting was fixed for July 1883.

Some interesting facts over the years:

- During the early days, all professional riders carried a penalty of 7 lb (3 kg).
- The Jockey Club sponsored special races for horses that were bred within 250 miles (400 kilometres) of Birdsville.
- For a £10 fee, owners could lead their horses into the saddling enclosure.
- The old course was 3 miles (5 kilometres) west of the township, and steeplechase races were part of the program. This course was later abandoned after regularly being inundated by floodwaters.

- Prize money for the Cup has varied from £5 in the 1880s to £500 in the 1940s. In 1982, the Centenary Cup was worth $5000, and now prize money is a very attractive $30,000 for the Birdsville Cup.
- As the horses left the saddling enclosure, a bell was rung, and if connections did not have their horses at the starting in five minutes, they were fined 10 shillings.
- Star Ace, the 1970 winner, was trotted up the Birdsville Track beside his trainer's vehicle, the reason being that there was no horse float available.
- Races were once started at the drop of a hat, then on to barrier strands, and later to the civilised barrier stalls.
- The Club was originally called the Border Jockey Club, later becoming the Birdsville Amateur Turf Club, then the Diamantina Amateur Race Club, and finally the name was changed to the Birdsville Race Club Incorporated.
- Unregistered horses were allowed to start in hack races.
- Prior to 1954, with the exception of the Cup, prize money was only ever paid to the first and second place-getters.
- The Cup distance has remained at 1 mile (1600 metres) since its first running in 1882. In 1949 and 1950, the Jockey Club raised money for the construction of the Birdsville Hospital by renaming the race the 'Hospital Handicap'.
- The annual race meeting is now held to raise money for the Royal Flying Doctor Service.
- Apart from World War II, there have only been two occasions that the Birdsville races have been cancelled. The first happened in 2007 due to the outbreak of equine influenza in Queensland and New South Wales. This saw a complete ban on horse movements in many places on the east coast of Australia. This happened one week prior to the race, so horses were unable to travel to Birdsville and the race meeting was cancelled. The second was in 2010, when hot and dusty old Birdsville experienced the unthinkable. Floods! But, of course, in keeping with an Aussie's lofty standards of respect, and working through the very worst of times, entertainment

and festivities did continue throughout the Birdsville Cup meeting. Despite the lack of the horse racing during the carnival, the show did go on.

Drongo

... the horse that helped change the English language!

This is about a special horse named after an extinct species of bird that lived on the island of Madagascar. By the end of his racing career, he became synonymous with the very Australian vernacular meaning somewhat slow and useless.

Drongo was a non-winner in his 37 race starts. However, he was a bit better performed than the 124-start non-winner of the 1980s, Ouroene. In all of Drongo's race starts, he was placed in some races that are now Group status:

- 1923: 2nd VRC Derby
- 1924: 2nd VRC St Leger
- 1924: 3rd AJC St Leger
- 1924: 5th AJC Sydney Cup

Equivalent prize money today in those races alone equates to around $420,000, which is not too bad for a bit of a drongo. He also contested the 1923 and 1924 Melbourne Cups but unfortunately, by running 11th and 17th respectively, he lived up to his name.

In 1924, a tipster for the Melbourne *Argus* commented, 'I think Drongo is definitely going to be very hard to beat on Saturday, as he keeps improving with every race start.' Unfortunately for Drongo, every other horse he raced against was improving with every start as well because, try as he may, he could never greet the judge as a winner.

In 1977, the VRC honoured the horse's contribution to the English language, by featuring a race at Flemington called the Drongo Handicap. It was open to apprentice riders only, and for any horse that had not won a race in the previous twelve months. It seems quite amazing how the Australian public warms to the underdog and supports the little Aussie battler.

Sometimes we tend to remember the fascinating stories of all the slow coaches, horses like Drongo and Ouroene, more than the great horses of the past.

... get out of the road, you bloody drongo!

Big Red, the Biscuit and the Iceman

... a long-lost saddle and the champions that made this story possible!

Some things in life are meant to be. Even fewer things are played out in such a way that creates a treasure trove of historical facts that begs belief. This is one such case that joins together three of the greatest names in thoroughbred racing history in Australia and the United States.

These are the players:

Phar Lap: the New Zealand–bred Australian thoroughbred champion whose achievements captivated the public's imagination during the early years of the Great Depression in Australia. Phar Lap dominated the Australian racing scene during his distinguished career, winning a Melbourne Cup, two Cox Plates, two Derbies and nineteen other weight-for-age races before he went to the United States. Nicknamed 'Big Red', Phar Lap was adored by the Australian public.

In 1932, he went to Tijuana, Mexico, to race in the Agua Caliente Handicap where he defeated Reveille Boy in track record time. Unbeknown to everyone, this was to be his final race. After a sudden mysterious illness that has been well documented, this great champion of the people died.

Seabiscuit: a champion thoroughbred racehorse from the United States, affectionately known as 'the Biscuit'. From an unremarkable beginning, this unlikely 'hero' went on to become a representation of hope for many Americans during the Great Depression. Seabiscuit and the great War Admiral went head to head in the Match Race of the Century in November 1938.

Seabiscuit was ridden by George 'the Iceman' Woolf on that day he won, and this great horse was named Horse of the Year in 1938. He was the grandson of Man O'War, while War Admiral was a son of Man O'War. Man O'War was often referred to as 'Big Red'.

George (the Iceman) Woolf: regarded as one of the best jockeys ever to be legged up on a horse in the history of American thoroughbred racing. He earned his nickname 'the Iceman' because of his steady nerves and his faultless sense of timing. He rode Seabiscuit in the Match Race of the Century against War Admiral, as well as other occasions when his regular rider, Red Pollard, was not available due to injury. George has been documented as saying that in his opinion, Seabiscuit was the best horse of them all.

George suffered from diabetes. Tragedy struck the jockey late one afternoon on 3 January 1946, when he fell mid-race from his mount Please Me and was killed. Some say he just slipped from the saddle unconscious from the symptoms of his diabetes. Because of his condition, his rides were limited, which highlights how good his rides to wins ratio was – he was still named the nation's leading stakes winning jockey from 1942 to 1944.

The unbelievable link ... *a saddle*

After the mysterious death of Phar Lap in the United States, his jockey, Billy Elliot, decided that Phar Lap's saddle was too important to be disposed of. He graciously presented the saddle to his friend and great jockey, George 'the Iceman' Woolf.

American saddles were generally made of cowhide, but this Aussie-made saddle was something special. It was made of kangaroo hide and trimmed with snakeskin. A real bottler! George affectionately referred to it as his lucky saddle, and used this saddle the day he rode Seabiscuit in the Match Race of the Century in 1938.

In the following years after the Biscuit had retired, George continued to use his lucky saddle on many occasions. After that fateful ride on Please Me where George lost his life, his good friend Seymour Willoughby had the job of cleaning out George's personal effects from his car. To his amazement, in the boot of his car, Seymour found the lucky saddle of kangaroo hide and snakeskin.

It is said that on that fateful day, George remarked to a fellow jockey that managing his diabetes and insulin was becoming increasingly difficult. George may have already been suffering from a severe episode caused by his diabetes that day he went to the races to ride Please Me, and forgot to take his lucky saddle with him to the jockey's room.

... the spirit of three great champions live on forever.

The entrepreneur

... and his legacy to the racing industry

Many a word has been written about former entrepreneur Christopher Skase. Here is a very brief overview of his business life.

In 1975, Skase purchased a small Tasmanian company, Quintex. Over the years he developed some of Australia's greatest tourist resorts (the Mirage Group), and his acquisitions included ownership of Channel 7 and a prominent Queensland football team.

However, the good times did not last, and it was not long before the proverbial hit the fan, and with many investors knocking on the front door, Skase fled to the Spanish isle of Majorca. The word was that he managed to squirrel away a vast fortune from the hands of his creditors. Unfortunately for the investors and despite the best legal efforts available, he never came back to Australia to face the music, his defence being that he could not fly because of a life-threatening lung condition. Skase passed away in 2001 from stomach cancer.

Now, what is Christopher Skase's legacy to the racing industry? It is none other than good old Aussie ingenuity, with horse owners using Skase's story as an inspiration in naming some of their racehorses:

- **Skase:** sire Secret Savings, dam Exotica
- **Exiled:** sire King Cugat, dam Quintex
- **Quintex:** sire Masterclass, dam Bunglung
- **Bunglung:** sire Yonder, dam Boardroom Gem

This was probably what a lot of investors at the time would have liked to hear:

- **Getemup**: sire Freeze, dam The Flying Bullet

The legend and the pretenders!

... our first Aboriginal Melbourne Cup winning jockey

A lot has been written about who was Australia's first Aboriginal jockey to win a Melbourne Cup. Research has shown that there were a couple of pretenders, however there is the one and only.

The first to claim the title was John Cutts, who rode the Melbourne Cup winner in both 1861 and 1862. But here are the facts.

When Archer won the inaugural Melbourne Cup in 1861, he was ridden by this very capable jockey. According to legend, Cutts, who was born near Nowra, was one of the many Aboriginal lads who replaced the white stockmen who left the area to join the great Australian gold rush. However, historical records and photographs show that John Cutts, also known as John Dillon and John 'Cutts' Dillon, was of English stock and did not have any Aboriginal blood whatsoever.

Cutts was the regular rider of Archer and won eleven of his sixteen starts, including Archer's first two Melbourne Cups. This Aboriginal jockey riding our first Melbourne Cup winner started out as a legend, but soon became a myth.

The second lad to put his hand up to claim the title was Peter St Albans, who rode the Melbourne Cup winner in 1876. The following day newspaper reports said that, 'before a crowd of 75,000, the filly Briseis, ridden by Aboriginal jockey Peter St Albans, brilliantly won yesterday's Melbourne Cup.'

The legend that young St Albans was Aboriginal arose from the fact that he was under thirteen years of age – too young to be allowed to compete in the cup – and so to allow him to ride in the Cup, it was argued that his birthdate and parents were unknown. With this in mind, the authorities took it as fact that he was Aboriginal. They just took the word of the young fella that he was indeed thirteen, the lowest age one could be to officially ride in horse races.

However, he was born Michael Bowden, and it was said that he changed his surname to St Albans as proof that his mother, who happened to live on the St Albans Stud's property, was Aboriginal. The story continues that he was left as a baby on the steps of one of the stud's grooms, Michael Bowden.

It was proven later that the young jockey's birth certificate showed his parents as Michael Bowden and his wife Cathleen Bowden. Further confirmation of his being white is seen in a painting by Frederick Woodhouse featuring the young St Albans standing beside Briseis and stable jockey Tom Hales.

Another myth debunked.

And the first Aboriginal jockey to ride a Melbourne Cup winner is …

… Frank Reys, who rode the champion Gala Supreme to victory in the 1973 Melbourne Cup.

Born in north Queensland in 1931, Frank Reys was one of fourteen children born to his Aboriginal mother and Filipino father. He had to be pretty tough to survive around the dinner table.

Early in life, the family referred to their heritage as being Filipino, because they were concerned about their family being broken up as part of the Stolen Generation. Frank's Aboriginal grandmother was from the Djiribul people of North Queensland, and she and her siblings were victims of that terrible practice.

Years later, Frank Rey's daughter Shelley said:

> It seems life would have seen far more struggles if the family was to acknowledge their Aboriginal heritage. Their instinct was to maintain their Filipino heritage, build their standing amongst the community, and only then could the family remain together. This gave the family the opportunity to be free from being removed from their parents and to feel safe from the many hardships that other Aboriginal families faced within the community.

Frank's small stature was due to his Filipino heritage, and this was the starting point for him to look towards being apprenticed as a jockey. It was a natural progression for the skinny little fella, who was a regular at pony races and gymkhanas around Cairns. Frank began his jockey apprenticeship in 1949, at the ripe old age of eighteen, and was indentured to Alfred Baker and later to Gordon Shelley.

At the end of his apprenticeship (with 45 winners), Frank was just like the Leyland Brothers, travelling 'all over the countryside'. So great was his determination, it wasn't long before he joined the select band of Australian jockeys who had ridden over 1000 winners. One of his best riding feats in Queensland was to ride four winners in one afternoon at Cunnamulla. He also rode the winners of three Cunnamulla Cups. Who knows, he may have been the inspiration for the old song 'The Cunnamulla Fella'.

In 1955, Frank Reys decided it was time to try his luck in the big smoke, and he relocated his family to Sydney where he enjoyed moderate success. However, in 1961, and with the burning desire that every jockey has to win a Melbourne Cup, Frank and the family moved to Melbourne. He became a very successful jockey in the competitive Melbourne scene, and was held in high regard by owners, trainers and fellow jockeys.

The years between 1961 and 1973 were pretty tough for the lightweight 'hoop', as he suffered many falls and a few horrendous injuries, and soon earned the not too flattering nickname of 'Falling Leaves'. But with the winning of the Melbourne Cup always on his mind, the little bloke soldiered on. Only then would he consider finally putting his saddle away.

Frank had built up a wonderful rapport with trainer Ray Hutchins, and together these two gentlemen achieved great success, including the 1962 VRC Oaks with Arctic Star. Through those tough years of injuries, Ray stood by the little bloke from north Queensland, and their mateship was about to lead them into the history books with a little horse by the name of Gala Supreme, which had been allotted 49 kg in the 1973 Melbourne Cup.

On Tuesday 6 November 1973, after a great second in the Caulfield Cup just two weeks prior, Gala Supreme, trained by Ray Hutchins and with his 41-year-old jockey in the saddle, lined up at the start of the Melbourne Cup. Starting from an outside draw in front of 103,170 people, Frank Reys did his Aboriginal heritage proud as Gala Supreme won the Melbourne Cup.

Back from injury and adversity, the diminutive and emotional Frank Reys made his victory speech. A hush came over the crowd. For those of us who were privileged to watch and hear what was said, it would stay in our hearts forever. There were not too many dry eyes watching the television sets that day. The next day, newspapers Australia-wide published Frank's exact words, words that we shall never forget: 'I thank my God, my prayers and my family for their encouragement. This is such a wonderful day. I kept picking myself off the ground and hoping I would win a Melbourne Cup. It's something every Australian jockey dreams about. I still can't believe it.'

In the mounting yard prior to going on to the track, Frank had told Ray exactly how he was going to ride Gala, and in his later recollections of the race, Ray Hutchins said, 'He was fantastic and it was the perfect ride. He went and rode the race of his life.'

Three years later, in 1976, after a career highlighted by winning a Melbourne Cup, Frank rode a winner at Flemington for his great mate Ray Hutchins, and immediately announced his retirement from the saddle. He had ridden 1329 winners stretching from north Queensland to Victoria.

After fighting a brave battle with cancer, Frank Reys passed away in 1984 at the age of 53.

Frank Reys was Australia's first Aboriginal Melbourne Cup winning jockey, and possibly our first Filipino Melbourne Cup winning jockey: two for the price of one!

Australia held a referendum in 1967 to vote in favour of granting Aboriginal people citizenship rights. That year the Reys family celebrated the birth of Shelley, their third child. We are sure that Frank would be incredibly proud of his daughter today. Shelley Reys is a successful businesswoman who has worked tirelessly to help bridge the gaps between indigenous and white Australians.

Frank and Shelley Reys, a father and daughter who have done their Aboriginal heritage so proud.

Our First Ladies

... and their right of passage!

There is a first time for many things, but here are some facts that are strictly ladies first.

2 January 1979: Queensland's Cheryl Neale became the first female jockey to win a race at a metropolitan racecourse. She was successful on Macluen in the Ladies Handicap over 1600 metres at Moonee Valley in Melbourne.

9 March 1979: Women were first given approval to compete against male jockeys, and from 16 March, trainers could apply to apprentice women under the same conditions as men.

7 May 1979: New Zealand jockey Linda Jones became the first registered female rider to win a race in Australia against male jockeys. She rode Pay The Purple to win the Labour Day Cup in Brisbane.

15 May 1979: Brisbane jockey Pam O'Neill was granted a country licence to ride against men after riding in ten barrier trials to the stewards' satisfaction. Four days later, she rode a winning treble at Southport. Her winners were Samoan Lady, Panahita and Gelastic.

23 June 1979: Pam O'Neill became the first Australian female jockey to win a metropolitan race against male jockeys. She won on Samei Boy, which was trained by her husband, Colin O'Neill. Later that year, Pam rode Consular to defeat champion Melbourne jockey Roy Higgins in the Unisex Handicap at Moonee Valley. When invited to Japan, Pam rode three winners to become the first Australian female jockey to achieve this great honour.

1981–82 season: Tasmania's Bev Buckingham became the first female jockey in the world to win a State premiership. She rode 63 winners.

1982: New Zealander Diane Mosely became the first female jockey to ride a Group 1 winner in Australia when she won the Doomben Cup on Double You Em.

October 1985: Debbie Stein was the first woman to train the winner of the Cox Plate, Rising Prince.

November 1986: Bev Buckingham became the first female jockey to ride five winners in the one afternoon on a metropolitan racecourse. She rode over half the program.

1987: Bev Buckingham became the first female jockey to ride in the Caulfield Cup, on Brave Tresspasser.

1987: New Zealand's Maree Lyndon became the first female jockey to ride a 3200 metre Cup winner when she rode Lord Reims in the then Group 1 Adelaide Cup.

1987: Maree Lyndon became the first female jockey to ride in the Melbourne Cup when she rode Argonaut Style to finish 20th behind Kensei.

1988: Iris Nielsen unfortunately became the first female jockey to lose her life in a race fall at Lismore.

1995–96 season: Tasmania's Bev Buckingham, by riding 109 winners, became the first female jockey to ride over 100 winners in Australia.

1995 Melbourne Spring Carnival: Gai Waterhouse, the daughter of legendary trainer Tommy Smith, became the first woman to train a Group 1 winner of the VRC Derby. The winner was Nothin' Leica Dane.

1996–97: Gai Waterhouse became the first woman to train 100 metropolitan winners in Australia.

October 1998: England's Lady Herries, wife of legendary cricketer Sir Colin Cowdrey, became the first woman to train the winner of the Caulfield Cup, Taufen's Melody.

2001: New Zealand trainer Sheila Laxon officially became the first woman to train a Melbourne Cup winner when she won with the all-conquering Ethereal.

2003 Melbourne Cup: Claire Lindop was the first Australian female jockey to ride in the great race. She rode Debben, which finished 19th behind Makybe Diva.

2004/2005 season: Claire Lindop became the first female jockey to win a metropolitan premiership on mainland Australia.

2005: Andrea Leek was the first woman to ride a Grand National Hurdle winner at Flemington, on Team Heritage.

2006: Adelaide's Claire Lindop became the first Australian female jockey to win the then Group 1 Adelaide Cup on Exalted Time.

2007 Melbourne Cup Carnival: Nikita Berryman became the first female jockey to ride a 100/1 Group 1 winner, when she rode Tears I Cry in the Emirates Stakes.

2008–09 season: Claire Lindop became the first female jockey to ride two Group 1 winners in the same racing season, both Derby winners. She rode Rebel Raider to win both the VRC and SAJC Derbies, with Rebel Raider starting at around 50/1 in the VRC Derby.

October 2009: Michelle Payne rode Allez Wonder to victory in the Toorak Handicap at Caulfield. This was the first time a combination of a female jockey and a mare were to win a Group 1 race in Australia. Allez Wonder, trained by Bart Cummings, started at 40/1.

2009: Australian punters nationwide heard an unusual race call from Alice Springs. What was so different was that the course broadcaster happened to be a woman by the name of Victoria Shaw. Many of us listened in earnest to hear how she went, and she did well. It was a very concise race call and Victoria did her craft proud.

8 October 2011: Claire Lindop on Perfect Punch officially became the first female jockey in the Southern Hemisphere to ride 1000 winners.

Last but not least . . .

1932: Precocious won the Grand National Steeple, giving Dorothy Sheil the distinction of being the first woman to train a winner at Flemington. However, the Victorian Racing Committee refused her entry into the mounting yard. They had quickly passed a resolution that 'trainers must hold permits which are denied to women'.

As the words to Bob Dylan's hit song said . . . the times they are a-changin'!

Australia's first winning female jockey

... she lived her life as a man!

Little was known about the occupant of the unmarked grave, number 25 in row six, of Herberton Cemetary. Council records state that W Smith, aged 88, died on 24 June 1975 and was of Church of England faith.

Pam O'Neill and Linda Jones are credited as being the first female jockeys to race against male jockeys and win. However, sometimes the truth is stranger than fiction. Here is the story of one jockey that fooled them all during his, or should we say her, career.

A small baby was born in a Sydney hospital in 1886 and was orphaned soon after. Baby Smith grew up with no known relatives and in later years found work on ships and in the mines under the name of Bill Smith. Later in Bill Smith's life, he had a 20-year term of employment at the Cairns Brewery in north Queensland.

During his travels, he ended up riding horses on some of the major racecourses in the north, including Cairns, Mareeba, Innisfail and Herberton. Bill was extremely quiet on the social front and because of his mannerisms and size, he was often referred to as 'Girlie'. He never got undressed in front of other jockeys and always wore his riding gear under his street clothes when coming to the track. After riding his card of horses for the day, not wishing to attract any more attention than necessary, he always put his street clothes over his riding gear and went home – never taking a shower at the course in front of other jockeys. At one stage Bill was tackled by some louts in the jockeys' room to strip him of his clothes and a struggle ensued. Fortunately for Bill, a race steward came into the room and saved him from any embarrassment.

Bill 'Girlie' Smith lived the life of a town hermit with no friends and no social outlet, only his riding. One can just imagine the loneliness he endured over all those years. When Bill called it a day and retired from the saddle, he took up residence in the small town of Hot Springs, right next door to the hotel.

Illness forced him into the Herberton Hospital in 1975, but unfortunately, he never recovered and died there in June of that year. When preparing Bill Smith's body, some very respectful nursing staff found out his secret, and so that he would not go to his grave as Bill Smith, they searched all records until they found the register of a birth in the Sydney Hospital in 1886, Wilhemena Smith, a baby girl who was then passed on to an orphanage.

It is not known when she changed her appearance and took the name of Bill, but it would have been around the turn of the 20th century, when there were better opportunities of finding work if you were a man.

We cannot move on without sincerely thanking the quiet dignity of Wilhemena 'Bill' Smith, and the respect given to her by the nurses at the Herberton Hospital, who gave her the recognition that she deserved.

Peter Christian Barrie

. . . a ringer of renown on both sides of the Atlantic!

Don't ever think that you have heard it all about the crooks and con men involved in our racing history. This gentleman will change your mind; you may well think at the end of this tale that any participants attempting to ring in a horse at the races would have to have read the handbook of the king of ringers, Peter Christian Barrie. This man dedicated his life to cheating the only way he knew how: at the nearest racecourse.

Peter Christian Barrie made his start born in the shadows of Edinburgh Castle early in 1888, and had a very colourful life. He came from a stable family background and his dad was the local butcher. Probably his earliest entry into the world of skullduggery was when, at the tender age of sixteen, he bought a grey mare from a local female identity for 16 guineas, then after careful colour selection and with the right tools of application, proceeded to paint the same mare brown and duly sold it back to the original owner for the princely sum of around £275. He made a handsome profit of 1617 per cent, which more than likely spurred him on to bigger and brighter purchases. Just to prove the success of his ventures, his bank account during 1919 and 1920 had over £100,000 deposited into it. In those days, that amount may have bought you the whole city of London.

The year 1920 was not a good one for Mr Barrie. He appeared as a defendant at the Old Bailey, at the London Courthouse, and surprise, surprise, he was convicted of turf fraud and sent straight to jail. After being released from jail, he completely disappeared from the face of the earth. We do know from some research by others that he visited Australia, England, Canada, Cuba, Mexico, South Africa and America, and it would not take a mental giant to guess what sort of tricks he would have been up to along the way. When he did come to Australia, he joined the Australian Army where he spent a very short time at Gallipoli. He was injured there, then spent many weeks on a hospital ship before being discharged from the Army while 'recuperating' in England.

In every country he visited, he was involved in, or the instigator of, ring-ins. Some of his partners in crime eventually became members of the Mob in the United States, and some shady bookmakers as well. The Mob would have been there to back that 'tainted, or should I say painted' winner and the bookies were there for the other side of the coin. In bookmaking, you can make a kill by not necessarily picking a winner; the big money could be made picking a loser. Yes, Peter Christian Barrie certainly had both sides of the coin covered.

His specialty was painting horses and ringing in the good one for the Mob, and then painting horses and ringing in the bad one that looked like the favourite for the bookmakers. It was not uncommon to see a 50/1 outsider backed into 2/1 favourite, making millions of

dollars for those involved in that race. On the other side of the coin, the bookies would take hundreds of thousands on the favourite expected to win, only having the punters' elect finishing way down in the pack and all of the money staying in the bookies' bags.

Not to appear as if he was a one-trick pony, our esteemed Mr Barrie then dabbled with drugs during his US campaign. He bought a horse and gave it a dose of cocaine, feeling confident that it would enhance the horse's ability and be a good little earner for him. Unfortunately, the horse, while being positioned in the starting gates, managed to chew through its reins, and in its agitated state bolted and could not take its place in the race. A lesson learnt, you would think, but no, it was simply a case of adjusting the levels administered to eventually reap his reward.

Some two-year-olds in 1913 in England never raced under their own name; in most cases they simply were known and raced as, for example, 'a filly by Amazing'. They would just nominate the dam, so you could see that Peter Christian Barrie was a man for these times. It was his antics that eventually brought about the tattooing of the horse's lip as a means of putting an end to identification fraud. Finally, microchipping was developed as the con men found a way around the tattoos by forging the identity certificates with the correct tattoo number.

Communication improved over the years from track to track, state to state, and eventually from country to country, and it was inevitable that he received his marching orders in 1945 and was never seen again. W Bubbington, Senior Jockey Club Supervisor of Racecourses in the United States, recognised our Peter Christian Barrie and warned him off the course, and with that, he disappeared again.

With some painstaking research, there was found a notice in England that Peter Christian Barrie died at the age of 85, in 1973, at Greenwich District Hospital. He suffered from senile dementia at the time of his death.

Hoofnote: JM Barrie, the author of *Peter Pan*, was born in Scotland in 1860. Peter Christian Barrie, the king of the fakers as the Americans liked to call him, was born in Scotland in 1888. Makes you wonder if there were any family ties between them, and if the ability of Peter Pan to remain in his childhood was a family trait woven through Barrie's mindset.

What do you reckon?

How many is too many?

... a race caller's nightmare

In 1885, 41 horses lined up to contest the Caulfield Cup, and it was inevitable that somewhere during the race there would be severe interference. On turning into the straight, there was a fall that sent jockeys and horses crashing to the turf. Sixteen horses fell, and 24-year-old jockey Donald Nicholson was killed. There is no record of any horse losing its life.

Grace Darling was the winner and unfortunately we remember her for all the wrong reasons.

The long and short of it all

... where the best bet was the alphabet!

Some horses have names that are nice and simple, while others have names that would do a short novel proud.

In Australia in the late 1970s, there raced a horse of very limited ability that eventually found his way over the hurdles. There was another stayer in New Zealand of great standing that won the 1995 and the 1997 Wellington Cup. The biggest difference between the two horses was not so much their winning record, but in the length of their names: the difference was eighteen letters.

The Kiwi's name was Ed, with just the two letters, and the Aussie's name was A Gentleman from Verona, with 20 letters. He had one of the longest names registered in Australian thoroughbred history. The rules have changed since then and the maximum letters you can now have in a horse's name is eighteen.

Let us now go back in time to the late 1800s and thank goodness there were no race callers to call this pair in races. In Shepparton,

Victoria, in 1889, there was a horse winning races that had 30 letters in his name. The horse was Reverend Zacariah Stockdollinger. But if you thought that was tough, think again. In the Inverell area of New South Wales in 1888, there raced a horse with 23 letters in his name; try and get your tongue around Googeedeegullageenullah.

Can you imagine the race caller's nightmare in having A Gentleman from Verona being chased by Reverend Zacariah Stockdollinger with Googeedeegullageenullah close behind turning into the straight? They just roll off your tongue, don't they?

You want what odds?

... you can't handle the odds!

Before the days of the photo-finish camera, judges had to make some very serious decisions. Did horse 'A' win or did horse 'B' win, or was it too close for a verdict, and should a dead heat be declared?

But what if there was one bookie on course who would, at the start of an eight- or nine-race program, give you odds of there being a dead heat during the course of the afternoon? Would you take 5/2, 5/1, 10/1, 20/1, 50/1, or any sort of odds? As true blue Aussies, I am sure many of us would have a side wager on that, but time after time those bookies would be well and truly in front.

Now what if there was a dead heat, for example, in any two races of an eight-race card; I think the odds would be quite incredible and I think the bookie who laid you some odds would be in the back of the course ambulance on a respirator praying to the Almighty, saying take me, take me, please take me.

Now if there were dead heats in consecutive races at the same distance, the odds would be more like 50,000,000/1 or, in all probability, Tasmania/1.

Could that happen? Surely not. Did it happen? It certainly did, and right here in little old Australia.

At Flemington on 10 March 1969, there were two dead heats in consecutive races. Luckily for the judge, he had the assistance of the photo-finish camera. In the Elms Handicap, Mateship and Camp David dead-heated for first, and in the following race, the Australian

Cup, Cyron and Yootha dead-heated for first. Both races were over 10 furlongs (2000 metres).

What are the odds of this happening again – the United States of America/1?

George Mulley and a street directory

... never the 'pane' shall meet

Jockey Athol (call me George) Mulley was a character of the Australian turf. He had the distinction of winning fifteen races in a row on the mighty Bernborough and at his attempt to rack up sixteen consecutive wins in the 1946 Caulfield Cup, Mulley could not get the great horse out to challenge the leaders until the race was virtually over. Carrying the impost of 10 stone 10 lb (68 kg), Bernborough ran a gallant fifth behind the winner Royal Gem, which had the luxury of carrying only 9 stone (57 kg).

At the horse's next race start in the LKS Mackinnon Stakes, Mulley was replaced in the saddle by Billy Briscoe and to everyone's shock that day, the mighty Bernborough faltered at the turn into the straight, and had to be pulled up. He had broken down and was never to race again. His great adversary, the mighty mare Flight, went on to win the race. You have to feel sorry for two champion jockeys of the day: Mulley, who was replaced that day on the great horse, and Briscoe, for being the jockey who had his one and only ride end in such tragedy.

But in Athol George Mulley, we have an unforgettable character who was a very forgetful bloke:

- One day he went to the Hawkesbury races to fulfil his riding engagements. Unfortunately he should have gone to Kembla Grange.
- One other day, he arrived at Rosehill only to find no-one there. He should have been at Canterbury.
- Before the days of jockey managers, Mulley on many occasions accepted for two rides in the one race.
- On one occasion, when selling his house, he sold it to two different buyers.

- On another occasion, Mulley received a phone call from his drycleaner who told him that he had better come down and pick up the £200 he had left in the coat pocket of his suit.
- How's this for a bizarre injury. The story goes that Mulley always slept with the bedroom window open. However, this night, before retiring, his wife decided to shut the window. Next morning, on awakening to go to trackwork, Mulley went to see if it was raining, and yes, he put his head straight through a pane of glass. Ouch!

Thoroughbred vs standardbred

... the difference between them

So often we accept certain terminologies without understanding the meaning behind the word. Following is a dictionary explanation.

Thoroughbred: The thoroughbred is a horse breed best known for its use in horse racing. Although the word thoroughbred is sometimes used to refer to any breed of purebred horse, it technically refers only to the thoroughbred breed. Thoroughbreds are considered a 'hot-blooded' horse, known for their agility, speed and spirit.

Standardbred: Standardbreds are a breed of horse best known for their ability to race in harness at a trot or pace instead of under saddle at a gallop. Developed in North America, the breed is now recognized worldwide for its harness racing ability. They are solid, well-built horses with good dispositions that are also used under saddle for a variety of equestrian activities, particularly in the Midwest and eastern United States.

Laurie Connell

... a story of a leopard and his spots

Now there are opportunists and there are opportunists – some back their judgement; others are too busy backing something else. Here is the story of Laurie Connell, who had the knack of creating opportunities.

Strike one

1975 Kalgoorlie Racetrack: It takes a lot of money to shorten a horse's price with the bookies. If you have the time, just position yourself in a betting ring and see what sort of money is required to halve a price on a horse that would be in commission – say a 10/1 shot coming in to 4/1. That takes serious money.

Just wonder then how much money Laurie Connell and his mates put on a horse called His Worship at the Kalgoorlie racecourse, to shorten the price from 9/1 to 1/3. This starting price of 3 to 1 on is Phar Lap stuff, unbeatable odds, and the bookies would use this fall-back price so no more money could be wagered on the horse.

The race meeting being bet on was a radio link of a Melbourne race coming over the loudspeakers on the Kalgoorlie track. Well, Laurie and his mates backed His Worship as a certainty, because it was a certainty. Someone had conveniently intercepted the landline broadcast of the race to the Kalgoorlie track and delayed the actual broadcast to the track for a full seven minutes. The race had been run and won by His Worship in Melbourne some seven minutes earlier, but their intercept team had created a way of cutting off the broadcast to the Kalgoorlie racetrack. They then waited for an appropriate time for the people in the know to hammer the bookies on course, and then replayed the race at the course. For his involvement in the Kalgoorlie Sting, Laurie Connell was disqualified from attending race meetings for two years.

Strike two.

AHA Cup, Bunbury 1983: The reasons for what happened at the AHA Cup are not well documented, but we think you can be pretty sure there was some sort of payday for Laurie Connell on his next misdemeanour.

He had a runner in the AHA Cup at Bunbury in 1983 – a horse by the name of Strike Softly, to be ridden by Jockey Danny Hobby. During the course of the race, it was very apparent that Danny Hobby took a swan dive from his mount, which automatically disqualifies the horse from any placing in the race. It must have been comical to the extreme, as all the punters had to do was look down the racing page and see who owned the horse that just lost its jockey, and the bells would be ringing – Laurie Connell.

The authorities did not act quickly enough as they did not believe the extremes that Connoll and Hobby would go to, just to escape scrutiny and the courts. Danny Hobby disappeared overseas and of course Laurie Connell could not shed any light on the subject.

It was reported that Connell funnelled in excess of $1 million overseas to Hobby for his years on the run, but after a while, the former jockey tired of this nomadic lifestyle, while Connell still enjoyed his hometown freedom in Western Australia.

On Hobby's return, he readily admitted that Connell gave him $5000 to fall from Strike Softly during the running of the AHA Cup. Connell was tried and sentenced to five years for trying to corrupt the course of justice during the investigation into this horse race. However, the courts found Connoll not guilty of fixing the race, and he only served one year in jail before receiving a work release. Hobby received three years for his part.

Strike three

Perth Cup 1987: This time of the year in Perth is always a nervous time for bookies, especially those who frame doubles charts on the Perth Cup and Railway Stakes.

Laurie Connell had Rocket Racer entered for the Cup, to be ridden by JJ Miller. Connell had backed his horse at long odds in the Cup, and coupled Rocket Racer with all of the winning chances with the doubles bookmakers fielding on the Railway Stakes as well. Rocket Racer was backed in from 25/1 to 2/1 favourite. Was it the weight of money that Connell had invested on the punt to shorten the pricing so dramatically, or were bookies getting wise, because it could be about history repeating itself when Laurie was involved.

The field jumped and soon after the start, Rocket Racer went to the front of the 3200 metre race, and kept going as if it was a dash for cash. The Laurie Connell–owned Rocket Racer won by nine lengths, and it took the jockey almost another full lap to pull the horse up. The horse was clearly very distressed when he was led back to the winner's enclosure, so much so that connections and helpers had to manhandle the horse out of public view, as it was a distressing sight for anyone to witness the state of this poor animal.

It has been said that the animal was far too distressed to be swabbed or any other test taken. Sadly, within a few weeks, the horse died and there was no subsequent post-mortem done either. It was generally regarded in racing circles that Rocket Racer was reacting to the banned substance called etorphine, or 'elephant juice'. Only a few weeks earlier, another Connell-owned and George Way–trained horse tested positive to etorphine. Unfortunately for Mr Way, this led to a lengthy disqualification. JJ Miller, the rider of Rocket Racer, was cleared of any wrongdoing in the race.

Needless to say, Laurie Connell picked up a bundle after the 16/1 shot Valley Of Carome won the Railway Stakes, which he had coupled with Rocket Racer to win.

Rothwells Merchant Bank: Laurie Connell's term at the helm of the Rothwells Merchant Bank is a matter for public record. Investors with any sort of knowledge of investment principles would have to have been very naive, because of Laurie's background, to invest any monies with him. But many people did believe the promise of significant returns.

It is no surprise that Rothwells' sudden emergence was overshadowed only by the merchant bank's sudden collapse. It would come as no surprise, either, to read that the WA Government at the time, and Laurie's acquaintance Premier Brian Burke, were instrumental in providing hundreds of millions of dollars to Rothwells to save it from collapse ... alas, to no avail.

Laurie Connell, merchant banker or gambler – you be the judge!

Tips from the spirit world!

... and the seance that rattled yours truly

I experienced my first and last seance in August 1972; it's quite amazing how some things vividly stick in your mind after 40 years.

On this particular night, three couples including yours truly and the bride, for some unknown reason, decided to get hold of a ouija board and have a bit of fun. You know – is there a spirit out there, or words to that effect.

As the night wore on and after an extended happy hour, accusations were flying thick and fast that one or two of the men were having some influence in moving the upturned glass around the board. With that accusation, I volunteered to take my hands from the table and I would ask the questions. Since I was the only one in the group who had any knowledge of the racing industry, I decided that the next couple of questions to the Spirit World would be about racehorses. All the players agreed, but I was only allowed two questions.

At that particular time, weights had just been released for the 1972 Melbourne and Caulfield Cups. The first question I asked was about Gunsynd, which had just been given equal top weight in the Caulfield Cup and close to top weight in the Melbourne Cup. I cannot recall the exact question but I think it was something to the affect of 'Is there anything you could tell us about Gunsynd'. Nothing specific, but I felt if I could cast a wide net with my first question then I could possibly come up with something that may just be relevant. The tumbler with all the other players' fingers on it spelt out T-H-R-E-E. Not really understanding the answer, I asked the same question a second time and T-H-R-E-E was spelt out again. At the time that meant absolutely nothing to me. By this time all players, including me, were in total agreement about what a lot of crap this was.

The second question I was going to ask would be more specific, about the Melbourne Cup. I knew who the early favourite was, and I was banking on the fact that if there was a remote possibility that someone else in that room had any idea whatsoever, they might not spell it right. The second question was, 'Who is the early favourite for the Melbourne Cup?' The glass tumbler, with all the other participants' fingers on top, started to move.

The glass spelt out L-L-A-N-A-N-T-H-O-N-Y.

Everyone looked at each other with very quizzical looks on their faces. Someone asked, 'What the bloody hell does that mean?' Once again I repeated the same question.

L-L-A-N-A-N-T-H-O-N-Y was spelt out again.

Same question, same result.

Well, the horse in question happened to be the Kiwi galloper with the unusual Welsh name of Llananthony, spelt with two Ls. I told everyone who Llananthony was, and quick as a flash, all fingers were off the glass tumbler. No more ouija board that night. It was definitely time to get back to the amber fluid and more Porphyry Pearl. That game was definitely off the agenda for me for the rest of my life.

Some fifteen years later, when looking through the Saturday form guide, something came in to my mind out of the blue regarding August 1972. It hit me like a tonne of bricks. The answer given about Gunsynd, T-H-R-E-E, was now crystal clear, even though it hadn't rung any bells back in 1972 because the Cups had not been run. Gunsynd went on to run third to Sobar in the Caulfield Cup and third to Piping Lane in the Melbourne Cup. That's what the spirit was trying to tell me – T-H-R-E-E!

I then went through the Melbourne form guide looking to have a bet. I noticed in one race, some fifteen years after the seance, that there was a horse running around sired by none other than Llananthony. Maybe after all this time it was an omen. With that, it was off to the local TAB to have my interest bet. One never knew.

Did it win? Sure did, and started at around 12/1.

Maybe the spirits that night back in 1972 were saying Barry, we're here!

Where it all began

... a punt, a pie, and the 1948 Morris Tourer

Many moons ago, when yours truly was a young bloke around seventeen or eighteen (1960–61), I would sometimes go to the races at one of the city race tracks in Brisbane, either Eagle Farm, Doomben, or Albion Park, affectionately known as The Creek.

At the time I lived at Hawthorne, which was only a five-minute drive to the ferry at Bulimba. On the other side of the river is the suburb of Hamilton, which is within walking distance of both Eagle Farm and Doomben. At that time, I owned a little 1948 Morris Tourer, a real classy little goer. The one problem with the car was that as a Tourer, you could not lock it up properly because it had a soft vinyl roof and removable acrylic side curtains. However, that did not deter me from parking at the ferry, because I had my own way of locking the car.

What was this simple but ingenious way of making my car theft-proof? On arrival at the ferry, it was up with the bonnet, unclip the distributor cap, out with the rotor, wrap it in cloth, and lock it in the boot – the only thing that the car key could lock up successfully. That was my method of locking the car whenever it was unattended. My theory was if someone decided to knock the car off, they would have to have a spare rotor in their pocket, and what were the odds of that happening? The second part of my strategy was to put 2 shillings (20 cents) in one of my socks, and I will explain that later.

With all that done, I'd get onto the ferry, form guide in the back pocket, and across the river, before a brisk walk to the races. Being only a five bob punter, your wishful thinking is all about how you will clean up on the first couple of races, giving you a nice bank for the rest of the day. Sometimes that goes completely out the window, and after a number of bets, it isn't long before you have to hit the cunning kick, and no doubt every punter has one hidden somewhere. As happens with many of us punters at the races, all of the best-laid plans go out the window so it is 'off with the head and on with the pumpkin'.

When the finances are just about completely exhausted, you usually put your hard-earned on your new special, which is your get-out bet for the day. As many of us diehards would know, there is nothing more sickening than seeing your original selection come down the outside to win, while the new special finishes among the cab catchers.

Time to go, and with your tail between your legs you set off on the slow, quiet and painful return home.

What if ... Why didn't I ... I shoulda ... God, I'm a bloody idiot ... and on and on!

The punter's lament is deeply etched in the brain of all who have been there.

Once outside, there on the footpath stands one of the greatest sights that one can behold, the famous pie cart. This is where the second part of my strategy comes into play, the 20 cents (2 shillings) in my sock. Back then, for 15 cents you could buy one of the greatest gastronomical joys that have ever been marketed by mankind, the famous meat pie and peas. In Brissie, the footpath pie usually has a great topping of mushy peas, thick enough not to spill as you walk, and tasty enough to take away the pain of a losing day.

Back at the ferry, and with the remaining 5 cents, it was across the river and back to the little Morris, which was always there where I left it. Then it was only a matter of putting the rotor back in the distributor cap, putting the cap on, kicking the engine over, heading off home and thinking about a new plan of attack next time I went to the races.

After eighteen months of driving a Tourer that always leaked when it rained, it was time to upgrade, or downgrade, whichever way you look at it. My next piece of joy happened to be a second-hand straight eight-cylinder 1936 Hudson Terraplane, the same model that held the uphill speed record at Pike's Hill in the United States.

Well, the petrol bill ended up being a bit steep for a second-year apprentice at 10 miles to the gallon, so eventually that had to go as well. But at least I could lock it up when I went to the races.

I still salivate over those mouth-watering footpath pies and peas.

Ah! such was life.

The darker side of our racing game

... and hopefully never to be revisited!

Where money is in big demand, unfortunately there are those around us who just don't have that work ethic to put their shoulder to the wheel and get the most out of life by putting the most into life, those who are after a quick return for very little effort. Here are just a few examples that fill our files.

Mel Schumacher's pulling Tommy's leg

Halfway down the straight of the 1961 AJC Derby, Tommy Hill's mount Summer Fair pulled narrowly ahead of Blue Era, being ridden by Mel Schumacher. Blue Era fought back tenaciously, with the horses passing the winning post locked together. However, on returning to scale, Tommy Hill quickly fired in a protest, claiming that Schumacher had grabbed his leg and held it for about 50 metres, retarding his mount.

Unfortunately for Mel, the head-on camera verified this claim. Summer Fair won the race on protest and the AJC stewards took the unprecedented step of standing Schumacher down from riding for the rest of the program, because he had been banned for life. Mel Schumacher, after a successful appeal against his life sentence, returned to riding after five years away from the track.

Unbeknown to the jockeys that day, it was the very first time a steward's front-on camera was used and had Mel's antics on tape for all to see.

Erbie: the king of ring-ins

Officially, the thoroughbred Erbie won a total of 23 races, mostly on the New South Wales tracks. However, in July 1934, the horse's double life was exposed in South Australia. A horse by the name of Redlock was entered in the Trial Stakes at Murray Bridge and after tumbling in price from 10/1 down to 5/2, he won easily. Present on course that day was a very astute journalist named Bert Wolfe, who wrote for the *Herald* in Melbourne under the pen name 'Cardigan'. Unfortunately for all connections, he was very familiar with Redlock.

Wolfe put this run down in his little black book, as he had his suspicions. A little later, after Redlock had another win at Kardina racetrack in South Australia, Bert then pressured trainer Charlie Prince to see if he could take a look at Redlock after that win. Erbie had a distinct white blaze, and Bert found dye had been applied to Redlock's forehead in an attempt to hide a blaze. It was later discovered that Erbie had previously raced as Duke Bombita at Holbrook, raced at Kyneton as Chrybean, and through all of this, was still racing and winning as Redlock.

While Erbie was running around in disguise, the real Redlock was leisurely eating grass in a paddock outside Sunbury. Prince was jailed and warned off racetracks for two years. It is believed that good old Erbie won at least another four races as a ring-in before the whole affair was exposed.

The Royal School/Regal Vista affair

At the Castleton racetrack in May 1972, a $350 purchase named Royal School was taking part in the main race of the day. The bookies were hit and not surprisingly, where there's smoke there's fire; Royal School won with ridiculous ease, a real shock considering its form.

An inquiry was immediately held and it was revealed the real winner was in fact the 1970 Liston Stakes winner and 1969 Stradbroke Handicap runner-up, Regal Vista. Royal School's owner, Rick Renzella, and trainer, Ross Affleck, were both jailed for two years, and disqualified for life from all racetracks. Jockey Stephen Wood was given a two-year probation.

Thundering Legion and the Electric Whip

It was a handicap race at Morphetville in May 1955 and Thundering Legion was reasonably priced at 33/1. He had drawn 18 out of 22 in the race, and had finished towards the tail of the field at his previous run. Then came the plunge from 33/1 down to as little as 5/2. Something stank in Denmark, or so thought the head steward, Fred Everest.

Prior to the jockeys taking mount, Fred confronted Thundering Legion's jockey Bill Attril about the plunge, and during the questioning, Fred Everest accidentally touched the whip to be used on Thundering Legion. He received a shock.

He immediately stood down Bill Attril and appointed another lightweight jockey, Des Coleman, to ride the horse. In the running, as soon as Coleman pulled the whip, Thundering Region shifted up a couple of gears before hanging on to win by a head – strange as it may seem, as this whip did not have any batteries. The horse had been conditioned to think that every time a whip was pulled, he was going to get a shock – and obviously did on a number of occasions during the weeks leading up to the race. Poor old Thundering Legion thought he was going to be stung again when Coleman pulled the whip, so he just got up and got going.

At a stewards' inquiry, Attrill admitted that he used a battery-charged whip to condition the horse to react once it was hit. For this he was disqualified for ten years. The batteries in the whip that day were simply insurance to get the steed to take notice, but in the eventual outcome, Thundering Region was not going to wait around to find out. *Shocking!*

Mackinnon and the weight scandal

In the 1920s and 1930s, LKS Mackinnon was the Chairman of the Victoria Racing Club and a pillar of society. He had a well-bred colt in Carradale, but unfortunately his horse ran up against the mighty Phar Lap in the 1929 Victoria and AJC Derbies and was well and truly beaten. It's interesting to note here that Carradale was a colt and Phar Lap was a gelding.

After these defeats, Mackinnon and some of his committee tried to have new penalties introduced in weight-for-age events, their aim being to penalise geldings more than colts. They indicated that these changes would bring about improvement in racing stock.

Amid the scandal over the committee's endeavour to put an end to the dreams of the battlers, was it any wonder that the Australian public established Phar Lap as their champion?

Horse sense

... different terms for different ages and different sexes!

For the uninitiated, the following terms are used to describe the gender of a horse or pony at different ages.

Filly: a young female horse under four years of age
Colt: a young male horse or pony under four years of age
Foal: a horse that is one-year-old or younger
Yearling: a young horse of either sex that is between one and two years old
Mare: an adult female horse

Stallion: a male adult horse that has not been castrated. (Stallions are also known as entires.)
Gelding: a castrated male horse
Ridgling or Rig: a colt with undescended testicles

SP bookmakers

... the origin of the species!

In general terms in Australia in the 1920s and very early 1930s, betting with bookmakers on-course was the only legitimate form of gambling. In 1931, Victoria introduced small on-course totalisators, which gave punters another alternative when having a bet. However, with the arrival of the wireless and the telephone, people who wanted a punt could now hear the race results off-course, without going to the races.

Midweek races as we know today were virtually non-existent back in the old days, so many a bet was placed on a Saturday, and many a bet was with the local SP bookmaker (for our young readers, 'SP' is short for 'stating price'). However, Melbourne Cup day was so well loved by the Aussie public that punters all over Australia had only one thing in mind: to get a bet on. Yes, this era was one of larrikinism and pretty good illegal times for the SP bookie.

While it was successful up until the early 1960s, it was still a complex business. It involved a bookmaker and people called runners and cockies. While the bookie was needed to take bets and pay up, the runner would simply run all over the suburb taking bets from people in the back lanes, at the local pubs, and even in their homes. Possibly the most important job was done by the cockies (short for cockatoos), who were posted at strategic points around the neighbourhood. They were usually positioned at some elevated spots or intersections, and if there were any approaching police, it was their job to warn the bookies and the runners.

Many a blind eye was turned, and in many cases bets were paid up in local bars and in general meeting places.

With so much lucrative activity going on that was not generating taxes, something had to be done. A Royal Commission was set up in

1959, and in 1961, the off-course TAB (Totalisator Agency Board) was set up and operated under the ownership of the Victorian Government. The concept was acceptable to most people, as it finally meant that some of the money wagered on racing would be returned to the racing industry. That also gave the punters a means of having a bet without lining the local bookies' pockets. With that, the pressure was also off the local police sergeant.

We can clearly remember our father telling us of one particular SP operation that was held in a well-hidden area at Albion Park. Punters would place a bet with the runner or SP bookie and their bet was written with sharpened chalk on the back of a good old Milk Arrowroot biscuit. If they were raided, the punter could throw his bets in his mouth and the evidence would be lost forever. If the bet was no good, well there were plenty of broken biscuits lying around the place, but no slips of paper on the ground – the local fauna just loved race days!

Now that the SP bookies in Australia could not operate from their local 'off-course shops', the majority of bets were placed on course with bookmakers. In the mid-1990s, the Northern Territory Government could see more and more revenue available and issued licences to corporate bookmakers, enabling them to offer services to the public for phone and online gambling. With the winning formula by the Northern Territory Government kicking things along, it

NO NO! I SAID "I BET YOU NEVER BIT A BETTER BISCUIT!"

wasn't long before other states of Australia followed. Australian and overseas customers can now bet with numerous betting agencies on all sporting and racing events.

A part of our colourful past gone forever ... or has it?

The wisdom of Solomon

... and his not so wise approach to winning!

It's every punter's dream to wake up one Saturday morning to see that the Sunday papers have just been delivered, with all Saturday's results in it, even though the races haven't yet been run. How good would that be? Well we know that's impossible, because it is only a dream.

Or you are at the TAB, you hear the winner of a certain race and notice that everyone is clamouring to get a bet on the winner, even though the TAB is still taking bets on a race that has already been run and won.

They certainly are far-fetched dreams. We know that it couldn't happen ... or could it? Well, it did happen, or pretty close to it.

On 16 December 1939, in the days before TV and TABs and only the good old wireless to listen to, something extraordinary happened. The last race at the old Ascot racecourse in Melbourne was about to get underway in the Berkeley Welter Handicap at 5.05pm:

'They're off in the last in Melbourne' – 3DB's Eric Welch.
'Away they go in the last of the day' – 3LO's Jim Carroll.
'They're racing' – 3AW's Fred Tupper.
'Yes ladies and gentlemen, we now have quite a few minutes before they jump, so I will go through the field and give you my thoughts' – 3XY's Harry Solomons.

As the field was about to jump, one of Solomons' cohorts cut the wires of stations 3DB, 3LO and 3AW, leaving no live radio broadcast from the stations. This was the start of a very audacious sting by young Harry. During his review of the field, Solomons kept mentioning one particular galloper by the name of Buoyancy, which was continually playing up behind the starting gate, causing the race to be delayed by just under five minutes. Before the race got under way on 3XY, there was a tremendous rush all over Australia to back just one horse. After a good while, Solomons then proceeded to do his phantom call, and yes, Buoyancy won at the very nice odds of 6/1.

Harry Solomons had played his part in the sting, and many thousands of pounds had been won. He already knew the winner, and it was very plain afterwards that the 3XY broadcast had not started until after the race had finished. Unfortunately for Solomons, there had been one minor problem. Eric Welch at 3DB had shouted 'They're off' before his line was cut. Also overlooked by the culprits was the fact that one of Fred Tupper's extra lines on 3AW to 2GB was still broadcasting, while the 3DB and 3LO lines were down.

Investigations soon led to 3XY's Harry Solomons, who fled the country just before his court case could be heard. In June 1940, Harry's luck finally ran out. Australian detectives found him hiding in Fiji, arrested him, and brought him back to Melbourne where he was sentenced to six months' jail in Pentridge.

So much for the wisdom of Solomons!

Husband and wife winners

... one for the record books?

History records that only one husband and wife have trained Melbourne Cup winners.

Laurie Laxon trained Empire Rose to win in 1988.

Sheila Laxon was successful when Ethereal won in 2001.

History also records that Sheila Laxon is the only woman to train a Melbourne Cup winner – or was she?

When Catalogue won the 1938 Melbourne Cup, the trainer was listed in the race book as Mr A McDonald. However, he was not the trainer. The horse was actually trained by McDonald's wife, HW 'Granny' McDonald, who held a trainer's licence in New Zealand.

At the time, the VRC forbade any women to hold a Victorian trainer's licence. Unofficially, the victory was credited to the trainer's wife ... Chauvinists!

The biggest loser

... a tale of a much-loved mare

In the late 1970s and early 1980s, there emerged a racehorse in the Land of Oz with a cult following; her name was Ouroene. She had 124 career starts spanning from 1976 to 1983, but Ouroene never won a single race. Owners George and Lorraine Chiotis loved this mare and were even prepared to race her against the mighty Kingston Town in WFA races, both times starting at 200/1 and 500/1. She was given no chance, even though both races had very small fields. Every time Ouroene went on to the track, the crowd cheered and applauded her, knowing that she was going to struggle to even run a place. Many a small punter would have a dollar each way just in case she got under their guard.

In the eyes of her trainer George Chiotis, she was his Phar Lap, his Bernborough and his Kingston Town all rolled in to one, and one day, George and his champion mare would stand in the winner's stall cheered on by the punting public.

Unfortunately, that was never to be.

We can all be dreamers, but in 1983 while being prepared for the Brisbane Winter Carnival as a lead-up to the Melbourne Spring Carnival, Ouroene had to be euthanased due to a track accident. This broke the heart of her trainer and his wife, who treated her like one of the family.

In 124 starts, Ouroene had no wins, two seconds and seven thirds, for total prize money of AUD$14,605.

Stop press

At the time of writing, Ouroene has just lost the distinction of being the Biggest Loser worldwide. Puerto Rican mare Dona Chepa has had her name written into the record books by completing her 125th race without a win. Her total prize money to date is US$12,971.

Here is the Roll of Honour of the most number of runs without a win:

1. Dona Chepa: 125 races (Puerto Rico)
2. Ouroene: 124 races (Australia)

3. Gloria Springs: 106 races (Japan)
4. Thrust: 105 races (United States)
5. Quixall Crossett: 103 races (Britain)

Bastards, buzzards, privates and pubics

... more cheeky Aussie contributions!

We often come across two very well-known acronyms, SNAFU and FUBAR.

For those who do not know, an acronym is described as a word formed from the initial letters or group of letters in a set phrase or series of words. For those who honestly reckon they have never heard of them, here are the meanings (they are believed to have originated in the armed forces):

SNAFU: Situation Normal All F***ed Up
FUBAR: F***ed Up Beyond All Recognition

And this leads to the horse racing in late 2009, by the sire Fubu, named Fubah. Does that mean F***ed Up Beyond All Hope? I wonder if this is another case of good old Aussie humour.

Not to be outdone, consider the Kiwi racehorse Fig Jam: F*** I'm Good Just Ask Me. *Beautiful!*

Sometimes odd-sounding names are registered for racehorses, and without the proper checking by authorities, they race once or twice before they have their name changed. In 2010, a two-year-old raced at one of the Toowoomba twilight meetings with a bit of an unusual name. Some of the on-course punters of Lebanese background were cheering and laughing as the horse won on debut. The whole Lebanese racing community in Australia must have found this one to be hilarious.

So what was so funny with having a horse named Aidee Fic?

Well it didn't take long before we all found out via blog sites, pubs and the bush telegraph that Aidee Fic was the loose translation of the Lebanese phrase meaning 'F**k you'.

Aidee Fic's name was changed to Journey On, which was basically the same meaning but expressed in a very polite way.

Privates and pubics

In the 1980s and early 1990s, Sydney medico turned racehorse trainer Dr Geoff Chapman trained many winners. Two of the champion racehorses in his stable were the multiple Group 1 winners Myocard and Dr Grace. However, back in 1983, the Doc also trained a little filly with a very unusual name: Merkin.

Merkin won at her first two starts, the second being the 1983 Silver Slipper Stakes at Rosehill. They were two very promising runs, and the Golden Slipper was now on the agenda.

Being such a great character, the Doc was probably grinning from ear to ear whenever his horse was mentioned in the press, and more than satisfied to hear the horse's name being called by the race broadcaster. However, it wasn't long before the authorities were alerted to the meaning of the name Merkin and the filly's connections were advised to change her name. She then raced as Giostra. Wonder why?

Well, back in the old days, a merkin was a wig made from pubic hair.

You can't help but feel Dr Geoff was still having a go at authorities because maybe Giostra was an acronym for Geoff Insists On Still Teasing Racing Authorities.

The bastard and the buzzard

In the 1920s, a stallion arrived on our shores, all the way from England. He was to stand at Lyndhurst Stud on the Darling Downs in Queensland.

In Australia he ended up having an amazing record as a sire of stayers, producing Melbourne Cup winners Old Rowley and Rainbird. He also produced Caulfield Cup winners Buzalong and Basha Felika and Sydney Cup winner L' Aiglon, and many other notable champions of their day.

His name was The Buzzard.

The Lord Roseberry-bred horse raced under another name in England, but the Australian racing authorities were fearful that if he was to retain his original name, the floodgates may open for some very Aussie interpretations naming his offspring. After all, we are talking about Aussies.

His English racing name was The Bastard. Yes, the bastard became a buzzard, but isn't Australia the home to a lot of silly old bastards?

The Fiji Flyer and me

... a true story of a champ, a chump and a kid just having fun!

In 1991, four couples including yours truly and the bride went on a two-week holiday to Fiji, which just happened to coincide with our 25th wedding anniversary.

When a group of business people and their wives go on holidays together, it is inevitable that the winding down of our stress levels usually begins on the very first night with good food, good wine, plenty of laughter and usually plenty of BS and bravado. A few nights into our relaxation period, and celebrating our 25th, it wasn't long after a great Fijian meal and 'more Ben Ean for my friends' that it was time for coffee and port. Coffee to put the grey matter back into gear and a cleansing port lovingly referred to as monkey blood, just to make sure that we appeared to be in control, to finish off a great night.

At the end of this very long evening, somewhere between a number of cleansing ports and finding our land legs, some fool suggested that we all go horse riding the following morning along one of the beaches. No doubt yours truly was probably the culprit who made that ridiculous statement, because on reflection, at that time I felt 10 foot tall and bulletproof, under the influence of a big night out.

The following morning, after a very slow breakfast with a symphony orchestra playing in my head, we four musketeers and wives headed off to the beach to enjoy our ride.

On arrival at the 'OK Corral', we were told by a huge mountain of a man to select our horses. We couldn't argue with the hulk and immediately I looked for the fattest, laziest horse I could see, hoping that walking and not cantering was its top speed. I happened to draw the short straw and was handed the reins of a horse that appeared to be quite a bit fitter than the other three.

Once mounted, and sitting in a saddle that seemed to have survived the World War I charge by the Light Horse Brigade, I wondered how bad this ride could be on such a beautiful and pristine beach in Fiji. It was only an 800 metre canter to the Point, a slow turn around and a dismount, followed by a nice walk back to the waiting wives. Silly smirks and all.

Now this is when my nightmare began.

After mounting, one of those cheeky little Fijian kids decided to give my horse a decent whack over the rump. That bloody mongrel of a thing took off at break-neck speed, and in my mind I was thinking he was probably running ten seconds to the furlong. As I was caught totally off-guard, it wasn't long before both feet were out of the stirrups, arms clinging to his neck and mane, and I was thinking, 'God, why me?' I vowed and declared at that point that I would never make any rash statements again while in a state of alcoholic euphoria, as one is prone to do.

Thank God 'Phar Lap' came to an abrupt stop at the 800 metre mark, right at the Point, when I finally fell off. Once on mother earth, I prayed to the Almighty for sparing my life; it was out with the rosary beads and all the Hail Marys.

No doubt the horse had done this hundreds of times before. Backing them, not riding them, was now the only thing in my life. That was one of the scariest things to happen to me and I think all jockeys should be paid a king's ransom for riding a 500 kg lethal weapon like that.

The escape from hell did not end there. Those bloody little Fijian kids were running up the beach laughing and cheering and treating the whole thing as a great joke. The kid who'd given 'Phar Lap' a good whack over the rump came up to me with tears in his eyes from laughter, and said, 'Sir, you are riding a very fast horse. He is a racehorse and is racing in Nadi tomorrow.'

I couldn't believe what I was hearing, and asked him to repeat what he had just said. 'Yes, sir, he is racehorse, and he is racing in

Nadi tomorrow. He is called Rocket, sir.'

At least that rotten little kid had manners.

The rest of the Mouseketeers, and that's what they were, mounted on their very fine slow thoroughbreds, soon caught up and we all headed back to the wives, who were laughing their heads off. I walked back and let those kids lead Rocket, the lethal weapon, back to the beach stable. I felt like a dead man walking. When you are crook, you are crook, especially after an early-morning gallop like that one.

When we got back to the 'OK Corral', I asked the 140 kg man-mountain in charge, who probably played rugby union for Fiji in his spare time, if the yarn that kid had spun me was true. 'Yes, sir, his name is Rocket and he is racing in race three tomorrow at Nadi. It is a very short race, sir.' Any wonder it was a short race, he has just left the training track with a bloody 48-year-old, 85 kg track rider on board.

As we were leaving, the 'head gunfighter' actually asked me if we were going to the races tomorrow to watch Rocket race. With a sickly polite reply of no, and with all of that port now turned into muscatel churning around in my stomach, I vowed and declared that the only horses I would be coming in contact with were the ones on the TAB screen, the ones that I read about in *Best Bets* and my form guide – never again will I sit astride such a giant lethal killing machine.

For many years, people doubted how fair dinkum I was about my story. Around 1995, a business colleague of mine took his wife and family on holidays to Fiji, and they happened to stay at the same hotel that we had stayed in back in 1991. He took his daughters horse riding on the same beach one morning, as we had, and unfortunately, one of them had a fall from one of the horses that had broken into a gallop, and she was hospitalised.

The x-rays showed a slight hairline fracture in her left hip. When my mate went back and confronted the new guard at the 'OK Corral' about the speed the horses were doing on the sand, he was told that they were racehorses and the local kids got some extra money to exercise them between race meetings.

Was this the same killer animal that went by the name of Rocket?

Motto: keep away from horse riding on the beaches in Fiji, because you too may get to ride a racehorse, possibly a direct descendent of the infamous Rocket.

So there it is – Rocket the Fiji Flyer, and me.

World champions: the most successive victories

... and what a wonderful habit to get into

The following horses, although beaten during their career, have the rare distinction of having the greatest number of successive wins. This list is correct as at 31 May 2012.

The top ten with the most successive victories are:

- 56 wins: Camarero (Peurto Rico), lost his first start then won 56 straight. He won 73 from 77
- 49 wins: Cofres (Peurto Rico)
- 44 wins: Condalo (Peurto Rico)
- 39 wins: Galgo Jr (Peurto Rico)
- 24 wins: Sicotico (Dominican Republic)
- 23 wins: Leviathan (United States)
- 22 wins: Miss Petty and Sava Jet (Australia), Pooker T (Puerto Rico), Rapid Redux (United States)
- 21 wins: Picnic in the Park (Australia), First Consul (United States)
- 20 wins: Shackle Bar (Australia), Fashion Filch (Ireland)
- 19 wins: Gloaming and Desert Gold (NZ), Zenyatta (United States)

Following are the lists of horses with the most wins in one season:

Northern Hemisphere: 1 January–31 December

- 29 wins: Camarero (Puerto Rico)
- 21 wins: Fisherman (Great Britain)
- 19 wins: Citation (United States)
- 18 wins: Hindoo (United States)

- 17 wins: Jamaica Princess (United States)

Southern Hemisphere: 1 August–31 July

- 22 wins: Top Ace (Australia)
- 15 wins: Clover Valley and Mainbrace (New Zealand)
- 14 wins: Ajax, Phar Lap, Tulloch (Australia), Desert Gold and Syntax (New Zealand)
- 13 wins: Gay Port (Australia), Grey Way and Gloaming (New Zealand)
- 12 wins: Eurythmic, Kingston Town, Prince Cortauld and Surround (Australia)

The Australian horse, Jorrocks, who raced in the mid 1800's, won 30 out of 31, but that was in a calendar year in Australia.

The top ten horses that are undefeated in the world as at 31 May 2012 are:

- 54 wins: Kincsem (Hungary) foaled in 1874
- 21 wins: Black Caviar (Australia) 2006
- 19 wins: Peppers Pride (United States) 2003
- 18 wins: Eclipse (Great Britain) 1764 and Katayal (Turkey) 1970
- 16 wins: Ormonde (Great Britain) 1883
- 16 wins: Prestige (France) 1903, Ribot (Italy) 1952
- 15 wins: Colin (United States) 1905, Macon (Argentina) 1922
- 14 wins: High Flyer (Great Britain) 1774, Nearco (Italy) 1935
- 13 wins: Barcaldine (Great Britain) 1878, Personal Ensign (United States) 1984

The top ten beaten in only one race during their career are:

- 21 out of 22: Native Dancer (United States) 1950
- 20 out of 21: Man O' War (United States) 1917
- 19 out of 20: Zenyatta (United States) 2004
- 18 out of 19: Hambletonian (Great Britain) 1792 (the galloper, not the trotter)
- 17 out of 18: Botafogo (Argentina) 1914, Brigadier Gerard (Great Britain) 1968, Gradisco (Venezuela) 1960

- 15 out of 16: The Flying Dutchman (Great Britain) 1846
- 14 out of 15: Sysonby (United States) 1902
- 11 out of 12: Alba (Germany) 1927, Invasor (Argentina) 2002

The twelve golden rules of successful betting

... Eric Connolly's betting bible, and it could be yours too!

Don't tell anyone that I told you, but just to reiterate what I have said previously, the large successful punters always did their homework. It may be tedious, but winners don't just happen; they select themselves if you have the Golden Rules to follow, just like Eric Connolly had in the first half of the 20th century. You will have your ups and your downs, but never stray from the path when you are on a slide. Keep the courage of your convictions as the greats have done. Here are Eric Connolly's golden rules:

Rule 1: Do *not* bet on all races. Follow the steps below and be patient. You can *win on a race* but you will *not beat the races.*

Rule 2: Punters who bet SP pricing should think again when having something each way where there are more than twelve starters. In SP betting it is generally accepted that the place is a quarter of the odds on the straight-out price for a win. The punter is not getting good value where it is a big field.

In a field of eight, each horse has three chances of running a place, which leaves five horses not running a place. With a field of 20 horses, you have three chances of running a place and seventeen of not running a place. Yet, your place odds do not change. By having a $1 each way on a horse in a large field, a punter would be better off having $1 straight out on two runners in the race. Is it starting to make sense?

Rule 3: This is extremely important for the average punter. Often you have not got the time to study the form the way it is intended and you should confine yourself to good horses, being trained by good trainers, where they have good jockeys on their backs. Too often your hard-earned money ends up in the bookie's bag because of your impatience and poor judgement in backing poorly performed horses, trained by sub-standard trainers and being ridden by poorly performing jockeys.

Rule 4: All punters should study the winning jockey's list. There are quite a number of jockeys who average one winner in every 20, 30, 50 or even 100 mounts, yet a number of racegoers will often take the short odds about one of them winning a race. However, this rule does not apply to every race and there may be races where inferior race jockeys have the field to themselves with no good jockeys riding in that race. Steer clear of ordinary riders as their winning percentages are very poor, and also steer clear of races where all hoops are apprentices unless there is a standout.

Rule 5: Backing a poor horse usually results in a poor bet. Poor horses are not as consistent as the better class of horse, and it is highly unlikely that such a galloper will turn in two successive good runs. If the horse is top class, and is trained by an astute trainer, it is more likely to run to form. A trainer that generally doesn't know his business will fluke getting a horse to its peak. Maidens and restricted handicaps for horses of all ages are generally a trap and well left alone. You have the improving younger horse against the aged horses that may have a couple of convictions to his name – steer clear.

Rule 6: Never back a runner on a heavy track if it has no history in the mud, and back only those that have proven heavy track form. When doing your form, never consider a performance by a horse in heavy going when assessing what might occur on a good track. Wet weather form should only be applied to races run in slow or similar conditions.

Rule 7: Class is extremely important. Backing horses in a higher class of race is generally flirting with danger. Quite a few times, a young horse, and even older horses who keep on improving, will overcome the rise in class, but when such a horse comes along and you have done your homework, it is generally obvious.

Rule 8: Always consider the course where a race is going to be decided. If a horse runs away with a 1200 metre race at Moonee Valley, for example, it does not mean it will beat the same type of field over 1200 metres at Caulfield or Flemington. Knowing that a horse that handles the course it is to race is extremely important. In other words, 'horses for courses' is critical in your selection.

Rule 9: Weights are obviously a great pointer to winners and losers. One of the greatest assets for a punter to have is the ability to handicap horses against each other. Doing your maths is absolutely vital. It requires knowing which horses can carry weight, which horses are lightly framed and which are unlikely to be able to handle a big lift in the weights.

In doing weights, Eric Connolly always allowed 3 lb (1.5 kg) to equal a length. However, in long-distance races, he estimated a length was 2 lb (1 kg). He also considered in long-distance races that every half-kilo over 57 kg was equal to 1 kg. In doing form on high-weight races, the rule of thumb usually pays to start with the bottom-weighted horse, then work up to the top-weight.

Rule 10: Barrier positions *must* be studied. Each barrier can present its own problems as to whether the horse is a fast or slow beginner. Backing horses from wide barriers rarely pays off. Inside barriers have a distinct advantage. For example, a fast beginner may start from barrier 13 over 1600 metres at Caulfield and you would count that against that horse; however, you may find that there are are a number of horses drawn inside that are slow beginners – in such circumstances, the handicap may not be as bad as first thought.

Rule 11: In having a bet, make it a rule not to bet odds-on. If you have \$5 on a horse at 2/1 to win \$10 and it gets beaten, you then have to bet \$5 again on two winners at 2/1 on to break even. However, betting a shade of odds-on is allowed on a stand-out bet.

Rule 12: Always treat your investment as a business. Never have a bet just for the sake of betting. Only invest your money when you believe you have a better chance than the bookie.

When you are having a game of poker, you don't play every hand that you are dealt. Betting is the same, so apply the very same rules when you are betting on the horses.

Well, there you go; those are the golden rules, but two of the most important things to remember are *always do your homework* and *be very patient*. After all, your money is hard-earned, so treat it with the respect it deserves. Put a plan in place, do your homework well, and I am sure if all of the above is put to good use, you to can be successful on the punt.

Good luck!

Our Aussie chocolate icon!

... and where our pride and joy got its name

This is a true story. Back in 1955 in the Calumet Farm in Kentucky, in the good old US of A, a colt was born. His sire was the great Tom Fool and his dam was the equally famous Two Lea. He had fourteen starts for ten wins, one second and three thirds.

His greatest achievements in the United States were the contests of the Triple Crown in 1958. In his three-year-old Classic year, he won the first leg, the Kentucky Derby, followed by the second leg, the Preakness. While enjoying what was a winning lead in the home stretch in the final leg of The Belmont Stakes, he fractured a sesamoid bone and hobbled the last few yards across the finishing line, tragically beaten into second place.

Strangely enough, his legend lives on with great popularity in Australia, thousands of miles from where he began and finished his career. From the tip of Cape York to the southernmost tip of Tassie, from Point Danger on the eastern seaboard to Steep Point, the westernmost tip of Western Australia, his name is always on someone's lips.

They named a very famous biscuit after him. No, he wasn't called 'The Milk Arrowroot', and no, not 'The Scotch Finger'; he was responsible for the name of our chocolate-coated biscuit icon. His name was 'Tim Tam' and so therefore he is loved, admired and digested in more ways than one, far, far from home.

And where did he get his name? It was said that he was named after the Yorkshire terrier that had the run of Calumet Farm at the time he came into the world. His name was Timmy Tammy. Tim Tam sounds so much better, doesn't it?

It started at what price?

... every punter's dream

Over the years, Australia has had some very long-priced winners that just keep you wondering, how could that bloody thing win?

Here are only a few to whet your appetite, because the list just goes on and on:

- Anntelle: 1982, Canterbury Park (500/1)
- Pablo Pulse: 1987, Warwick Farm (500/1)
- Magic Wind: 1956, Doomben (330/1)
- Disseminate: 1969, Rosehill (330/1)
- Leonotis: 1976, Randwick (330/1)
- Chiamare: 1982, Canterbury Park (330/1)
- Dulcify: 1978, Morphetville (300/1)

Yes, there have been literally hundreds over the years, but this one may be the granddaddy of them all. His name: Zulu Gold.

Zulu Gold won at Cheltenham, South Australia on 10 September 1977, officially starting at 400/1. One gentleman must have labelled this horse to be his absolute best bet special of the day. Why? Well, this lucky punter claimed one bookie for $10,000 to $20 each way at 500/1, and the horse duly saluted the judge in first place.

One can only imagine the scene when correct weight was declared – one very ecstatic punter and one extremely sick bookie who probably called for a bucketload of alcohol just to take the pain away. It must have felt like being kicked in the kahunas by a 2 tonne horse.

Do you think that bookie ever set that punter again? I don't think so.

Dopes and doping

... the underbelly of our industry!

There have been many reported stories and actions against criminals, trainers and connections when plans have been concocted to interfere with the running ability (or inability) of a racing thoroughbred. Some have been blatantly obvious and others remain unsolved. Here are just a few incidences where man has endeavoured to line his pockets in the easiest way possible. After all, it always comes down to money, doesn't it?

The further we remove ourselves from the rules and regulations of an industry with underhanded and illegal practices in mind, the more we must rely upon those guardians appointed to scrutinise that behaviour and impose that rule of law to ensure a proper operation.

It was common knowledge in the isolated race meetings in outback Western Australia in the 1950s that because of an insufficient number of officials on the course, stewards only had the time to swab one winner per meeting. This opened the floodgates because the racing public on course would then be aware that if that winner was swabbed in one of the early races, then it was 'Rafferty's Rules' for the rest of the card. That led to every man and his dog watching for anything untoward in the latter races; for example, big plunges on outsiders and little money for favourites.

At one such meeting, a local thoroughbred (which shall remain nameless) was given a magic potion just before his start in Race 3 on the seven-race program. The first two winners for the day had not been swabbed so they took their chances.

Race 3 was away and the horse in question bolted away on the turn to unexpectedly win by four lengths. The trainer's legs turned to jelly when after unsaddling his steed and correct weight being announced, a steward walked up to him and said, 'Swab, mate.' Accompanying the trainer and the horse back to an area behind the race stables so the necessary urine sample could be taken, the official was blissfully unaware of what was about to happen. On the way, the trainer's thoughts were going at a hundred miles an hour – how in the hell do I get out of this?

Well he sure had the answer, because as he turned the corner with the steward following him, he quickly gave the horse a solid slap on the rump and away the steed galloped into the scrub. The two men looked at each other and no further action was taken – the horse found its way back to the racing stables some two days later.

When at first they don't succeed ...

There was a very handy horse running around the United Kingdom in the early 1960s named Pinturischio. He had two starts for one win, but so convincing was his win that he was quickly installed as the early favourite for the 1961 English Derby.

One of the lead-up races for the Derby was the Dante Stakes, and this is where some mystery men instigated their plan. They had backed another horse to win the Derby and regarded Pinturischio as the only danger. Thinking this was a qualifying race to run in the Derby, they slipped Pinturischio a concoction that led to his being distressed, and his connections had to scratch him from this race. Apparently, it wasn't a qualifying race to run in the Derby, and Pinturischio quickly recovered and sentiment from his followers kept him a firm favourite to win the Classic.

It wasn't long before the mystery men realised their mistake, and decided to to add another concoction to the poor horse's feed. However, on the eve of the 1961 English Derby, with poor Pinturischio in a very distressed state, the connections had no option but to withdraw him from the Classic. Would he have beaten the eventual winner, Psidium?

The sad part about this is that this very promising young colt never recovered fully and never raced again, going to stud in his later years with minimal success. Obviously the second concoction was much stronger than the first and affected this good horse quite severely.

When binoculars are not just binoculars ...

The King George V Stakes is a classic race held during the Royal Ascot meeting in England during the month of June every year. It is what they call a Heritage Handicap for three-year-olds run over 10 furlongs (2000 metres).

It was in the year 1988 in the King George V Stakes that the leader in the straight, Ile de Chypre, looked as though the race was safely in his keeping, when all of a sudden he veered sharply away from the winning post and subsequently threw his jockey, Greville Starkey, out of the saddle.

The reason remained a mystery to all who had witnessed the event; some pundits put it down to an insect sting or just something that spooked the horse at this very unfortunate moment. The connections were devastated and were at a loss to explain what had happened.

However, during an unrelated nobbling inquiry months later, evidence was heard of the use of an ultrasonic gun that had been designed to spook horses in running. The gun emitted a high-frequency sound that when pointed at the horse, distressed the animal so much that it became uncontrollable. It was later admitted that this device was used on the horse Ile de Chypre during the running of the King George V Stakes.

You would think that it would be obvious to onlookers if they saw a member in the stand pointing an unusual device at a horse in running, but it was admitted during the inquiry that the ultrasonic gun was camouflaged as a set of binoculars – and no-one would have known the difference.

... and dear Lady Melwyn

This is one nobbling gone wrong with the worse possible eventuality. It is one thing to rob someone blind where there is no pain inflicted, but to harm an animal for your gain just highlights what sort of people we have running around the place on the fringe of the great industry that we all support.

It happened at a race meeting at Brisbane's Albion Park in the mid-1930s; the day was just coasting along like any other race day with the long-suffering punters in attendance, the bookies doing battle to earn a quid, and the horses going round and round as they do.

Then a race started that included a filly called Lady Melwyn. Everything was going as scripted after the start, but unfortunately not for Lady Melwyn. She lost all interest in the race and, while chasing the field down mid-race, went absolutely berserk. Her jockey, after many attempts to settle her in running, was finally able to pull her up. However, her behaviour only got worse. The filly was completely out of it and crashed into the fence on the grandstand side, badly injuring her leg. Racecourse staff and connections managed to lead her back to the stable area, but she continually lashed out at all and sundry, something totally out of her character. Someone had got at the poor bugger, and unfortunately she died the very next day.

No extra money in the kick is worth that, and one can only hope that those responsible eventually got their just rewards.

CHAPTER 6
Horse Names

Wot's in a name
... where it all began!

My fascination with the naming of thoroughbred racehorses started in the 1960s. I had always accepted the name as a given but then started to realise the thought, ingenuity and immense scrutiny the owners put themselves under to identify their charge in a manner that explains, in most cases, who they are and where they came from. That journey of delight and obsession started with the naming of just one horse – it made me think. He was racing in Sydney at the time and was named Pink Elephants.

The penny fell when I saw that the sire was Tip the Bottle and the dam was Circus Act – very clever – and that, my friends, is where it all began for me.

The following Australian examples of ingenuity and originality are some of the pearlers that I thought deserved a mention. I am sure some of the owners burnt the midnight oil to ensure that their horse, in some way, represented the lineage from which he or she had come from. Many people will probably say, 'That can't be the name of a horse, surely,' but all horse names are registered in the Australian and New Zealand Stud Book. In each case the offspring's name is first, followed by the sire 'x' and the dam (and any little comment that is appropriate). Enjoy!

Wilander: Exceed And Excel x Scandinavia *(brilliant)*
Tickle My Pocket: Coincidence x Grease My Palm *(out of the politician's handbook)*
Tickle Me Quick: Urgent Request x Make Me Giggle *(please hurry, can't wait)*
Punch Up: Sunday Knight x School Blue
Knight in Tights: Sunday Knight x Overtight *(feel the squeeze)*
Wanted Man: Untouchable x Free Kick
From the Terrace: Untouchable x View *(Jimmy Stewart and Grace Kelly's famous movie)*
Wecanbeheroes: Honours List x The Baggy Green *(Australia's finest)*
Sly As: TV Heart Throb x Supertart
Kevinoseven: Secret Savings x Most Excellent *(yes Kev, but watch out for the auditors)*
Go Forest Go: Mr Innocent x Tough Assignment *(run, Forrest, run)*
Codeword: More Than Ready x Vocabulary
Hand Up: Pupil x Stand up
Wojinski: Exceed And Excel x Cat's Cradle *(one of Geelong's finest premiership players – go the Cats)*
Bodgie Business: Key Business x Our Rhodes Scholar *(Bob who?)*
Trade Me In: Wily Trader x Be My Bride
Defrock: Canny Lad x Excommunicate
Hybeam: Racer's Edge x Visibility
Ponder: Strategic x Brainwork *(thinking, thinking, thinking)*
Maybe Nadal: Masterclass x Spaulding *(a tennis classic)*
Divorces: Domesday x Family Breakup *(that will do it)*
The Jackal: Bite The Bullet x Positive Surprise
Put the Boot In: Youthful Legs x Ouch *(that hurt)*
Every Man's Dream: Charge Forward x She's Game
The Fangsta, Impaler and Fangsforthememory: Three brothers by Dracula x Catecombe *(I want to drink your blooood)*
Once a Week: Dr Johnson x Honeymoon's Over
On Bail and Offenders: Canny Lad x Parole
Off Shore: Dash for Cash x Swiss Franc
Seesawing: Easy Rocking x Playground

Somewhere Safer: Postponed x Security
Orchestra Stalls: Centre Stalls x Keep Us Laughing
Idoovoodoo: Pins x Abracadabra
Every Other Sunday: Any Given Sunday x Are You Serious *(a part-time Christian)*
How Fairdinkum: Genuine x No Mukkin 'Round
Staccato: Rapid Man x All Tune *(we all know someone who talks and sings too fast)*
Spilt Milk: Over x Crying *(one for the ages)*
Bob And Dolly: Untouchable x Pickabox *(yes they were, back in the days of radio and early TV)*
Left for Dead: Marooned x Corporate Writeoff
Preparetostop: Dangerous x A Red Light *(by Danger)*
Smart Punch: Shrewdy x Puppet Strings *(remember Punch and Judy?)*
Dubai Fling: Dubai Destination x Kissing Cousin
First Man: Adam x Crystalize
Headline Affair: Halo Homewrecker x United Press *(you brought it on yourself, Tiger)*
Slip of the Tongue: Dangerous x Secret Speech *(a politician's nightmare)*
Any Minute Now: Exceed And Excel x Dim Sim *(love the Chinese food, don't you?)*
Forehand: Exceed And Excel x Set Point
Sixtyfour: Exceed And Excel x Ateates *(have a think about this one)*
Overindulge: No Slip x Very Long Lunch *(know the feeling well)*
Gargle: Untouchable x Mouthwash
Whippy Van: Street Cry x Absolute Lure *(we can all remember this)*
Unknown Soldier: Medal of Honor x Sister Who
Neversaidit'seasy: Easy Rocking x Never Said a Word
Not So Coy: Not A Single Doubt x Thank You Ma'am
Forge: Counterfeit x Stylish Title
Useless Attorney: Lawyer x Stumbling *(you're fired!)*
Under The Counter: Real Quiet x Millions
Blameless: No Excuses Needed x Facing the Music

Chess: Strategic x Slow Motion *(a lot of strategy involved, but not the fastest game in the world)*
Break The Habit: Hong Kong Stopover x Obsessive *(gee, go somewhere else)*
Unwanted: Youthful Legs x Passion *(a father's lament)*
She's Dangerous: Dangerous x Punched *(one of Charlie's Angels)*
Home On the Wife: Home On the Grange x Wife Exchange *(wow)*
Noisy Scooter: Clang x Gotta Scoot *(every kid's dream)*
Circled: Strategic x Periphery
Maywyn On Tuesday: Partner's Choice x Monday Eve *(bet you don't)*
Our Baby Bonus: Dash For Cash x Mother to Be *(many thanks to the government)*
Makes Cents: Dash For Cash x Just a Little Bit
Five Aces: Real Cash x Dead Lucky *(you certainly would be)*
Ringside Ron: Festival Hall x Babble On *(the good old days)*
Auditor: Untouchable x Total Whisper
We Are Happy: Lucky Owners x Little Bit Happy
Calm Before: More Than Ready x Storm At Night
Big Birdie: Exceed And Excel x One Under *(a golfing classic)*
I'm a Single Lady: Not A Single Doubt x Silk Pyjamas
New Recruit and Pass It On: Inflate x She's Swell
Boxing Bride: Festival Hall x Take the Veil *(she wanted a quick stop on the way to the reception)*
Decision Time: Foreplay x Daunting Thoughts
Tiger Won't Tell: Hold That Tiger x Willy Tell *(obviously 'Willy' was the problem)*
Carlton Forward: Charge Forward x Carlton Ace *(go Jezza)*
Teasing: More Than Ready x Turned On
Justonetwomany: Happy Giggle x My Highball *(that will certainly do it)*
Treasury Notes: Special Bond x Financial Rescue
Beach Model: Footstepsinthesand x National Star
Playing to Win: Strategic x Golf Circuit
Playful Miss: Foreplay x No Fear Here
Youknowtherules and Out for Lunch: High Rolling x Dare to Flirt

It's Not Me: Mr Innocent x Going Higher
Hanzoff: Untouchable x How Sweet She Is
Showimyacross: Dracula x Casket *(good old Vlad again)*
Take Your Seat: Commands x Season Ticket
High Aspirations: Exceed And Excel x Career Start
Too Good: Honours List x Clearly Best
No Hesitation: Not A Single Doubt x Three Cheers *(good on you, mate)*
Bleaching: Not A Single Doubt x Barrier Reef
Bettawatchout: Dangerous x The Wife *(don't forget to duck)*
Zigzag: Domesday x Hairpin
Itoldyouso: Legal Opinion x Love Thy Neighbour
Gyrocopter: Dangerous x Flew
Bushranger: Dash For Cash x Take to the Hills
Callmewhatyalike: Foreplay x Schoolies
Are You Awake: Foreplay x Midnight Monday *(well are you?)*
Lazyboy: Comfy x Anywhere There
Bells: Clang x Happy Thought *(a wedding in the air)*
Bye Bye Bruce: Springsteen x Wings of Time *(a rock star follower)*
Wanna Play Doctor: Dr Johnson x Goodbye Cherry Pie *(hmmm)*
No Monica: Conatus x Yes Hillary *(careful, Bill)*
She's a Sure Thing: Not A Single Doubt x Vital Curves
Let's Misbehave: Foreplay x Hell It's Hot
Bad Boy Roy: Over x Banned (*Australian cricket history)*
Lucky Move: Lucky Owners x Gone Yonder
Mydadjumpedefence: Isle Of Rum x She Got De Butcher *(Wow!)*
Verballed: Conatus x Accused
Weekend Intent: Key Business x Uncanny Action
Get Closer: Easy Rocking x Smoochie Smooch
Blurred Vision: Half Hennessy x Optometrist *(maybe give up the grog instead)*
Be Afraid: Dangerous x Cunning
Wine and Wickets: Runs to Win x Miss Bollinger
Six Empty Wallets: Inventory x Count the Silva
Sentoff: Arena x Expelled

Soliciting: Street Cry x Sunset Stripper *(surely you're not going to arrest me, officer!)*
Cracked Pitch: Scaredee Cat x Top Spinner
Won't Take Long: Barely a Moment x Yahtzee *(if you've played it)*
Grab That Tiger: Hold That Tiger x Escapada
Now What: No Excuses Needed x Some How
Maximus Gladiator: Arena x I Will Survive *(bring them all on!)*
Refuse the Ring: Refuse to Bend x Double Carat *(all yours, girls!)*
Sergeant Major: Commands x Sounds Assertive
Quick Thoughts: Barely a Moment x Recollection
Point Pain: Exceed and Excel x Acupuncture
Short Term Trader: Inflate x Rogue Trader *(one for the Stock Exchange)*
Give Me Room: Footstepsinthesand x Cover My Tracks
Sure Larceny: Undoubtedly x Plunder
Wayward Attack: Dyslexia x Shark *(well thought out)*
Junket: Bureaucracy x Fun to Fly *(three cheers for the pollies)*

. . . and the winner is:

All we can say is that the tennis buffs must own a lot of horses because the winner of this category is a reference to a great champion and all things tennis.

Maybe Nadal: by the sire Masterclass out of the dam Spaulding. I think Rafael Nadal would love being mentioned in the same breath as Masterclass and Spaulding, and the tennis sponsor would just love the association.

Where Dad was the influence

... and no correspondence to be entered into

Following is another honour roll that is deserving of mention and praise. These, as you might say, are the one-liners that the owners have concocted or stumbled over and given their horse that appropriate derivation, naming him or her after the sire with no reference to the dam.

It may just mean that the dam's name did not in any way contribute to the thought process, but nevertheless, it's ingenuity at its best – we shall let you be the judge. Once more, in each case we spell out the offspring followed by the sire *(followed by any remarks that grab our fancy)*

Australia

Some are Bent and **Follow the Leader** by Distorted Humour
Went the Trolley by Clang *(for all us oldies, great song Judy Garland)*
Ringa Ringa Rosie, Stephen Got Even, The Skater, Theyallfalldown and **All Fall Down** by Bradbury's Luck *(remember Steve Bradbury in the Winter Olympics?)*
Skating Past by Bradbury's Luck *(Go Stevo)*
Charlie Won't by Carry the Crown *(maybe the Queen knows something here)*
Ideal Centreman by Three Legs *(it really doesn't matter what code)*
Bail Me Out and **The Mongrel** by Lawyer *(apologies to the legal profession)*
Acquits and **Wasnt' Me** by Mr Innocent *(what else could you call him)*
Cramps by Refuse to Bend
Million Pound Note by Reassure
Looselipssinkships and **Sensational News** by All Chatter
The Sixties by Grandera *(if you remember through the smoke haze)*
Backwards Forwards by Dyslexia
Snatch the Cash by Break the Vault
A Little Knowledge, Got Nuthin Ta Fear and **I'm a Soldier** by Dangerous *(sounds like someone I know)*
Howgoodisthat by Seven Figures
Cantakitwithyou, Kunninkick, Skase and **Inatin** by Secret Savings *(for all those retirees)*
That's Cricket by Over
King Shane by Spinning World *(well done, Warnie)*
He's a Wonder by Colossus *(have you been working out?)*
Cockles'n'mussels by Street Cry *(was that Eliza Doolittle calling out?)*

Shoot Out by High Chaparral
Tram or Train by Good Journey
Knock Knock by Anyone Home
A Grade and Head Prefect by Pupil
Treasury Agent by Untouchable
Richard the Brave by Lion Heart
Liquid Nails by Special Bond
To the Keeper by No Slip *(the owners must be cricketers)*
Snug by Comfy *(as snug as a bug in a rug)*
Pass the Ace by Final Card
Wrigley by Bubble Gum Fellow
Youeffoh by Starcraft *(UFO – think about it)*
Goalattack and **Try Time Billy** by Quick Score *(netball players)*
Jumpinmycar by Hillman *(now we're going back in time)*
Hewho by Commands
That's Not It, Magic Carpet Burns, Beataroundthebush and **Ohmygod** by Foreplay *(fumbling and stumbling)*
Unanimously and **Ratbag** by Not a Single Doubt
Radio Pleasure by Stay Tuned
Pure Merino by Platinum Scissors
Fighting Fury by Festival Hall *(for all of the old fighters out there)*
Brain Explosion by Mind Games
Backinfive by Postponed
Mugging by Street Cry *(unfortunately, today's society)*
Bloodline, Thirsty for Blood and **Fangsforthememory** by Dracula
Flying Bails and **Copy That** by Over
Sayahailmary by Keep the Faith
The Majority by Quorum *(only in a democracy)*
Girl Friday, Rake the Bunker and **Beachcomber** by Footstepsinthesand
Playawedge by Sandtrap *(take a bow, golfers)*
Detector by Speeding Fine
Freemason by Grand Lodge
Bedbug by Ring for Nurse
Guarantees by Howbaddouwantit
Cutlet by Snitzel

Garfield by One Cool Cat *(love it)*
Blades by Oarsman
Sandler by Adam *(for the movie buffs)*
Eucalyptus by Timber Country
Prowl by Marauding
Howkudai by Don't Forget Me *(don't worry, I won't)*
Robert the Bruce by I Conquer
Era by Menzies *(and what an era Bob made it)*
By the Ears by Hold That Tiger *(enough said)*
Igotitfrommymumma by Natural Act
Planet Watcher by Galileo
Lucky Hand by High Rolling
Thirsty for Blood by Dracula
View the Stars by Galileo *(a classic)*
Chicago Hood by Untouchable
Tasty by Lunchtime
Lumpa by Forbetoo *(typical Aussie slang)*
Mr Biggs by Break the Vault *(no, it was the train)*
Where to Now by Good Journey
Honey Roll Over by Shagny
Souls by Amen Brother
Kings Rescue by Colonial King out of Lifesaver Lass
Costello by Bureaucracy (Peter Costello was once the Treasurer for the Liberal Party)
Al Zimer by Forgetful
Casino Evil by Final Card

New Zealand

He's Glovin It and **Twoeezy** by Keeper
Straightothepoolroom and **Lame Excuse** by No Excuses Needed
Bad Enough, Howbaddouneedit, Again 'N Again and **I'm Back Jack** by Howbadduwantit
Big Boy by Something Special
Lawsuit by Justice Prevails
Double Vision by Pupil
Pleasure And Pain by Pins

Lacquered by Painted Black
Just Right by Before Breakfast *(woowoo!)*
Take a Raincheck by Postponed
Three Fingers by Occidental Tourist
Quick Log On by Reset *(IT has made its mark)*
Duckworth Lewis by Postponed *(one for the cricket lovers)*

… and the winner is:

Many are impossible to separate for the winner, but one that both Monarchists and Republicans would understand and one that obviously was given a lot of thought is this one:

Charlie Won't – by the Sire Carry the Crown. Poor old Prince Charles, destined with Camilla to sit in the bleachers forever, or so some would think!

THAT WON'T HELP… HE SAID GELDED NOT WELDED!

Mum has the last say

... and we all know what that is all about!

There appears to be more to say when naming your charge using the dam's name only. Maybe it's that mums always have the last say and are far more gifted with their use of the English language than we mere male mortals.

In any case, who are we to criticise the lineage of mums, because after all, 'she who must be obeyed' is the love of our lives, the stars in our skies, the purpose in all we do and, more importantly, 'I've got to live here'.

Once more, the name of the offspring is be followed by an X designating the dam. *(We will then add any little comment that we are game enough to put to paper.)*

Jantzen x Ossie Cossie
Shatter, Prang and **Crunches** x Smash
Hush Up and **Hear No Tears** x Hide My Grades
Monaghetti x Just a Runner *(don't think so)*
Finding Neverland x Faraway Places
Bowled Lillee x Courtmarsh *(brilliant cricket combo)*
Stop the Traffic x Let Me Thru
Voice Coach x Drama Class
Dealers x Many Hands
Horlicks and **Brew** x Malt
Van Gogh x Timeless Art *(it certainly is)*
Nullabor Crossing x Born Western
Race the Shadow x Ta Ta
Adoptme Two x Adopted *(instant family)*
Ontick x Need the Money
Munch x Let's Do Lunch
General Confusion x Misunderstanding
Often Wrong x Brave Word *(the male's lament)*
Kayowed x Blew His Top
Whitehousewhispers x Impeachable *(good old Monica)*
Truce x Love Not War
Professor x Research

Luvbite x Does She Bite
Coroner x No Finding
Magnificent Pair x Maewest *(come up and see me some time, big boy!)*
Retrenched x Refuse to Quit
Low Cut x Perfect Cleavage *(well, hello there!)*
Friend x Pals
Change of Light x Dusk
Scorching x Badly Burnt
Button Up x Still Bragging
The Catwalk Star x Fasting *(only the ladies could pick that one)*
Willigobung x Insomniac *(hope not)*
Quadruple x Treble Your Bet
Owzat x How About That
C'mon Now x Just Do it Now
Wire Tapper x Lots of Secrets
On the Mend x Recover
Sosueme x Don't Delay *(well go on then)*
Time to Change x Change Over
Panic Button x Cradlesnatcher *(Dad's got the shotgun)*
Tread Lightly x Egg Shells
Arcades x Penny *(yes, a classic by the Beatles)*
All I Need x One Good Reason
Peg That Lease x Secret Handshake
Biona Winner x Winning is Best *(now think about Biona)*
Cabinet x Wardrobe
Nokin x Not Related . . . by Family Ties *(all related)*
Guessed x Brilliantdeduction
Rollem x Winning Table
El Cheapo x Not So Rusty
Pray for Me x Hymn
More Than Words x Jargon
Clothing x Rompers
Kindy Kid x Show and Tell
Freedom March x Liberty Walk *(a history lesson)*
Sir Walter x Turf *(nothing but the best)*

Banana Kick x Cunning Kick *(one for all you footy fans)*
Mr Eisenhower x True Peace
Cut the Tears x Weeping
Aim High x No Fear Here
Calendar Lass x Februarytwelve
Light Saver x Switches
Function x Office Party
Glass of Bubbly x Fair Occasion
Keyboard x Piano
Carry on Doctor x Repercussion
Backstabber x This Era *(a politicion's excuse?)*
Another Takeover x Soft Target *(we see a lot of it today)*
Lock It in Eddie x Believable *(McGuire pops up everywhere)*
Morrison x Brown Eyed Girl *(Van Morrison, a classic rocker)*
Chronic x Migraine
Shout Out Loud x Hit Your Kick *(and get your money out)*
Last Rites x Blest
Comma x Pause *(grammar with a grin)*
Blow My Candle x Happy Birthday
King of the Sling x Bonus for Me
In a Jam x Sweet Marmalade
Wow x Pretty Special *(hubba hubba)*
Morosi x Political Pet (by Bureaucracy) *(shades of Juni and Jim Cairns back in the 1970s)*
Miss Campbell x Arrest *(now, now, Naomi)*
Livin' on the Edge x Wysiwyg *(What You See Is What You Get)*
Tracksuit x Something Casual *(see, they have to bring fashion into it)*
Cinderella Girl x Midnight
Time Has Come x Chief Testimony
Giteau x Nimblefoot *(one for all you Rugby fans)*
All I Need x One Good Reason
Purge x Save Time
On the Carpet x Saviour *(wow! Too much information)*
Lonesome Tonight x Dateless
The Apprentice x Career Start
Tongue Tied x Tongue Twister

The Reporter x Newsworks
Cooperative x Unwilling
Rolangarros x Advantage Venus *(by Clay Hero – well done, another French Open win)*
Lines and Miss Detention x Chalkboard
Seeohtoo x Pollution
Might Make a Grand x Mighty If
Lifter x Put Me Down
Photograph x Glossy Print
Nosugar x Latte *(ah, a true coffee drinker)*
Yell and Loudest x Vocalist
Not a Pretender x Mimes
Perfect Days x Days Like This
We Betcha x Wager
Forty Eight Crash x Suzy Que *(we all loved Suzi Quatro)*
Teary Eyed x Theseeyesadoreyou
Doubly Sure x Pyjamas *(did you pack them?)*
Nothin' Better x Life's Rosie
Quicker Than Me x For Granted
Special Verdict x Grand Juror
In the Cards x Straight Flush *(for all the poker players)*
War Ends x Good News
The Comedian x How Funny
Lotsa Land x Don't Fence Me In
Redford x Best Picture *(who else could it have been?)*
Grasshopper x Cricket It Is
Appetizer x Sherry
Comatose x Napping *(they are bringing up our little naps again)*
Broadleaf x Lilypad
Crafty Lodger x Tennant
Promiscuous Girl x No Flirting *(you go girl!)*
The Blimp x Above the Crowd
Share Trader x Suspicion
Alltalknoaction x Youhadyourwarning
Thankgoditsfriday x Free Friday
No Fixed Address x Nomadic

Conanthebarbarin x Raid and Pillage ... by Marauding *(another movie classic, Arnie)*
Ofcourseican x Yes She Can Cancan
Turning Wicket x Vettori's Charm *(one for the Kiwi cricket enthusiasts)*
Curtseyed x On Bended Knee
Only for You x Academy Awards
Lotsa Grunt x Constant Pressure *(keep it clean please)*
Ten Day Special x Girls Get Physical ... by Let's Get Physical
Wong Man x Octical Sillusion *(now you see him, now you don't)*
Catch My Attention x Almost Blonde
Tell Us When x Aerobics
I'm Going Alone x March
Dr Grace x English Wonder (*absolute cricketing classic)*
Sweepshot x Dr Grace *(well done WG)*
Googly and **Crease** x Leg Bye ... by Dr Grace – *(missed bat, pad and keeper)*
Jigsaws x Picture Puzzle
Just Say Sumthink x Make a Statement *(if you're game)*
Never Sad x Laugh and Be Happy
Dispensed x Prescribed *(owned by a pharmacist obviously)*
One Eyed x Mrs Nelson
Just Make It x Teamaker
Display x Exhibit
Don't Come Monday x Firing Time *(good old DCM)*
All Australian x Simply Marv
Wouldn'thaveaclue x Too Smart ... by Knowledge
Public Holiday x Thanksgiving ... by Generous
A Boy Called Sue x Duck And Weave ... by Dodge *(well, wouldn't you?)*
Midnight Romp x Miss Midnight
Renouf x Susan (Susan Renouf was once married to a former Liberal Party politician)
Stuck Fast x Quicksand
Nip of Cognac x Spirit of France
Row Boat x Dinghy

. . . and the winner is:

There are two winners in this category, one for the sports minded and one for the oldies.

Rolangarros: the dam is Advantage Venus. When you analyse this further, it covers everything and the owners have put in a lot of thought. Roland Garros is the home of the French Open tennis tournament. Advantage is a term used in tennis and Venus Williams also won this prestigious event. To go one step further, the dam Advantage Venus is by the sire Clay Hero, which is a direct reference to the surface on which the final is played – brilliant!

Magnificent Pair: the dam is Maewest. As the older brigade would know, there is absolutely no reference or explanation needed. What a magnificent pair!

The quirky, the pseudo-jumbled anagrams

. . . and the ones that can do your head in!

Now here is a list of horse names that will make you squirm, think, and say, 'What the?'. Some owners have simply taken the easy way out, some have presented us with the answer and we have to look for the question, and others have simply tried to do our heads in with the naming of their thoroughbred.

In each case the first name you see is the name of the racehorse, and the word (or letters or phrase) beside it is the where the name originated. You can only imagine what they were thinking at the time. To those responsible for the 'originality' shown, we have to say, why bother!

Lemarac and Caramel
Revoc and Cover
Iruklam and **Malkuri** *(two old Brisbane racehorses with a mirror reverse solution)*
Esroh and Horse *(a lot of thought in this one)*

Eripsni and Inspire
Kisrak and Karsik
Arwon and Nowra *(Melbourne Cup history)*
Taws and Swat
Rovert and Trevor
Nepro and Orpen
Mik Yelrow and Kim Worley *(the horse is owned by the Worleys)*
Buriton and Rubiton
Retlaw and Walter
Reizarb and Brazier
Nosteppins and Snippetson
Fracs and Scarf
Racso and Oscar
Rab and Bar
Civelb and Blevic
Naes and Sean
Sedecrem (New Zealand) and Mercedes
Stun On and No Nuts
Sutanoc and Conatus
Tartoor and Rootrat *(enough said!)*
Rentrap and Partner
Nailati and Italian
Eris and Sire *(so original – not)*
Neslo and Olsen
Mr Tarneet and Mr Teenrat *(maybe he was)*
Nobragnow and Wongarbon
Enakram and Markane
Moozama and Amazoom
Our Yendor and Our Rodney *(obviously Rodney was at the table)*
Erewhon and Nowhere
Nerak and Karen
Sirrah Nashira and Shanira Harris
Rehctub and Butcher

and the ones that you have to think about ...

Youkay Teevee and UK TV
Wip and Work In Progress
Roygbiv and Red, Orange, Yellow, Green, Blue, Indigo, Violet
Aytozed and A to Z
Elkayel and LKL
Double You Em and WM *(obviously WM was at the table)*
El Be Double You and LBW *(sorry mate, but you're out. That's cricket)*
Are Pee Gee and RPG
Geejayhaitch and GJH
Sea Eye Pea and CIP
Arbeecee and RBC
Emteevee and MTV
Gee Eff Cee and GFC *(Global Financial Crisis)*
Ay Dee Bee and ADB
Bee I En Gee Oh and BINGO *(you got it in one)*
Tee Emar and TMR
Karbee and KRB
Peekay and PK
Essbeew and SBW
Areteare and RTR
Be Em Cee and BMC
Elljay and LJ
Jay Kay Tee and JKT
Lionssixchristiansnil
Footfullabindies
Mydadjumpedefence
Rhymes With Banker (NZ)
Pistol Knight *(repeat over and over again and you will get the message)*
Wear the Fox Hat *(repeat over and over again and you might get a slap)*
Euro Merly *(repeat over and over again and she may be glad to see you)*
Home on the Wife *(wow!)*

Efinpee (NZ) *(whoops!)*
Thong and Pushbike *(can you believe these?)*
Mince Pie
He's No Pie Eater
Shrunk in the Wash
Far Call *(typical Aussie humour – similar to 'Far Que')*
Fatty Finn's Dog
Little Dick *(what the?)*
Richard Cranium (NZ)
Slugsbrothernugget
Slugsisterkate
Toldyaiwastrouble
G'Day Old Mate
Foneeleven (NZ) *(F-111, it's a plane, it's a plane)*
Suchabimbo
The Cookie Monster
Snowy on the Tram
Tuppence Halfpenny
Aldidhavabrother and **Alcarntspell**
You Can Call Me Al *(told you so Baz)*
Bad Boy Bazza and **Big Bad Barry** *(named after me no doubt)*
Mybigfatgreekhorse
Harry Dehorse
Horsewifnoname (NZ)
Harry the Drover
Sleep and Snore
Bornintheuessay *(remember Bruce Springsteen's song?)*
Mickey Drippin *(a golden oldie)*
Fly Off the Handle *(as you would sometimes)*
Coodawoodashooda
Chuckawheely
Hewentwoosh
Aracingwewillgo
Karma Gutza
Karma Getya
Notafullquid

Sheez Zocay (NZ)
Imacatostrophe
Warts and All
Willhaveahundred
Dozintmateranyway (NZ)
Takincareofbizniz (NZ)
Australia's Finest
Quick Thinking
C'Mon Now
Left Behind
Bazza's Dream
Long Road to Glory
Don't Stop Believin'
Are You Kidding
Decision Time
Take the Risk
Takeachance
Itoldyouso
Lots of Money
Every Man's Dream
Onestepatatime
Hardacttofollow
Neversaidit'seasy
Yabigorse
Maythehorsebemagic
Pane in the Glass
Yousnoozeyoulose
Givethegirlsago
Frankoo Verymuch
Forcryingoutloud

And the two American contributions are:
Mywifeknowseverything and
Mywifedoesn'tknow *(get out of here!)*

… and these were obviously named at a barbie!

Chilli Mud Crab
Fangin' Around
Five Lobsters
Six Crownies
Downa Crownie
A Quiet Shandy
Carry On Drinking
Imabarmaid
Justonetwomany
Slow Talking Walter
Bandy Legs
Running Dry
Beerwineandspirits
Liquid Amber
Jaydeeandcoke
Smooth Drop
Another Frothy

… and the winner is:

The choice of Grand Champion was unanimous and was taken out by an Australasian trotter. The name needs no explanation. Why? Because it defies any rhyme or reason.

Lionssixchristiansnil – please tell me how, when, where and why.

We couldn't think of a name

… you are kidding, aren't you?

Were the owners lazy in naming some of their horses in the late 1800s and early 1900s? Maybe they were, as they were registered with letters only. Just imagine if we had a race where every horse was represented by just initials, as we see below. The race callers might appreciate it.

LL: 3rd 1867 Victorian Derby
JL: 3rd 1872 Queensland Derby
AT: 3rd 1878 Epsom Handicap
ABC: 3rd 1880 Victorian Sires Produce Stakes
DOD: 1st 1881 South Australian Goodwood Handicap
EK: 1st 1892 Williamstown Cup (Sandown Classic)
TMS: 1st 1901 Villiers Stakes
FJA: 1st 1903 Victorian Derby
IOU: 1st 1929 Queensland Stradbroke Handicap
Ar: 1st 1884 Bagot Handicap

One would think the next progression would be to actually name a horse, but no, some thought that merely adding a numeral was less time consuming.

Here are two examples:

J5: 1st 1895 Geelong Cup, Victoria
A1: 3rd 1909 RJ Peters Stakes, Western Australia

CHAPTER 7
Trivia Teasers

'Trivia' is defined in the dictionary as the following:

- Unimportant matters of detail
- Of very little importance

Whatever its true meaning, trivia is that treasure trove of little-known facts or figures that are slow to evolve and combine at the crossroads of a mental state to create a whole new world.

Horses

... and some little-known facts of the matter!

- One of the oldest horses recorded in history was an English barge horse, Old Billy, who lived to 62 years of age.
- The oldest pony reliably reported was named Teddy E Bear; he lived until he was 55.
- The oldest winning thoroughbreds were eighteen-year-old Revenge at Shewsbury, England, in 1790, Marksman at Ashford, Kent, England, in 1826 and Jorrocks at Bathurst in Australia in 1851.
- The Falabella of Argentina is recognised as the smallest breed in the world. The tallest of this breed stands about 74 centimetres (29 inches) at the shoulder.
- A miniture stallion by the name of Little Pumpkin is recognised as the smallest pony in history. He stood 14 inches (35 centimetres) and weighed only 20 lb (9 kg).

- The tallest horse ever recorded was a Shire named Sampson. He stood 21 and a half hands at his withers, (7 feet 2 inches, or approximately 218 centimetres tall).
- Sampson was recorded as being the heaviest horse, weighing 1524 kg (3360 lb).
- The record for the highest jump is 8 feet 1¼ inches (247 centimetres) by a horse named Huaso. He was competing at Vin del Mar, Santago, Chile on 5 February 1949, ridden by Captain Alberto Larraguibel Morales.
- The record of the longest jump over water is 27 feet 6¾ inches (8.4 metres) by Something, in Johannesburg, South Africa, on 25 April 1975, ridden by Andre Ferreira.
- We have nearly 400 different breeds of horses and ponies on earth.
- A great number of foals are born undercover of darkness to protect them from other hunting animals and the danger that represents.
- Horses expend less energy standing up than they do on the ground.
- The British racehorse Humorist won the English Derby in 1921 but should never have raced at all. He died shortly after his win and after performing an autopsy, it was discovered that he only had one lung.
- Because of their long limbs, horses find galloping a natural part of their lives; on the other hand, when they are confronted by an obstacle, most will not jump over it and will go around because running, not jumping, is what they are bred to do naturally.
- If a horse's nostrils are blocked, they can suffocate because they cannot breathe through their mouth.
- The Republic of China has the most horses on earth, estimated to be over 10 million.
- Horses cannot vomit.
- Hippophobia is the fear of horses.
- Equinophobia is also a fear of horses.
- If a statue in a park is of a person on a horse and the horse has

both front legs off the ground, it means that that particular person represented died in battle.

- If the statue of a horse has one front leg in the air, it signifies that the person died as a result of wounds received in battle.
- If the statue of the horse is in a jumping position with no legs on the ground, the person represented died naturally.

Bits and pieces

...from racing's archives

- In 1865, one of Australia's most prominent jumps jockeys and greatest poets, Adam Lindsay Gordon, penned a verse about a horse race. It included the horse names of Tim Whiffler and The Barb. How was he to know that The Barb would win the Melbourne Cup the following year, in 1866, and Tim Whiffler would win the Cup in 1867?
- A punter betting on every race in a typical nine-race meeting will have to review approximately 24,000 pieces of information if he wishes to review the record of each participating horse – and people think that you're not too bright!
- Never Mind II holds the record for the slowest winning time ever recorded for a race. When he won a 2 mile jumps race (3200 metres) in 1945, he finished in 11.28 flat. Never Mind II refused to jump at a fence and was abandoned by his jockey, only for that jockey to find out that all the other runners in the race had been disqualified or had fallen. The jockey quickly returned to Never Mind II, mounted, and finished the race at his leisure.

Our glorious racing past!

- Who is the prominent Queensland religious figure whose father was an SP bookmaker? **Answer:** The Catholic Archbishop of Brisbane, Archbishop John Battersby
- Who was the jockey at the centre of The Great Phantom Race Call Swindle in the 1930s? **Answer:** Scobie Breasley
- Who was the gentleman who coined the phrase in tight finishes,

'I will bet London to a Brick On'? **Answer:** Sydney racecaller Ken Howard

- Who was the jockey who won eleven Victorian premierships, won two Melbourne Cups, and the pundits say was robbed for his third? **Answer:** Roy Higgins and the horse Big Philou
- Who was the jockey who jumped off his mount (Strike Softly) mid-race during the running of the 1983 Bunbury Cup in WA? **Answer:** This incident eventually saw horse owner Laurie Connell jailed and the jockey doing some time as well. Danny Hobby
- Who was the jockey who started riding at places like Cunnamulla, Thargomindah and Brisbane in the 1950s and 1960s, and ended up riding for the very rich owners and very best trainers in Europe, but still could not vote in his own country? **Answer:** Darby McCarthy (he was an Indigenous Australian)
- Who was the great racing journalist who couldn't help but follow the horses because his dad owned the Doncaster Hotel at Randwick (and this little bloke grew up beside a race track as well)? **Answer:** Max Presnell
- Who was the legendary jockey who was outed for life in the infamous leg-pulling incident in the 1961 Derby? It was recorded that the great racing journalist Max Presnell said, 'Though it was a foul ride, it was the best ride I have ever seen.' **Answer:** Mel 'The Shoe' Schumacher
- Who was the trainer responsible for sending a local TAB Agency broke? **Answer:** She trained Time Frame, which was from the small rural town of Wagin. All of the locals backed the local steed and when it won the TAB agency in town ran out of money. Angela Smith
- Who was the gentleman supposedly responsible for bringing out the first thoroughbred, Rockingham, on the First Fleet? **Answer:** His family name today remains embedded in Australian racing history. Henry Waterhouse
- Who was the biggest bookmaker during and after World War II and was subsequently banned from the track over the Fine

Cotton affair? **Answer:** Big Bill Waterhouse

- Who was the jockey a parochial female was yelling to when the jockey announced his intentions of riding overseas and possibly the United States and she yelled out, 'Look after yourself. Be careful of those Yanks because they killed Les Darcy and Phar Lap'? **Answer:** Edgar Britt
- Who was credited with saying, 'I put too much trust in human nature – my friends are the horses'? **Answer:** Bart Cummings
- What was the name of the horse that in the 1840s ran over three heats of the Melbourne Town Plate with one hour's rest between each race – and won them all? **Answer:** Petrel
- The connections of Petrel issued a challenge to the connections of the Sydney champion Jorrocks to decide who was the best horse of all time. What was the horse's name, and who was the winner? **Answer:** Jorrocks, and Jorrocks
- Who was affectionately known as The Iron Gelding? **Answer:** Jorrocks
- Which horse won 60 of his 113 starts, and was also credited with equalling the most wins by any thoroughbred worldwide in a calendar year? **Answer:** Jorrocks, with 30 wins from 31 starts in 1846. The courses included Sydney, Bathurst, Goulburn, Maitland and Mudgee.

And when big meant big . . .

When Kelso won the 1897 Rosehill Cup in Sydney, there were 43 starters, the largest field ever to assemble for a registered race in Australia. Thank goodness the race callers of today do not have to contend with fields like that.

Just imagine a field of that size in a 900 metre sprint. Talk about interference.

Some little-known facts about our sport

... everything you wanted to know but were frightened to ask!

- Chariot races run in ancient Rome are the earliest known example of organised horseracing. However, it is likely that horses raced as long ago as 4500 BC in central Asia.
- The lowest weight recorded by a jockey is 49 lb (22 kg).
- The average race horse weighs about 500 kg.
- Over $100 billion is bet on horseracing every year.
- The thoroughbred horses of today are almost double the size of the Arabian racehorses that competed over a thousand years ago.
- The term 'big hearted' has an anatomical basis in horseracing, where horses with large hearts have a distinct advantage over horses with regular-sized hearts.
- The relatively high casualty rate for horses in the United States is in the main due almost entirely to the use of legal and illegal performance-enhancing drugs.
- One of the United States' most famous jockeys, Eddie Arcaro, rode 250 losers before winning his first race. Arcaro then went on to win 4778 races through his illustrious career, including each of the three races that make up the Triple Crown.
- Jockey Levi Barlingume raced competitively until the age of 80. He participated in his last race in 1932, during which he fell and broke a leg.
- Tango Duke set the record for thoroughbred longevity in 1978 when he died at the ripe old age of 42.
- Australia's champion and second-highest-rated local Timeform rated horse, Kingston Town, actually ran last in his first race. He was gelded, after a spell, went on to win fourteen Group 1 races, including three WS Cox Plates.
- Bart Cummings as a youngster was diagnosed with asthma and had an allergy to horse hair, lucerne, oats and hay. The doctor said that all would be well if he stayed away from the gee-gees. I wonder what the specialist would have said today.
- Never back odds on and 'never run upstairs' – a truer phrase was

never invented for the sport of kings. It was said that on the day Ajax started at 40/1 on, people turned up at the track with the deeds to their houses and would get a bet from the bookie, 'your house to X number of pounds'. Of course as we all know Ajax was beaten at that price and some people lost their homes, while some bookies entered the real estate market.

- We can all appreciate how dangerous the sport of kings can be for jockeys, so the story of the great American hoop Willie Shoemaker is ironic. In 1990, a crowd of over 60,000 people came to bid him farewell after a lifetime in the saddle, riding more than 8800 winners in 41 years. Incredibly, just twelve months after retiring out of the saddle in one piece, he was involved in a car accident and was paralysed from the neck down, and was subsequently wheelchair bound with very limited mobility. The make of vehicle he was driving the day of the accident, believe it or not, was a Bronco.
- We often joke about our great Melbourne Cup being run in another capital city in Australia besides Melbourne ... well, we have at least made a start. The Melbourne Cup trophy awarded to the connections every year is made in Brisbane, Queensland – one for the Sunshine State!
- Talk about the one that got away, especially for someone who could talk to the animals. Famous horse whisperer Monty Roberts bought a horse for US$40,000, broke him in, educated him, and then on sold him for a tidy profit for US$125,000. Job done, pay the bills with a few dollars in the kick. Well, the end of the story is a bitter pill to swallow for Monty. The horse went on to win nine races out of ten, with one place. He won two Prix de l'Arc de Triomphes and, with prize money totalling over US$636,000, was then syndicated to stud for a paltry $16 million. He was the great Alleged. Bad luck, Monty.
- One that all owners and would-be owners should *not* read. Did you know that 60 per cent of all horses foaled do not make it to the racetrack?

OMG… WHAT'S HE TALKING ABOUT… DOG FOOD?

Repeat winners of the same race

… you won't believe how many and who!

You would have thought that rarefied air was reached when we brought you the stories of two horses that had won the same race five times. The great American Kelso won the Jockey Club Gold Cup in 1960, 1961, 1962, 1963 and 1964, and equally the great Aussie Champ Manikato, which did the same to the William Reid Stakes in 1979, 1980, 1981, 1982 and then again in 1983.

But we haven't reached the top by any stretch of the imagination, as there were three horses that went one better with six wins, and five horses that went one better again with seven wins in the same race.

Unbelievably, there is one horse that has gone beyond this elite group.

Here is a countdown of these amazing animals.

Six wins:

- Beeswing: Newcastle Gold Cup 1836, 1837, 1838, 1839, 1841, 1842
- Brown Jack: Queen Alexandra Stakes 1929, 1930, 1931, 1932, 1933, 1934
- Gods Solution: Race Around Yorkshire Handicap* 1985, 1986, 1987, 1988, 1989, 1991 (*The Race Around Yorkshire Handicap was renamed the Gods Solution Handicap in 1990.)

Seven wins:

- Al Capone II: Prix La Haye Jousselin, 1993, 1994, 1995, 1996, 1997, 1998, 1999
- Doctor Syntax: Preston Gold Cup, 1815, 1816, 1817, 1818, 1819, 1820, 1821
- Franc Picard: Grand Steeple Chase de Dieppe, 1853, 1854, 1855, 1856, 1857, 1859, 1861
- Risk of Thunder: La Touche Cup 1995, 1996, 1997, 1998, 1999, 2000, 2002 (there was no race in 2001)

... and drum roll please ...

Eight wins:

- Leaping Plum: Grasmick Handicap 1995, 1996, 1997, 1998, 1999, 2000, 2001, 2003. You will notice that he did not win in 2002; however, he did come second.

Unbelievable!

How could a greyhound possibly become a trotter?

... well he did!

Greyhound was actually the name given to a grey standardbred born in 1932, being by Guy Abbey out of Elizabeth, by Peter the Great.

His most outstanding achievement was when he won the Hambletonian in a record time for the mile of 1:55.25, a record he held for 31 years. Nicknamed the Grey Ghost, he trotted 25 two-minute miles during his career and at one time held fourteen world records. He was so popular that after his retirement, his owner, Colonel Edward J Baker, allowed visitors to see the horse up until his death in February 1965 at the grand old age of 33.

Greyhound was honoured as Trotting Horse of the Century.

A Greyhound who became a trotter ... first class!

Great Aussie barbecue trivia

... and some facts that highlight the best

- In the history of the Triple Crown races for three-year-olds in Australia, only one grey has been successful: Martello Towers in 1959. He won the Canterbury Guineas (now the Randwick Guineas), the Rosehill Guineas and the AJC Derby.
- In 2002, Helenus became the only horse in history to win the 'Big 4' of the Melbourne three-year-old Spring Racing Carnival. He won the MVRC Stutt Stakes, MRC Caulfield Guineas, MVRC AAMI Vase Stakes, and the VRC Derby in four consecutive starts.
- When Tulloch won the 1957 MRC Caulfield Cup over 12 furlongs (2400 metres), his time for the race was 2.26.9, considered to be the fastest time ever run by a three-year-old in the world over that distance on turf.
- In the 1970s Australia changed from imperial to metric distance measurements, and the 12 furlongs became 2400 metres. Tulloch's time of 2.26.9 is still recognised as the fastest 12 furlongs ever run in Australia.
- In May 1957, the American colt Gallant Man equalled the world record of 2.26.6 when he won the time-honoured 12 furlong Belmont Stakes, run on dirt. This record stood until the mighty Secretariat clocked 2.24.00 when he won the Belmont Stakes by 31 lengths in 1973. His time for that race was a new world record for a horse of any age, breaking the previous record by a staggering 2.6 seconds.
- Up until 2011, the fastest times for 2400 metres by a colt and filly in Australia were both established in the QTC Queensland Derby. The colt De Gaulle Lane ran 2.25.2 in 2001, and the filly Dariana ran 2.26.49 in 2010.
- As at 1 January 2011, Australia had 68 Group 1 races with prize money of over $56 million – nice if you could win some of it...
- As at 1 January 2012, Australia has 20 races worth $1 million or more. The Melbourne Cup is the richest, with prize money in excess of $6.2 million.
- Since the Cox Plate's inception in 1922, only two full brothers have won the great race. No, they were not horses, but jockeys:

Darby and Jim Munro. Darby rode five: Rogilla, Young Idea, Mosaic, Beau Vite and Hydrogen. Jim rode one, Chatham.

... now on a more serious note!

- Alsop ran second to Rain Lover in the 1969 Melbourne Cup. Vansittart ran second to Baghdad Note in the 1970 Melbourne Cup. Maybe poor old Vansittart was destined to run second, and here is why. He was owned by none other than Mr and Mrs Alsop.
- Why was the flying two-year-old filly that won the 1958 Group 1 Stradbroke Handicap named Wiggle? Apparently, when the owners purchased her at the yearling sales, they must have seen something in the way she walked – they named her after the legendary screen actress Marilyn Monroe.
- In naming some horses, we are educated not only in their history and the story surrounding how they were bought, but also in the slanguage of the cutthroat world of the stock market. These three half-brothers certainly have names to think about: Takeover Target, Preditory Pricer and Wilful Default. Then there is Deadcat Bounce. If you ask any share trader they will give you a clear definition of its meaning on the stock market floor. The dead cat bounce had its origins in the East around 1985. It simply refers to when a stock is in severe decline and suddenly it has a sharp bounce from the low, but then returns to its downward spiral. One wonders how a poor cat got involved in the first place.

The Caulfield Stakes

... some great stats about our great race with a twist in the tail

First run in 1886, the Group 1 MRC Caulfield Stakes has been won by some of the great champions of the Australian turf.

Seven horses have won it twice:

- Wakeful: 1901, 1902

- Artillerie: 1909, 1910
- High Caste: 1939, 1940
- Lawrence: 1944, 1945
- Sky High: 1961, 1962
- Kingston Town: 1981, 1982
- Lonhro: 2002, 2003

Three horses have won it three times:

- Eurythmic: 1920, 1921, 1922
- Lord: 1958, 1959, 1960 (dead heat in 1960)
- Winfreux: 1965, 1966, 1967

However, when Eurythmic won in 1920, 1921 and 1922, he was part of a record that may stand for another 100 years. Eurythmic and Tangalooma are the only horses in history to quinella the same Group 1 race in three successive years:

1920: 1st Eurythmic	**2nd Tangalooma**	3rd Queen Comedy
1921: 1st Eurythmic	**2nd Tangalooma**	3rd Amazonia
1922: 1st Eurythmic	**2nd Tangalooma**	3rd Harvest Knight

How Tangalooma's owners must have detested the name and backside of Eurythmic.

WS Cox Plate

... some little-known facts

- In the history of the Cox Plate, Tommy Smith has been the most successful with seven winners: Redcraze, Tulloch, Gunsynd, Kingston Town (three times) and Red Anchor.
- Five horses have run second in two consecutive Cox Plates: Whittier (1923–24), Hall Mark (1934–35), Winfreux (1965–66), Filante (1996–97) and Defier (2002–03).
- The only filly to win a Cox Plate was Surround, in 1976.
- Only one jockey has won three consecutive runnings of this race.

Brent Thompson won on Family of Man in 1977, So Called in 1978 and the ill-fated Dulcify in 1979.

- Six mares and fillies have won a total of nine Cox Plates: Tranquil Star (two), Flight (two), Surround (one), Dane Ripper (one), Sunline (two) and Makybe Diva (one).
- In the history of the Cox Plate, Darby Munro has been the most successful jockey with five winners: Rogilla (1933), Young Idea (1937), Mosaic (1939), Beau Vite (1941) and Hydrogen (1952).
- When Kingston Town won his three Cox Plates, he had a different jockey on each occasion: Malcom Johnston in 1980, Ron Quinton in 1981 and Peter Cook in 1982.
- Only champions or soon-to-be champions win the Cox Plate, and some have won it more than once. While Kingston Town is top of the tree with three wins in 1980, 1981 and 1982, the following elite won the Plate twice: Phar Lap in 1930, 1931, Young Idea in 1936, 1937, Beau Vite in 1940, 1941, Tranquil Star in 1942, 1944, Flight in 1945 and 1946, Hydrogen in 1952, 1953, Tobin Bronze in 1966, 1967, Sunline in 1999, 2000, Northerly in 2001, 2002, Fields of Omagh in 2003 and 2006, and So You Think in 2009, 2010.
- In 1975, Fury's Order ran 2.20.4 on a heavy track to record the slowest time in the history of the Cox Plate. When Might and Power won in 1998, he ran a track record for the 2040 metre race in a track record of 2.3.54.
- In 1946, the Cox Plate was run in two divisions. Flight won the first and Leonard the second.

A horse's tummy

... I bet you didn't know this!

The stomach of a horse is very primitive – it was designed so horses could feed on foliage made up of grass and leaves from trees. However, when the grain-fed diet for thoroughbreds was introduced, it was totally foreign to their digestive system so colic became a common problem, all because nature never intended the thoroughbreds and standardbreds to be fed this way.

The Melbourne Cup

... some little known facts about the race that stops a nation!

- The Melbourne Cup was first run on 7 November 1861 with a field of eighteen. Archer was the winner at 6/1 with first prize a gold watch and £710.
- Archer's time was the slowest ever recorded for a Melbourne Cup: 3.52 flat.
- The very first Melbourne Cup in 1861 attracted 4000 people and within 20 years, it was attracting a crowd of around 100,000.
- The largest crowd recorded was in 2003, when 123,000 people saw Makybe Diva win her first Melbourne Cup.
- In 1972 the famous race was converted to metric distance. From then on it was 3200 metres, which is really 16.68 metres or 61.3 feet short of the old imperial distance of 2 miles.
- Kingston Rule holds the record in 1990 of 3.16.3.
- The biggest winning margin was eight lengths, by Archer in 1862.
- The highest winning weight was Carbine, carrying 10 stone 6 lb (66 kg) in 1890, followed by Archer with 10 stone 2 lb (64.5 kg) in 1862, and then Poitrel in 1920 carrying 10 stone (63.5 kg).
- The lowest winning weight was Banker in 1863, carrying the postage stamp of 5 stone 3 lb (33.5 kg).
- The highest weight carried without winning was the mighty Phar Lap, with 10 stone 10 lb (68 kg). In 1931 he finished eighth – no wonder with that weight.
- After the running of the 2011 Melbourne Cup, the most prolific age of winners is five-year-olds, with 43 winners, and the least is eight-year-olds, with just two winners.
- The most prolific winners are entires, followed by geldings.
- The shortest-priced favourite was Phar Lap at 11/8 on, when he won in 1930. The other two shortest-priced winners were Revenue at 7/4 in 1901 and Archer at 2/1 in 1862.
- The longest-priced winners have been The Pearl in 1871, Wotan

in 1936 and Old Rowley in 1940 – all started at the dream price of 100/1.

- Dual winners have been Archer in 1861 and 1862, Peter Pan in 1932 and 1934, Rain Lover 1968 and 1969 and Think Big 1974 and 1975.
- The only triple winner was the great Makybe Diva in 2003, 2004 and 2005.
- The smallest Melbourne Cup field was in 1863 with seven runners. The winner was Banker.
- The largest field was in 1890 with 39 starters. The winner was Carbine.
- The most winning saddlecloth numbers are 4 and 12, with eleven wins each. Number 1 has ten wins, and numbers 6 and 8 have eight wins.
- The trainer with the most wins is Bart Cummings, with twelve.
- Prize money was £710 ($1420) and a gold watch in 1861, $5.1 million in 2005 and $6.2 million in 2011.

Now for a spicy ending!

... they did what? ... you've got to be kidding!

After a brief but brilliant racing career, triple Group 1 winner Mouward, the younger brother to Octagonal, was sold to China in 1998 to continue his somewhat lacklustre stud duties. However, the Chinese racing industry collapsed in 2005. Was Mouward put out to pasture or shipped back to Australia? Neither, he 'came and went like a rocket'.

Unfortunately, poor old Mouward ended up on a platter at a Chinese restaurant – waste not, want not.

... his life was sort of sweet and sour.

THANK YOU

Thanks to our friends and family, especially our wives, who have encouraged and supported us throughout this rollercoaster of a journey.

Special thanks to Rolf Westin, who in August 2009 said, 'Gee, Baz, you should write a book!', and to Peter McGuiness for his support and direction.

The tales contained within these covers are the product of a keen interest in, or some would say obsession about, racing facts; all have been read or seen, or have attracted a keen ear when the storyteller made his mark. Some of the books and magazines that have told similar stories are long gone, but we have managed to confirm the events where we could with what is available today.

We discovered the internet as a source of checking facts, but it became obvious to us in our journey that not all information published is accurate or credible. This led us to cross-checking many events and details in an effort to confirm whether the information we had ended up with was fact or fiction.

There are over 250 short stories in our compilation, and our thanks are directed at too many sources, some quite obscure, to nominate individually*. The tales, both old and new, are a product of our memories and generally confirmed research on the internet, books and magazines. They are told in our words and have not been directly extracted from any reference source. Many facts are just part of the public record of our great industry, and we are deeply

* The definitions we have used are from *The Free Dictionary* by Farlex and *Merriam Webster Learner's Dictionary*

indebted to those wonderful animals and identities for making our journey possible.

If any of our readers do find any fact that they believe is inaccurate, could they please make it known to the authors for future reference.

Barry and Alan Wood